Portland Place

Portland Place

Secret Diary of a BBC Secretary

Sarah Shaw

Constable • London

CONSTABLE

Some names and details have been changed to protect the privacy of others.

First published in Great Britain in 2015 by Lulu Enterprises Inc.

This edition published in 2016 by Constable

1 3 5 7 9 10 8 6 4 2

Copyright © Sarah Shaw, 2015

The moral right of the author has been asserted.

A CIP catalogue record for this book
is available from the British Library.

ISBN 978-1-47212-468-5 (hardback)

Typeset in Great Britain by SX Composing DTP, Rayleigh Essex
Printed and bound in Great Britain by CPI Group (UK) Ltd, Croydon, CR0 4YY

Papers used by Constable are from well-managed forests
and other responsible sources

MIX
Paper from
responsible sources
FSC® C104740

Constable
An imprint of
Little, Brown Book Group
Carmelite House
50 Victoria Embankment
London EC4Y 0DZ

An Hachette UK Company
www.hachette.co.uk

www.littlebrown.co.uk

For those who were there, with thanks.

Acknowledgements

I owe an enormous debt of gratitude to Robert Gwyn Palmer of DCD Media, who made this book possible; Andreas Campomar and Claire Chesser, copy-editor Jane Donovan and all at Little, Brown for their time and expertise.

Thanks also to Gill, Valerie and Penny. Despite their past lives being unexpectedly exhumed, they have generously answered questions, shared memories and, as ever, offered sensible advice. I am also very grateful to early champions of the diary Elaine Day, Sarah Harrison, Rod Cooper, Deirdre Hyde, Andy Priestner, Gina Ferrari, Katie Turner, Helen Burrows and others, including those on Twitter and Facebook.

I would especially like to thank my husband Ray for his encouraging involvement throughout.

Contents

Portland Place

Prelude

I found my diary for 1971 when we cleared out the loft, buried at the bottom of a cardboard box, covered by old papers and notebooks. I hadn't seen it for many years, and no one but myself knew that it existed. Holding it in my hands again brought back a chilly discomfort. I could remember roughly where I was, and what I was doing that year, and that I had deliberately destroyed other mementos from that time. Yet I had hung on to this diary, and it had travelled with me from loft to loft through various house moves. Now I was curious to read it, but at the same time I dreaded what embarrassing truths it might reveal.

I decided that if I was going to finally throw it out, I had better check first. So I opened the diary. It is 8 x 5 inches, with a red cover, and has a page dedicated to each day. Most are crammed with writing and occasional shorthand phrases, and some spill over on to sheets torn from notebooks, inserted with long-dead strips of yellowing Sellotape. I was astonished by what I read. Here were work crises, lunchtime discussions, shopping trips, evenings out, even whole chunks of conversation ... Of course here too was the story I had wanted to bury and forget. Old emotions resurfaced: frustration, confusion, anxiety; excitement, happiness and desire. Sudden images appeared: half a face, a tabletop, a bedroom ... Gill in the BBC canteen, putting the green ceramic salt and pepper cellars together to demonstrate the line you cross in a relationship when you have sex with someone. My father in his tie and tweed jacket, dismissive, argumentative ... Then Frank's pink and white face, dimly lit in the lift, tilted back to gaze up at me.

Immediately, and without understanding why, I was gripped by a compulsion to transcribe it all. As I progressed, I realised my initial anxiety had been absolutely wrong. By the time I had finished, I knew that I had something quite special in front of me, and that whatever people might have thought about my behaviour then, had they known what I was up to, I had nothing to be ashamed of any more.

This story demanded to be set free.

Introduction

I grew up in the Surrey suburbs in the 1950s and 60s, just as Britain emerged from the weariness and austerity of the post-war world. In 1971, home was a four-bedroom house in Chipstead to which I returned most weekends to see my father and stepmother, but it wasn't an altogether welcoming place. Let me explain why.

My brother Oliver had died, aged twenty, from Hodgkin's lymphoma in 1961, when I was nine. Born during the war while my father was in the army, he and my mother had inevitably formed a close bond. My mother's health had never been good and, after losing him, the Crohn's disease and pernicious anaemia from which she suffered worsened. She developed a chronic depression. Effectively, she lost the will to live and died in 1965, leaving just my father and myself.

We put on brave faces and got on with things, and never mentioned my mother again. My school friends – Georgina Fox, in particular – did a good job of not letting me become too miserable. However, it felt as if losing a normal family life had diverted me down a track that was different from others my own age. A couple of years after my mother died, my father had married my stepmother, Vera, because we needed someone to shop, cook and clean for us and he feared that if he employed a housekeeper, the neighbours would gossip. Vera expected to be part of a normal marriage; my father did not. A retired journalist, he spent much of his time shut away, researching and writing articles.

It was not a recipe for happiness.

After attending a private girls' school, whose academic achievements were more aspirational than actual, and with less than impressive A levels, I failed to get into university. This was a great relief to me. In those days, careers for middle-class girls were barely discussed. It was understood that you would become a teacher, nurse or secretary for a few years, and then you would get married. I was unable to think ambitiously because I was still subconsciously sorting out the elephant in the room of our family tragedy, and no one in my family had ever gone to university. Moreover, the popular image of the day was one of long-haired, free-loving, drug-taking students protesting about virtually everything. Vera had no time for such things and my father was very worried about what I might get involved with. The prospect scared me too. Instead I spent nine miserable months at a smart secretarial college in South Kensington, which eventually redeemed itself by getting me a job at the BBC because someone on the staff knew someone in their personnel department.

In 1971 I was in my first job, working as a junior secretary in the School Broadcasting Council (SBC), one of the BBC's more remote outposts. It had many such administrative departments to support programme-making. The BBC in those days was a vast, sprawling empire, with departments all over London and the rest of the UK, as well as overseas. Its very size was both inspiring and intimidating. No one seemed to know quite how it worked but on the whole it was a happy place if you didn't pay too much attention to the management. It was notorious for its civil service bureaucracy, initialised job titles and acronyms, but was serious about its commitment to public service and generally took care of its staff. I was lucky to get a job there, and always felt proud to walk over the zebra crossing to the main entrance of Broadcasting House, and to pass through the heavy front doors beneath the statue of Prospero and Ariel.

The SBC was the policy-making and advisory body for the BBC's TV and radio schools programmes. Its officers were educationalists and former teachers, each of whom was supported by at least one secretary and other clerical staff – I think there were about fifteen of them altogether. There was a clear division between the officers and the secretaries. They called us by our first names, we called them 'Mr' or 'Miss' (my boss was the only 'Mrs' but she had divorced her husband). Secretaries were not involved in the real work of the department, such as educational theory and how to interpret it in programmes; we were there to answer the phones, open the post, take dictation, type up documents and arrange meetings. As my annual interview with Mr Roberts (21 July 1971) suggests, it was expected that we would spend a couple of years in the post and then move on. So through the diary trudges a procession of disenchanted secretaries, permanent and temporary. This wasn't typical of the BBC, though: other departments, such as production offices, tended to be more egalitarian places, where everyone was encouraged to pitch in with contributions.

The SBC's offices were located on the top floor of the former Langham Hotel in Portland Place, London. At that time the building languished in a state of benign neglect, occupied by a random bunch of departments. It was a sombre place, with lino-clad floors and vertiginous stairwells. One office still had a bath in it! The cavernous corridors were filled with the sound of tapping typewriters, hurrying footsteps and trilling telephones. The inside of the building was shabby, painted in the sort of green that made you feel as though you were permanently underwater.

I was designated to help Louise, Assistant (Information & Recordings). Her job was to handle all the incoming letters and phone calls about programmes for schools and to run a small library of recordings (film and audio) for schools to hire. In 1971 the bulk of unsolicited correspondence related to the sex education programmes for primary schools that the BBC had begun to broadcast in the previous year. This had caused a furore that, despite the publication of a carefully evaluated report (the draft of which I so disdainfully typed in the February), continued to rumble on throughout the year.

January

1st – Friday

The prospect of having to think of something reasonably intelligent to write every single day this year to use up all the space in this diary is more than daunting. I suppose I'd better begin by making some corny resolution, the best I can think of being to eat less. That's not a good beginning to a diary, but it will have to stand.

The Langham was quiet and the SBC as dead as a dodo. Louise, my boss, is on leave and there are very few people about. Carol, who is secretary to Mr Jones, is thinking of getting married, and there we were, all pitying her inevitable fate as a spinster. Good for her!

In the afternoon I got some work done for Gill's boss. It was a bit scary as he is second only to Mr Roberts, the Head of the SBC. It also involved smarming up to the Copying Services woman to get it done in time. Anyhow, I got off early to battle home by train.

God, it's cold here in the Deep South! Still, a mighty supper warmed me up a bit. Vera, my stepmother, seems a bit low today, which is bad.

2nd – Saturday

At home with my parents in Surrey. The weather is on the cold side, with snow still on the ground. Cat looks fed up.

Road conditions delayed Vera and me on our weekly visit to the shops in Purley, and later I had to go back there again with Father to buy some wine (as I am the only one who can drive the car, any taxi duties fall to me at weekends). I let slip that I thought it would have been better had I attended a co-ed school.

Just managed to get into the public library before it closed at 5 p.m. and borrowed a *History of Coulsdon*, a lengthy tome of 29 pages, in which my former English teacher launches herself into print.

Father was in quite an intelligent mood, although I had to explain to him at lunchtime that not all Beatles' songs sound alike. He could only remember 'Yellow Submarine'! Taped pieces from my borrowed records of Copland, Barrelhouse and Boogie-woogie.

3rd – Sunday

Because of thick fog and ice, I wasn't able to drive over to Purley to see my old school friend, Georgina Fox. Instead I played records, and read Leavis's *Revaluation*, most of which was beyond me.

I listened to John Lennon on the radio talking about the break-up of the Beatles. Sad that the Lennon/McCartney partnership is no more – it's about the best song-writing team this country has produced, and neither has been so original on his own since.

4th – Monday

Snow. Got up in the cold, dark morning and walked over the golf course to Chipstead Station to get the train to London. It was eerie in the dark, and I nearly fell over. The commuters are an odd lot, all *freightfully* jolly. They come in two types – thin, cold and distinguished, or round, warm and fond of a pint.

Louise is still on holiday so there wasn't a lot for me to do today.

Gill [secretary to the Senior Education Officer] was back at work but busy, so I had lunch with Adrienne, who works for one of the officers. She comes from New York. As I am a fan of George Gershwin, I really wanted to ask her if she knew anything about him or his family, but I lost my nerve as I didn't want to bore her or sound stupid. I think we both see each other as specimens of a type: she is a New York Jewess and I am a solid old English girl. Her earrings and clothes tickle me. It's amazing how Americans dress – you can spot them a mile off.

For lunch we usually go over to the canteen at Broadcasting House, which is open twenty-four hours a day. The food is OK; their salads with chips are good. During the day we get tea and coffee from the BBC Club on the ground floor of the Langham; in the evenings they open up a bar in the rooms beyond, which smell of booze and cigarettes. In both places there's always the chance of spotting a celebrity; only being so close to BH, the home of radio, you find yourself ignoring someone until he speaks and then you recognise the voice. I've seen John Timpson from the *Today* programme in the Club, also Pete Murray and David Jacobs [Radio 2 DJs], and a few months ago I saw Cliff Richard talking to someone in Portland Place outside BH.

The BBC has lots of societies staff can join, all of them free of charge. I'm thinking about the Film Club. Gill and I have already joined the chess section, which meets every Monday after work downstairs in the Langham. Several tables are laid out with boards and pieces, around which various middle-aged men, mostly with beards, sit like cats watching mouse-holes.

Gill and I have a different approach. We play our games at two or three times their speed, and wash them down with a few glasses of wine. Gill is very good at chess, and she kindly pointed out to me when I had won a game. Her husband Kaz, a Hungarian artist, came along as well, but he is of a better standard so he plays with the mouse-hole men. He has a slightly nauseating sense of humour. Still, that's a first impression.

Back to the hostel in Francis Street, near Victoria Station. This is run by something called the Girls' Friendly Society, which sounds alarming. The rooms are strung along the corridors like prison cells, all smelling of disinfectant and boiled vegetables. When you need to go to the bathroom, there is always the possibility you will run into a shuffling old woman with bits of last week's breakfast down her jumper.

Each room has a cream door with its name in black paint, like Badges, Heartsease, Charles and Olivia, Peace, Hope, Suffolk Archdeaconry and my favourite, The St George and Hanover Square Bourdon Lodge Committee. My room is called Robinson. It has a bed, a small wardrobe and chest and my little bookcase, and is so narrow that I can stand with my arms outstretched and touch both the side walls.

5th – Tuesday

Got a prospectus from the City Literary Institute. Decided to leave it until the Whitsun term as I seem to be too late for the current series of classes.

Did some work for Miss Handley in the Publications Office. She must be about forty and is quite funny. She's pleasant-looking, but her eyes never seem to be firmly fixed into her face. She keeps saying how I am being so helpful, but actually I am just pleased to have something to do. Or maybe she is simply being polite.

Lunch with Gill and Adrienne, then went shopping with Gill in British Home Stores.

In the evening I went to the cinema to see *Start the Revolution Without Me* with a couple of old school friends. One of them is going to work at the British Film Institute in the stills archives. Funny, because that's the sort of job I would like to do, but I'm probably better off in the long run at the BBC. I might leave the SBC in a year or so – I don't think it would be healthy for me to stay for too long. I might die of boredom.

6th – Wednesday

As neither of the two girls I know at the hostel, Liz and Meg, were up and I felt unable to face a hostel breakfast without them, I walked to work from Victoria to Portland Place. Execution thereof not perfect as I got lost just north of the Burlington Arcade and missed both the Malls.

Today, I was given some work by Miss Sharp, who is Louise's boss. She constantly generates letters, memos and especially 'aide-memoires' to be dictated to whoever is avail-able, with little regard to the time of day or anything the secretary might already have in her in-tray. She is always the first in, in the morning, and the last to go home at night. However, I didn't object to working for her today as it gave me something to do.

At lunchtime Gill and I went shopping but all the clothes at the moment are in pink, mauve or grey. They are the same colours as Vera's fruit puddings.

Went to Charing Cross Library and borrowed an LP by Louis Armstrong and Pergolesi's *Stabat Mater*, stopping off to inspect the grubby little record shop nearby. I suppose the crime rate will have increased so much in a few years that it will be impossible to visit Soho in the dark, so I'd better make the most of it now.

On my return to the hostel I had a laugh with Meg and Liz about Miss Axe, the incredibly thin woman who is in charge of the hostel canteen. We reckon she is kept deliberately thin because she's put on a set of scales and weighed against the portions of food for each meal. That way they keep the food bills down.

7th – Thursday

Read the telephone directory. 'Religious Organisations' in the Yellow Pages is always worth a look. Typed a letter to an old school friend and then got into a panic because I left it in the machine while collecting work from Miss Sharp's office. I hope nobody read it, as it included some choice remarks about my colleagues.

Two hot chocolate drinks from the vending machine on the fourth floor. Duncan from the Recordings Library appeared in the office to regale me with tales of how he got a bloke drunk and started a fight with him. Poor lad, he is the only boy in an all-female department so I suppose he has to show off a bit.

At the hostel, Meg and I chatted about her boyfriend. She said I have the tastes of an older person, which made me laugh.

8th – Friday

Breakfast with Meg in the hostel, consisting of tea only because the food was, as usual, inedible. The bacon was grey.

Despite warnings that the heating would be off due to the oil strike [an unofficial tanker drivers' strike in early January 1971], the office was boiling hot. Did some work for Miss Sharp and then spent the afternoon typing envelope labels for Miss Handley, who was very contrite about asking me to do it (well, she *had* to be). Miss Handley is jolly but has a rather soft look at times – she might well have been pretty in her youth.

Went hunting for shoes with Gill in the lunch break, but found none.

After work I went home to Chipstead by train.

9th – Saturday

Took Father to Coulsdon (what a dreary place!) and bought a reel of recording tape. After lunch Vera and I went into Purley. Listened to radio – *Round the Horne* – and watched TV.

10th – Sunday

Got up late. Had breakfast (Ryvita and Marmite). Played the guitar. Had lunch, cleaned the car; listened to the radio. If all that sounds boring it is because it *was* boring. Penny rang. She is now working at a bank in Piccadilly and not enjoying it at all.

I want something to happen in my life.

11th – Monday

Travelled on the train with Sue Moriarty. She lives in Chipstead and went to the same secretarial college as me. We only ever meet on Monday mornings on the train.

Arrived at the Langham to find my boss, Louise, back from leave. She is about mid-thirties, small, dark, neat and usually rather chic but today, at least until she had been to the hairdresser at lunchtime, she looked like the Wild Man of Borneo. She has been on holiday to Majorca and explained she only sent postcards 'to parents'. She was satisfied with the work I had done for the other people last week, and I overheard Miss Handley cracking me up [praising me] to her.

Miss Sharp was still generating masses of 'ORJUNT' work for me so Louise sat in her office, scribbling drafts. At 4.30 p.m. she said she couldn't last out the day without a ciggie. It was the start of the slippery slope, I warned her.

I rang the BBC Film Club as I'd been thinking about becoming a member. The woman who answered my call immediately asked if I would like to take over as their secretary, which suggested the state they were in, so I hastily declined and retracted my application.

Went to Chess Club. Kaz has failed his driving test, and thrown a spanner in the works of any re-take by swearing at the examiner, which made a colourful story. Scores: Gill 3, Me 2. Not bad. Got the giggles about 'mating with two bishops and one (k)night'.

12th – Tuesday

Woke up to hear George Harrison echoing down the corridor, very much hoping to see his 'sweet Lord' but it takes so long. As do so many things, George!

Louise has succumbed to the fags again, and admired my sheepskin jacket in a slightly odd way.

I had to check a long document with Gill for a couple of hours. This can be a very boring exercise – one person reads the original draft out loud, while the other checks the final, typed version. However, Gill and I made it more entertaining by imitating the voices of the officers who wrote each section.

Back at the hostel, Liz and Meg both told me that they are going to move out, which came as a shock. Liz is off to a flat in North London and Meg is going back home to Suffolk. They invited me to go with them to a dance at St Bartholomew's Hospital on Saturday. Apparently you just tell people on the door you are a nurse from St Thomas's and they let you in for free. No one checks.

13th – Wednesday

Finished checking the document with Gill, who will now have to retype some of it because, in true SBC style, Miss Sharp and Mr Jones wish to rewrite their sections.

As I had a dental appointment in Purley, I left work at 3 p.m. and headed off, reading *Photoplay*. It is cheaper than *Films and Filming* and has colour photos. I arrived too early so I wandered around the town a bit, peering at the old houses. So many looked sad and ashamed of their gardens.

My dentist is my Uncle Rupert, my mother's brother, so an appointment is a family as well as a medical occasion. He did a filling for me and then we came back together on the bus. He told me stories about the family including how, in the 1910s when he was a boy living in Purley, and they used to hoist a flag over Reedham Orphanage to show which university team had won the boat race, he would run upstairs to his bedroom to watch out of the window for the signal.

Can't imagine anyone being that excited about the boat race nowadays.

Stayed at Chipstead overnight.

14th – Thursday

Back to London. Louise was in a leather midi-skirt, looking a bit kinky. She told me about jobs she did before she came to England from Tasmania – market research, teaching – and spent a lot of the day talking. She sent me out in the late afternoon to do a bit of food shopping for her at British Home Stores. It was torture as I was so hungry myself. Didn't see much of the others.

15th – Friday

Work proceeded well but not so jolly as yesterday.

To carry out my tasks, I am armed with a stalwart Adler manual typewriter and plenty of sheets of carbon paper for the many multiple copies – sometimes I have to do as many as twelve! I'm really pleased to have the Adler. Gill, who is senior to me, only has an old Remington.

Louise and I have separate offices with a connecting door. Most days I take down Louise's dictation in shorthand and then I go back to my desk, read it back and type it up. If I can't read my shorthand back, I put down what I think she probably said. Very occasionally, I am allowed to answer basic correspondence myself, but we keep this between ourselves because Miss Sharp wouldn't approve. When we need more copies of something, I take the papers down to a Copying Services room on the floor above the ground floor called the Entresol, where a nice lady called Mrs Chambers runs off stencils or does multiple photocopies.

Lunch with Gill, another secretary called Anne and 'Anne's

little sister', who turned out to be almost my age and twice as precocious – that's what a Sherborne education does for you.

In the evening I went to Charing Cross library and then on to see my friend Penny (she used to work at the SBC, but left last year). Penny has a room in a flat overlooking the side of the Garrick Theatre. The scene from her window is strange, and gives the impression of having been the same for decades – there is a sickly smell from the cafes, flashing lights from the theatre across the roof, crowds chattering and a violin player busking in the alley outside. We talked about the SBC and psychic matters.

16th – Saturday

I am staying in London this weekend. Went shopping in Oxford Street with Liz and had lunch at the canteen in Broadcasting House (BH). Then down Tottenham Court Road to see *Paint Your Wagon*, which was a good laugh. Following this, we went to catch a bus to Victoria. Liz got on as it moved off; I chased after, leapt and did a spectacular dive into a puddle just outside *Abelard and Héloise*. A Swedish bloke offered assistance, but apart from a stiff knee and feeling a bit shaken, I was all right.

Later on we went to the dance at St Bartholemew's Hospital. Fairly quickly, I acquired a young man who seemed at first OK, although it is always difficult to examine your victim thoroughly, with flashing strobe lights turning him puce and music deafening everything he says. As things progressed, I learned more than I will ever need to know about car engines and pinball machines. After about an hour of it I escaped to the loo, where I lingered for ages reading the graffiti, but he was still waiting for me when I came out. Unable to shake him off, I said I wasn't feeling well and left.

Oh, it's hopeless! I'm nineteen. I've never been kissed (unless you count a peck from a spotty youth round the back of the village hall when I was thirteen) and I don't know any boys at all. Meanwhile, all the girls I read about, or talk to, seem to be on the pill and sleeping with their boyfriends. Sex is on the TV and in films and magazines and we're supposed to be living in a permissive society. So what's wrong with me?

As I understand it, these are the rules of the game:

1. Having a boyfriend is something that outclasses O- and A-levels, the Senior Sports Cup and a Queen's Guide Award.
2. In order to get one, you have to pretend that you are someone else. That means putting on make-up and wearing funny clothes that you don't like but they might want to see you in, and saying things to them, like how wonderful they are, even if they are totally dull (e.g. obsessed with pinball machines).
3. You also have to pretend you are less clever than they are.
4. And if you really fancy them, you have to pretend you don't care for them one bit.
5. After a while you have to ask them, 'Where do I stand?' I'm not sure what this means.
6. All the time you must remember that boys are only out for One Thing, which is to Have Sex with you.
7. You have to keep yourself pure for your husband on your wedding night otherwise no one will respect you.
8. You can break this rule, go on the pill and sleep around, but then you risk getting a reputation and then no one nice will want to marry you. There is also a chance you will get a disease or pregnant. Or a broken heart.
9. If you fail to find a husband, you will end up a spinster, like Miss Sharp or Miss Handley.

I find these rules bizarre and confusing, so even if a Nice Young Man fell down a chimney, I wouldn't know what to do.

17th – Sunday

Most of the morning was already gone by the time I got up. I had breakfast and went down to find Liz in her room. We did some sewing (oh, very matronly!) and washing; then Liz did some hectic packing. Meg and I helped her take her various bags and suitcases on the Underground to Turnpike Lane. It wasn't a cheap expedition, and as Liz couldn't afford it, I paid her fare. The flat seems a nice place but damp.

Came back to watch *The Six Wives of Henry VIII* on the hostel TV and had a quick nosh of yoghurt, cheese, apple and a Haliborange vitamin pill. No fattening food today.

18th – Monday

Not much correspondence for Louise and me because there is a postal strike [it ran until 8 March] so I spent an hour or so typing invoices for the Recordings Library because Duncan has left and absconded with most of the stationery.

Father rang up to find out whether I needed anything. He thought I was going to be at home yesterday. Of course, I didn't need anything, he was just checking up on me.

Gill and I played some thoroughly inebriated games of chess. I think(!) the score was about three-all so I'm slowly catching up with her.

19th – Tuesday

Bought two poetry books at Mowbrays bookshop on my way to the Langham.

Lunch with Gill and Adrienne. Gill and I were arguing the case that innocence is bliss and medieval man was nearer to God and therefore more stable and happy; Adrienne arguing with intensity against us.

After work, Meg and her boyfriend picked me up and we drove to Liz's flat in Hornsey. We took a circuitous route as we were caught in traffic. I was navigating, but as I couldn't read the small print in the *A–Z* in the dark, I sent us via Stamford Hill.

We met Liz's flatmates, a pair of slightly snooty girls who both went off to their rooms as they had colds (I said the flat was damp!). I didn't think much of them – they kept going on about their furniture being 'twendy' (I thought it was kitsch) and how the latest thing was eating individual baked beans off needles. Liz told us they wanted her to smoke pot with them. We left fairly soon and came back to Victoria for a drink in The Cardinal, next door to the hostel.

Bed at 11.30.

Glad to be in London.

20th – Wednesday

At breakfast Meg and I had a good laugh about the trendy types Liz has moved in with.

Spent the morning typing a stencil, somewhat hampered by inexplicable errors.

Stencils are a bit of a pain because if you make a mistake you have to paint over it with some pink stuff, wait for it to dry and then type over it again. (You can use nail varnish if you don't have a bottle of the right stuff.) Make too many mistakes and you have to start the whole sheet again.

Louise was in her Left Bank outfit today: black jersey, black midi-skirt with slits and an Indian incense holder casually slung around her neck.

Still no incoming correspondence.

I began to think I might be going down with a cold so I had oranges at lunch.

After work I sat in Meg's room in the hostel and ate more oranges while she packed to leave London on Friday.

21st – Thursday

Crawled down to a farewell breakfast with Meg. I said goodbye to her because I could tell I wouldn't be well enough to have supper with her and Liz tonight. Snivelling, snuffling and sneezing, I took a train back to Chipstead, phoned Louise and then sat around reading until Vera came back from the shops. Then I went to bed feeling rubbish and wishing I appreciated good health more when I had it. How could George Gershwin have played the piano to his friends when he had a cold? How could Louise's friend have endured *three* colds so as to strike up an acquaintance with a man she fancied at the Centre for Cold Research?

22nd – Friday

Father came into my room at 9.30 a.m. and offered me tea. Ye Gods, I haven't drunk tea since I was at school! Read a book by Auberon Waugh and had a chat with Vera. She thinks Father should sell the house so they can move to Dorset.

23rd – Saturday

Argued with Father about the merits of George Gershwin as a composer but then we never do see eye-to-eye on artistic matters. Cold is improved, but a skin problem has broken out on my fingers so I have bandaged them up. I think it might be eczema.

24th – Sunday

Vera and I went for a walk after lunch to discuss her Big Plan
further. We agreed that we would have great difficulty in
dislodging Father from Chipstead, even though by staying
there, Vera thinks Father misses out on a lot. It is callous to sit
like vultures waiting until he kicks the bucket, but that's what
it feels like.

25th – Monday

My cold was much better. Went up on a crowded train reading
F. Scott Fitzgerald. The day was dawning as we went through
Clapham.

Saw Louise briefly and was then pounced on by Miss Sharp.
Her secretary has gone sick and by all accounts is unlikely to
return quickly. She drove me up the proverbial wall.
Everything, of course, was ORJENT, and in rushing to get it
down, I performed some technical disasters on the typewriter.
In the middle of it all, while Louise was in a meeting with
Miss Sharp and a couple of the other bosses, a man rang for
her. I didn't know who he was but he said the call was urgent.
But I wasn't sure what to do. Should I interrupt a work
meeting for a personal call? I thought probably not, but then,
what if she'd been burgled? I didn't like to ask him what it
was about, so I played dumb and left Louise a message when
I went to lunch. Luckily, it was OK.

Chess Club score 2–1 in Gill's favour, with two stalemates.

Back to the hostel, but of course Liz and Meg are not there
anymore. I must meet more people.

26th – Tuesday

Walked to work, which took a time but was very pleasant.

I worked very hard for Miss Sharp all day, especially in the morning, and saw nothing of Louise, who is off on a course somewhere in Broadcasting House.

Penny rang Gill, who suggested we three go out together sometime, which I would very much like.

Met Liz after work in the pouring rain and had supper in the BH canteen. However, it turned sour afterwards, when I told her I didn't approve of her not paying her fares on the Underground. We wandered down to Oxford Circus and, although she told me I was being quite ridiculous, I insisted on buying her ticket. I don't know why I did that – actually, I think I just wanted to embarrass her.

27th – Wednesday

Still working for Miss Sharp. Louise asked her not to give me more work, but apparently I am asked because I get things done quickly.

Finger exploded in the afternoon so I hope this is a sign that it's getting better.

Lunch with Gill and Adrienne. Discovered that the latter has (a) been shot in the foot at a New York Chinatown New Year celebration, (b) lived with several men before marrying her husband, Doug and (c) is now twenty-nine. I thought she was about twenty-five.

Went to the library and then called in at Penny's for a chat, which was mostly about spiritualism but also our first impressions of London and how to be detached from worries.

28th – Thursday

Still labouring with decreasing enthusiasm for beloved Miss Sharp, now mistyped as 'Miss Shrap'. She gave me a load of work, nearly all memos. She actually dictates, 'FROM Senior

Assistant, SBC ...' each time, rather than just the message itself. Good grief! I know who she is! I haven't come across anyone else who does that.

Louise had been to a radio drama recording, where she saw Ian McKellen rehearsing *Henry VI*. Apparently they had trouble getting the right noise for a stabbing so they used a cabbage.

Didn't go for lunch but nipped out later to get Louise's antihistamine tablets for her.

It's a long way from the top of the Langham to the front door – you wouldn't want to walk up and down those stairs each time. Fortunately, there are two pairs of lifts. The pair on the east side are automatic and I used them a lot last year when Penny was working at the SBC because her office was at that end of the building, but since she left, I've changed to the ones at our end.

I used to be shy of using these lifts because each is driven by an old bloke, but Gill said I needn't worry. Had a lecture from Frank, the Irish lift man, about not getting married in a hurry (why me?). Mr Roberts asked me where my John Lennon leather hat, which I wear most of the time, came from. (He thinks it's Dutch.)

Went with Carol to the V&A exhibition in the evening, the press (literally!) showing of the costumes from the *Henry VIII* TV series. Had a meal in a Wimpy Bar; discussed various members of SBC staff.

29th – Friday

I told Frank first thing that I dreamt about him last night but couldn't remember what happened. This amused him no end. In the evening he tried to kid me he could type because he had sensitive fingers (!!!), while digging me in the ribs. But he was most sympathetic about mine, especially after the nurse over at BH had bandaged them. He asked me who Louise was – 'Is she your lady-in-waiting, then?'

Beautiful Miss Sharp was a little disenchanted with some of the work I did for her yesterday, and returned about half of it. I didn't think the retypes were much of an improvement. Felt a bit guilty because Louise and I are now insisting we have masses of our own work to do in the hope that it will stop her giving me more, although of course this isn't entirely true.

Louise talked about some obscure Polish critic who has a new thesis on *Hamlet*, which was a bit beyond me.

Had lunch with Carol and Gill. Apparently Miss Malcolm (Personnel Officer) told one of the secretaries who is leaving today, 'If you were getting married, I'd stay here in a steady job; if not, as you aren't, I'd move on.'

Back home to Chipstead.

30th – Saturday

Weather absolutely miserable. Did some shopping and went to the doctor about my fingers, but she was a right swine and told me to come back on Monday. Felt like kicking her teeth in. Went to Swinging Coulsdon with Vera in the afternoon, read *The Beautiful and Damned* and started *Herzog* again. There is a writing competition in *The Spectator*, which I would love to enter, only I can't think of a subject to write about and I don't think it would be good enough.

31st – Sunday

Listened to a recording of T. S. Eliot reading the *Four Quartets*, following the words in the book. I'm not sure I understood them any better afterwards but I like the sound of the language.

Uncle Ron, who is Father's oldest brother and a widower, came to lunch. Father bellowed at him in his usual banal, bigoted fashion, every sentence a declaration of war. He'd sweep dandelion heads off with an axe! He then vanished into the garden.

Vera and I walked round Chipstead and moaned about Father, not moving to Dorset, etc.

February

1st – Monday

No post = no work. Office deadly dull, and I spent the afternoon at my desk eating ¼ lb mixed nuts and reading Mr Jones's memos and files of old correspondence. The majority of the letters were about the sex education programmes for primary schools, which the BBC started broadcasting last year. It caused a big controversy, and Louise was brought in to deal with it all. I know we have to be very careful about anything to do with the subject. Some of the letters were quite disturbing, written in weirdly coloured ink. One even had diagrams, which were interesting to look at but I don't think they were very accurate.

At lunch we had a serious discussion about stealing from shops. I said I thought it was wrong in any circumstance. Adrienne and Gill both thought it was justified if the price of the item was exorbitant but Gill also said people should be punished if they were caught. I said there should be absolute laws; Adrienne thought there should be exceptions (e.g. murder is OK in some cases).

Trying to quash an affection for Little Frank, who has taken to not-so-concealed winks and profound stares whenever

I enter the lift. He is a really cute fellow, very cuddly and good-looking, but he is also shorter than me, middle-aged and walks with a Byronic limp.

Chess score: 3–2 to Gill. The last game was a disaster and I felt a bit depressed.

2nd – Tuesday

Weather still on the cold side and zero to do at the office. Gill and I took an extended lunch hour to formulate a complete reorganisation of the SBC. She told me Mr Roberts has a romantic history – he had an affair with one of the female officers. There's a scandal for you!

Little Frank, the lift man, was very chatty. He asked me with some awkwardness what my name was, where was Louise, how are my fingers, and how much did the apple cost that I bought in the Club for my tea. He is getting quite friendly and I find I almost quite fancy him in an affectionate way. He's amusing.

Walked down to Leicester Square to see *The Railway Children* with an old school friend. It wasn't as good as the book or the recent TV version. Bernard Cribbins and Jenny Agutter were both very good, as was the scenery but the direction and editing were flat and the end was dreadful. On the way back I got the blues over the absurdity of the situation with Little Frank. Crazy, but it is OK now, thank you.

3rd – Wednesday

The day passed strangely. Each Wednesday I collect free copies of the *Radio Times* for Louise and myself from the BBC Club office in Chandos Street. Today, Little Frank said he could show me a quick way to get there. He took me down in the lift to the Basement and, saying he wanted to help me, pointed out that the Goods Entrance goes straight out on to Chandos Street. When I said I thought Louise would have a fit if she knew he was spiriting me away below stairs, he said, 'Well, she's married, isn't she?' (Isn't *he*?)

The man who drives the lift next to Frank's is not at all prepossessing. He's almost bald and wears thick spectacles. We call him One-Eyed Jack. He asked me my name today, like Frank did yesterday. I wasn't sure I wanted him to know my name, so I said 'Field Marshal Montgomery.' 'Blimey!' he said. 'No,' said I, 'actually it's Stanislaus.' 'Sunny glasses?' he asked.

In the afternoon a secretary who works for the Nottingham Education Officer was brought round to my office. Apparently I had been given the job of looking after her and showing her around, but nobody had told me this. It was a bit pointless as she already knew how the SBC functions and I had no idea what to do with her. I was cross with Miss Malcolm, our Personnel Officer, who was supposed to have organised her visit. Anyway, I took her round the offices and introduced her to people. She said she would look after herself tomorrow (probably going shopping in Oxford Street).

As I put her in the lift towards the end of the day I said to Frank, 'Look after her, she's a visitor.'

'Oh,' he said, 'but it's you I would like to look after.'

Huh?

Supper with Penny, who is currently looking for a job, and Gill, and then Kaz joined us, fresh from further chess victories. Got sloshed on wine and laughed a lot.

4th – Thursday

As Gill observed, it was a peculiar day. The heads of departments had a big scare because the *Daily Telegraph* published a letter about the sex education programme, which includes a bit about masturbation. Then no one knew exactly what it said. Gill had a hell of a job trying to locate a copy of the programme so her boss could check.

Although I sort of know what masturbation is, I am not sure how it works and didn't want to say anything silly, so I pretended I knew what everyone was talking about. I hoped I might find out more, but didn't.

With no incoming mail, and Louise engaged in deflecting the abuse of self-abuse, I did nothing much all morning and joined Gill for lunch to deplore Miss Malcolm's inefficiency yesterday. We saw Thomas Cranmer (Bernard Hepton) in the BH canteen.

Typed a stencil for Miss Sheridan, and helped Gill to make up the nameplates for a committee meeting. We had quite a laugh rearranging the letters. You have to be careful with some of them, especially Dr De'Ath.

I asked Little Frank which part of Ireland he came from. He said Southern Ireland, so I asked him about the Irish not liking the English. 'All in the past,' he said. 'I lost t'ree brothers in the war.' (He meant the First World War.) 'Live and let live – and leave when you're tired of it.' He made solicitous enquiries about my fingers and was very helpful about coffee.

Went shopping, had a revolting meal at the Golden Egg and then came back to the hostel.

5th – Friday

Rather a slow-moving day. Did a little work for Miss Sheridan, who is the secretary to all the various committees. This consisted of getting copying copied and addressing things. Had a chat with Carol and Gill. I was going to the Albert Hall with Gill at lunchtime but decided against it, and we had a long lunch in the BH canteen, discussing her parents and mine.

Little Frank was in a joyous mood. 'Oh, me darlin'!' he enthused, giving me a huge hug as I went into his lift, which was a surprise to say the least. I was praying nobody would come by. Hearing I was going over to the BH Cashier's Office to cash a cheque for the weekend, Frank asked if I would change his pay packet into smaller denominations. I said I would. 'Oh, bless you,' he said, and beamed. (He pronounces BH 'Bee Haitch'.) He invited me to go for a drink with him but I politely declined. When I told Carol about that she looked at me pointedly and said, 'I must keep an eye on this situation.'

Miss Handley went down to the BBC Club at intervals to watch the moon landing.

Carol and I were chatting in my office when the door opened. We both jumped because we thought it must be Miss Sharp, but it was only Miss Handley so the three of us carried on chatting. After a short while the door suddenly opened again and we all jumped out of our skins. But it was only the wind. The Fear of Miss Sharp is a dreadful thing!

So I have had a boring week, apart from the chats with the others and fooling around with the lift man.

Back to Chipstead.

6th – Saturday

Rent due.

The house is cold and damp, and so am I. Went shopping in Purley, talked to Vera and played the guitar. There are pictures on TV of what look like Michelin men pushing wheelbarrows across a blow-up of the brain, but it is the moon. I have concluded the landings are devoid of romance. The moon, it seems, is made of dust.

Frank has crept insidiously into my mind. I don't know if this is fooling around or something more serious. I wonder if he has asked other secretaries out before, and with what result. Anyway, he is probably too old to cause any damage and I am more mobile than he is. Perhaps a kind man with experience might be useful.

I'm not sure where we go from here.

7th – Sunday

Wrote a song, went for a stroll, taped a record by Ethel Waters. Saw *The Six Wives of Henry VIII*. Took exception to Father trying to organise next weekend for me.

8th – Monday

Moseyed down to Coulsdon to see the doctor for five seconds about my fingers, which are still bad. She grunted, coughed and scribbled a prescription with her dark, hairy paw. I collected the ointment from John Bell & Croyden and arrived at the Langham to find Little Frank had had a haircut.

I told Louise I wasn't happy about the Nottingham girl's visit and she seemed to understand what, or rather whom, I am blaming. She agreed it had been pointless.

Saw very little of Frank, which was more distracting than I had thought it would be. However, at the end of the day he wished me a somewhat meaningful 'Good night'. Gill said that when he talks to me, he speaks so quietly no one else can hear it.

Chess a disastrous 5–0 to Gill (I wasn't concentrating).

9th – Tuesday

Not an exciting day. Saw virtually nothing of Frank, apart from him giving me a little hug when I descended on an errand at 10.30.

Spent a large part of the day typing the 'terribly ORJUNT' draft of a report called *School Broadcasting and Sex*

Education in the Primary School for Miss Sharp, which was an almighty bore, and then checked it with one of the clerks.

Gill was in a state of terror about going to dinner tonight with her father, poor girl.

After work I wandered down to the Houses of Parliament and saw Robert Carr and Barbara Castle debate the Industrial Relations Bill. It was a bit technical and I didn't understand what they were talking about, to be honest, but they were well-practised speakers. Ate a Kunzel cake and sang 'Jerusalem' to myself as I walked back down Horseferry Road.

10th – Wednesday

Spent most of the morning typing a stencil – I seem to be typing stencils non-stop of late. The one I did today was a list for trainee teachers of recommended books about educational broadcasting. Then in the afternoon I typed the draft for a Study Unit of the TV programme *Words and Pictures*. The final version will go into our Loan Scheme, i.e. the Recordings Library, with the tapes of the programmes, notes and pamphlets, so that it can be borrowed by schools.

Frank did ask me in the morning where I had been (so he noticed my absence).

'Hadja nose to the grinding stone?'

I had a ride down in his lift together with Miss Sharp, during which she apologised to me for the rush about the sex education draft report as it wasn't 'ORJUNT' after all. I avoided looking at Frank in case I caught his eye and got the giggles. It seems Frank is no more keen on Miss Sharp than the rest of us.

Spent the evening drinking with Gill and was joined briefly by Kaz. We ended up in hysterics about two drunken businessmen at the other end of the bar, who were arguing loudly.

11th – Thursday

Spent most of the day typing a stencil for the *Words and Pictures* Study Unit.

The Frank situation took an unexpected turn. He took me up to the sixth floor and, perched on the little tip-up seat of his by the door, started grumbling because his boss had told him he must 'improve his productivity'. Apparently it's BBC staff policy. 'So how can I create, or produce?' he asked. 'All I can do is work efficiently, and I'm doing that already.'

When I went down to get cups of tea from the Club for Louise and myself at 3 p.m. (my only break in the afternoon), he was talking about fire regulations; but on the return journey I mentioned to him that I had some of the new decimal coins and was trying to remember what they were. He said, 'Let me look at them.' He took the coins, pointed to each one and explained their value. As he handed them back to me he said, 'So, is that wort' a kiss?' I didn't twig what he was saying so I didn't reply, but when we reached the sixth floor he leant over and gave me a little kiss on the cheek.

I was surprised, but it was rather sweet.

In the evening he made a mysterious remark, which I misinterpreted as meaning he wanted to meet me after work, or he thought I always went to the BBC Club after work, or something. So I went into the Club and sat by the door so that I wouldn't miss him. I watched the television and ate a sausage roll and felt very strange. What on earth was I doing there? Anyway, it didn't matter because he didn't appear, so at half past six I gave up and strolled down to Penny's place. We talked about the possibility of going on holiday together.

I am having serious doubts about this Frank thing.

12th – Friday

I was awake from three to five in the morning, not pleasant. I was wondering why I'd gone and sat in the Club yesterday – that was silly of me. It was nice of Frank to kiss me, though. It feels as if I am in the middle of a Thomas Hardy novel.

I finished the stencil and told Louise I had seen Barbara Castle. In the afternoon she went off to an ILEA [Inner London Education Authority] film show, so I made myself useful to the other offices in the department by getting cups of coffee from the Club, delivering photocopying to the Entresol and collecting money from the Cashiers' Office. This meant taking a lot of trips in the lifts.

I didn't say anything about yesterday evening to Frank because I had obviously misunderstood something he said. I certainly didn't want anyone to know I had sat in the Club for half an hour waiting for a lift man.

Frank told me he lives in the Harrow Road and has a daughter in Basingstoke (no wife, it seems). He asked what I was doing at the weekend and I told him I went home to Surrey. I mentioned the problems I was having with my father, and Frank made some obscure comment about I can't help you there because I don't know about him. He wished me well and gazed at me as I departed. It was a bit uncomfortable, but it's a change to be the person who is being looked at, rather than the person doing the looking.

Came home to Chipstead to have supper with Vera. Father not in (thank God!) and I went to bed late. Frank said something about me going out with him at the end of next week, so now I have to worry about next Friday.

13th – Saturday

I drove to Croydon and collected a Mr and Mrs Holmes, whom

Vera had invited to lunch. Father knows Mr H through journalistic connections. They are stalwarts of the Moral Rearmament Association. Despite that they were quite nice, and not stuffy or priggish at all. The atmosphere was a bit stilted at first, but it got better. After lunch Vera and I took them for a walk to Chipstead church and back for tea. They left about 6.15.

Found myself thinking about Frank. Should I go on with it? Or tread water? What is he after?

House is cold and damp. Father sounded distressed when I told him I would stay up in London next weekend, but honestly, he doesn't do much to make me feel welcome when I am here, does he?

Have decided to take guitar with me to London, feeling a bit more inspired.

14th – Sunday

Nothing is happening, apart from the mortal wounding of pounds, shilling and pence. I like The Scaffold's jingles about the coinage. Sebastian Head, the 'Decimalised Child' on the radio, ties my intestines in knots. Ah, the 'killing of the shilling', like parting with the farthing.

Bored.

15th – Monday

Day went well. Had a chat with Louise about my parents. She said her father was as difficult as mine, which was encouraging.

I was disappointed to discover that Frank's surname is Browne. I had hoped it would be something more romantically Irish, like O'Shaughnessy or O'Toole.

Frank: Are you in love?
Me: It depends on who with.

He took the lift down to the basement and asked me for a kiss, which I declined. He asked why. I said, 'Because it's Monday' (bit of an odd excuse, I know). However, by the end of the day he was happy, being sixpence richer because someone dropped a tanner in the lift. Or should I say, two and a half pence richer.

Chess not too bad – I won two games quite well. I think the score was about 4–all, but Gill and I lost count. Kaz found a friend to beat 4–0. Everyone was laughing at the guy on the PA system in the Club and his exaggerated pronunciation – 'Cawling Mistah …'

Decimalisation not too bad. You have to check your change all the time because the people on tills aren't as efficient as I had expected they would be. Mind you, I feel sorry for them as I thought we would all be given proper instruction and shown what to do, but we haven't. The current joke is 'Two p or not two p'. I suppose we will get used to it soon, and everyone is having a laugh about it anyway.

16th – Tuesday

Weather turned colder. There wasn't much to do in the office, which was draggy. Louise not chatty and disappeared into Miss Sharp's office most of the afternoon.

The Frank situation is a bit more complicated. I didn't sleep well again – I only got about four or five hours' sleep. I told him I played chess last night and he promptly challenged me to a game of draughts.

I'm still curious about his surname, and said he should have been called Sinatra as he is often singing in the lift. He said I could always call him 'White' instead of 'Browne' if I wanted. I told him my surname was Shaw, and he said, 'Oh, like George Bernard?' and asked if I was Irish too. I said no, I had never been to Ireland. As for being called Frank, he was named after St Francis of Assisi.

When I returned from the Club in the afternoon, armed with a banana, he asked how were my fingers. The skin is peeling on my thumbs because of the ointment the doctor gave me. He asked to see, so I held out my hand. He took it, looked at me and said quietly, 'Why are you shaking so much?' I looked down and my hand was, indeed, trembling. I couldn't think why and didn't know what to say.

'What's the matter?' he asked. I panicked. It felt as if I was floating upwards into a space where the air was so thin all possible answers had disintegrated. Something needed to happen. So I smacked Frank, not very hard, on the face, made a dive for it and ran out of the lift.

Oh God! Head spinning, I got into my office, shut the door and thumped down on my typing chair. What on earth had happened? Why was I shaking so much? I don't shake ... It must be him, but why? How? He's just this funny little old Irishman. Terror struck me because I thought I had revealed all, or perhaps he would think I was afraid of him. It's so confusing. I wanted to do something but I couldn't think what. I'm not sure what is going on. Anyway, you can't go around smacking innocent lift men in the face, especially when they have been concerned for your well-being, so I owed him an apology for that.

When it was time to leave, I waited until I was sure there was no one else going down from the sixth floor and pressed the button for a lift, hoping he would come up to collect me. Which he did. As I went in, I said, 'I'm sorry I hit you.' He looked at me blankly as if he didn't understand, but I wasn't going to say any more about it. Anyway, I don't think he had any hard feelings because as I got out of the lift on the ground floor, he winked at me.

I think I have strayed beyond my depth. What happens now?

17th – Wednesday

Workwise, everything was OK – apart from Louise discovering that she had messed up the Study Unit.

Frank seemed quite nonchalant about yesterday so I didn't mention it again and we chatted in the morning about holidays. He is going into hospital soon as he has a plate in his hip, having fallen off some scaffolding in 1958.

At 2.15, I went on my weekly quest for the *Radio Times*, and was conveyed down to the basement. He stopped the lift there, but didn't open the doors. He glanced out through them for a moment, his fingers twitched, and then he turned to look straight at me. After a couple of seconds he stepped closer, put one arm around me and kissed me a couple of times – real kisses, on the mouth. I was astonished at first, and then a bit disappointed because I didn't feel swept off my feet or anything, but I suppose there's bound to be a gap between romance and reality. Still, I felt incredibly smug.

I had arrived in the adult world.

Frank:	You won't tell anyone about that, will you?
Me:	No, of course not.
Frank:	Only I'd be losing my job if it was found out.
Me:	I imagine I might lose mine too.
	(Pause)
Me:	Can I ask you something? Are you married?
Frank:	Yes, a long time ago. I'll elaborate in the future, I promise.
Me:	And have you got any other secretaries in tow?
Frank:	One or two.
Me:	Yes, well, I know the Irish.
Frank:	Bein' in a lift all day can be dull.
Me:	A bit like a morgue, I suppose.

Frank: Oh, 'tis better than dat. At least in here I see people, and most of dem are alive.

(It wasn't true about my knowing the Irish.)

In the evening Penny, Gill, Vera and I all went for a drink in the Club, and Kaz put in a brief appearance. I got back to the hostel around 9 p.m.

18th – Thursday

I woke up with a swollen left eye. I didn't want Frank to see me like that so I avoided him and went up to the office in Jack's lift. Louise took one look at me and said, 'Go over to the surgery at BH.' There, the nurse took one look at me and said, 'Go to Moorfields Hospital in Holborn.' In a corridor I waited there on one of those green cloth and bent metal chairs, listening to pneumatic drills and a march past by striking postmen. I saw a nurse walk by who sneezed, wiped her nose on her hand and then went on to deal with a patient. I wasn't sure whether to say anything or not.

I was inspected by someone who looked like David Frost's twin, had a sight test and then some other tests conducted by a nurse and a doctor. These were quite painful – they pulled my eye about and wiped cotton buds over it. When they had finished, I felt awful and burst into tears. They looked surprised, said I only had conjunctivitis and could go back to work.

Trotted back to the office and spent the afternoon working on some Letraset.

Frank was very sympathetic about my eye and Moorfields too – 'I once had to go dere furra paira glasses and bloody hell, I nivver picked dem up!'

He leaned forward and said conspiratorially, 'Dere are spies waitin' on every floor, Sarah. I can't kiss you today.' I wasn't sure I wanted him to kiss me today anyway, and if he caught anything from my eye, it would look very suspicious.

Gill told me she has found out from Frank that he sometimes arrives at 8.15 to start work at 9. She asked him why he got in so early and he simply said, 'Household chores. Syringe.' Goodness, is he on drugs?

19th – Friday

My eye has improved after bathing it in warm water as instructed, and no bandages on my fingers today (only Frank noticed they were gone). He said we both have tender skins.

Big scare at work because the *Daily Telegraph* is attacking us again. Finished the Letraset.

I had a bandage over my bad eye today so I looked like a pirate. Frank laughed at me and warned me not to strain the other one. I went down to the Entresol with some copying and he waited for me while I delivered it. When I got back to the lift, we had a little kiss and then he realised he had left the lift doors open, cursed himself and we had to stifle giggles because we heard footsteps coming. He shut the doors quickly so no one could get in and drove the lift away, still holding on to me.

He is bothered that people can always see what is going on inside the lift. It is what is called a birdcage lift; the doors are open metalwork and there is very little floor/ceiling between each stage.

'We can't go on meeting like this, Frank,' I said solemnly, much to his amusement.

Remembering what he had said last week, I wondered if he would ask me out this evening, but he didn't and I was a bit disappointed.

Had fish and chips for supper. Back at the hostel, I got talking to Zelda, who has the room opposite mine. She is a small, dark-haired Yorkshire girl, who works as a primary school teacher in East London. We played a fortune telling game of hers. The predictions were: I will have many lovers, marry someone on a cold day in November, the marriage will be precarious and I will have two children. Oh, and by the time my secret is discovered the situation will have changed.

20th – Saturday

Phoned Vera, said goodbye to Zelda and paid the rent. Took the train home, arrived 11.30. Vera seemed depressed and I have hardly spoken to Father. The house is cold and damp. Not sure whether to be bored in London or here.

I miss Frank – he's a thoughtful, kindly man. And of course he's sexy. Not sure what to do about it all though, especially as Friday on the Entresol shows that we can't do it in the lift.

21st – Sunday

Got up at 10 o'clock, having had a dream about finding on the bedroom floor a powerful magnet shaped like a large tuning fork. Attached to it was a flat disc. When I threw the disc it whirled around in an elliptical orbit and when it came near the magnet, the magnet vibrated strongly and I was afraid it would be too powerful to hold on to. Eventually the disc flew off on a tangent. The whole thing was done with my eyes closed and the walls seemed much wider apart than normal.

I would interpret this dream as referring to Frank.

Argued with Father. He said I should come home more often as the country air did me good. I said it wasn't country air in Chipstead. He protested. I said Chipstead was dull. He said the Holmeses said they liked it. I said they would hardly say otherwise, and anyway, they liked living in Croydon. Father said, 'Well, at least Mrs Holmes cares about Mr

Holmes.' I got up in arms, saying it was mean and insulting to suggest that Vera didn't care about him, which it was.

Father snorted.

Went for a walk with Vera.

22nd – Monday

Louise in good humour. Chatted with Gill about how mechanical and unsympathetic Miss Sharp is. Celia, the older woman who is secretary to Mr Roberts, pulled a fast one on the girl who shares her office. She got Mr Roberts to sign a note she had written herself with the instruction that their office window should be kept closed at all times. The girl isn't speaking to Celia anymore.

Frank is very interesting to talk to. He asked about my weekend, and I complained about my father being cruel and said he wanted to dominate me. Frank said that dominating wasn't necessarily cruel, and I replied OK, but in the case of my father it wasn't good for me.

'Well, life is more about give and take,' said Frank, 'and you must do both to be happy.'

When I got on the lift the next time he said, 'You know, probably your father loves you too much and is jealous.' He said it had happened to him with his daughter (who is his only child). He asked me about my family background and queried, 'Are you out of control?' I said no, I wasn't. (At least, I don't think I am, am I?) He told me to 'be steady'.

It was interesting to hear a father's point of view.

We had a quick kiss on the Entresol, and then he put his arms around me and kissed me, very gently, on the collarbone. As he lifted his head, we looked at each other and he said quietly, 'I will run all over you.'

I was a bit taken aback. I mean, I know about people kissing on the lips, but to have someone kiss your body is different. It was extraordinary, and wonderful. I had never thought about that before, not in terms of it ever happening to me.

When I had my brains back, I asked him whether he ever worried or got annoyed at working all day in a lift. He said no, in the past he might have done but now he ignores it.

> Frank: My only worry is gettin' to you wit'out being seen. Do you have a boyfriend?
> Me: No.
> Frank: Oh, so you prefer older men?

Chess 4–1 to Gill but close games (this score ignores one game in which Kaz played my hand for me and won in about ten moves).

Drunken men again in the Club.

23rd – Tuesday

Weather quite sunny. Spring has begun, I think.

Frank successfully put his lift out of action at 9.40, so that stymied any activity. Actually, it wasn't him – Jack's lift and the automatic ones at the other end of the building were out too.

Lunched with Gill, discussing the books we read as children – Mary Mouse, Rupert Bear, Billy Bunter, etc. Nothing to do in the office as the postal strike is still on. From 3.30 I spent my time reading files and wandering around the offices chatting to people, keeping an eye on the lifts.

On taking me down to the Club for tea, Frank said he was tired. He is supposed to have an hour's lunch break but the relief man turned up late so he had less than an hour off today.

'Dey don't care one iota, but I don't like leavin' him more than one hour.'

I found out that he is employed directly by the BBC, not by an agency, and he doesn't work on Saturdays. He also said he gives his overtime allowance money to Jack. I got the last confession under hilarious circumstances as he was holding and tickling me.

Me: What would you give up for Lent?
Frank: You.
Me: Impossible!
Frank: Ay, dat's true.

To enjoy the warmer evening I went for a long walk after work, down Charing Cross Road, Leicester Square, Trafalgar Square, Victoria Embankment and Victoria Street. It gave me plenty of time to think.

Listened to Beethoven's Violin Concerto on the radio.

24th – Wednesday

Went back to Moorfields for a check-up, clutching my current reading: *The Golden Bough*. The doctor examined my eye and said it was better.

Louise had a ghastly morning. She was blown asunder by Miss Sharp about something. When I went in to take dictation we talked about Esperanto. She called me a Conservative, which isn't entirely true.

More information on Frank … He ran away to England for two weeks when he was sixteen because he was bored with Ireland, but was scared of London so he went back again.

'I was a kid then, I didn't understand nuttin'.'

He is (I think) about forty-eight to forty-nine years old and a Roman Catholic (no surprise). He asked me if I was too. I said, 'No, I am a heretic.' 'It makes no difference,' he said.

He came up to the sixth-floor landing and hung around for

a bit 'killin' time'. As I was too, I joined him and together we leant on the balustrade by the stairwell, gazing down into its vertiginous depths. I said, 'I suppose you could commit suicide by throwing yourself down there.' He said it would be a messy death. Carol appeared, dispensing apples. Frank wouldn't have one but I did.

On the credit side, before lunch we exchanged a beautiful glance across a crowded lift, and after lunch, two kisses in the basement, one of which was interrupted.

'Huh! 'Tis all too open!'

I'm enjoying this with Frank. I love putting my arms around his shoulders when he kisses me. Although he is a bit shorter than me, they are broad and strong and I feel protected. Being with him makes me feel so light-hearted too.

Why the hell doesn't he ask me out? Please? Friday? (Remember last week.)

Chatted to Gill in the evening about anti-communism and elites.

25th – Thursday

Oh God, what a day!

I turned up at work early (about 9.10) and got into Frank's lift. We went up to the sixth floor and he asked how I was. I said OK, but I had slept badly. He told me he went to bed at 9, woke at 12, and stayed awake. He said he could have gone to sleep, though 'if I were sleepin' wid you'.

At first I thought I had misheard him and then that he was joking. When I realised he was quite serious, I was speechless. He sat there, looking at me.

Me:	But you're married.
Frank (shrugging):	It doesn't matter. Lots of people are married and have others, you know.

Me: Why did you get married then?

Frank: Well, to get married.

Me: Oh, that's very sad.

Frank: Why?

Me: It just is.

Frank: D'ye know what I mean about … sleepin' wid me?

Me: Yes, of course I do. Well, in theory.

Frank: 'Tis no great mystery – you get halfway and it does it for you.

      (Pause as I consider this)

Frank: And d'ye know how to take precautions?

Me: Yes, in theory.

      (But he is so much older than me. How can I point this out to him without being rude?)

Me: Look, Frank … I know how old I am, and …

Frank: I don't know how old you are. You don't know how old I am, neither.

Me: Yes, but I know how old *I* am …

At this moment, Jack came sailing up in his lift, singing.

'Tis payday,' said Frank drily.

After a bit more confused dialogue we finally agreed that we should just continue to have a 'carry on', as he put it.

I walked into the office completely stunned. Fortunately Louise was out all morning so it didn't matter that I couldn't do a stroke of work. Eventually I went down to Gill's office and confessed to her what had been going on and what Frank had suggested to me. She was very surprised, but gave me a few words of caution and then fished out a BBC sex education pamphlet. This contained the helpful advice that 'Girls should know boys get excited more quickly and think girls will go further than they will'.

I wasn't entirely sure what to do with that information.

At lunchtime I walked down Regent Street as I was going to a lecture on Queen Victoria at the National Portrait Gallery with Louise. I expect it was very informative but I was unable to concentrate at all, although I noticed Sir Kenneth Clark of *Civilisation* fame there. Taller and browner than I had expected, and he has quite a sharp nose. I must remember to tell Vera, because she likes him.

Carol is to be engaged on Saturday.

When I got back to the Langham, Frank was most subdued. He said, slightly bitterly, 'Why don't you find yourself a nice boyfriend and get married?'

'That's easier said than done. It depends on where you are, and who you meet.'

'Well, I'm no good to you,' he sighed.

He recited some old doggerel about 'birds of a feather' which ended up with 'don't cross me or I'll break you'. Also, 'leave to me what's mine' and 'I can't give you gold, I can only give you love'.

I didn't know what he meant by any of it and wondered if he was losing his marbles.

In complete turmoil I left work and in the twilight walked around Wimpole Street, Oxford Street, Regent Street, Anywhere Street ...

Why didn't I see this coming? OK, so we'd had a few kisses and hugs, but it was just a bit of fun. I wasn't expecting to be in this position so soon ... if at all.

Is it me? Have I been leading him on? Did he think I was a pushover?

Of course he's attractive, but the situation has no future. I'm not going further as I shall only embroil myself in deeper emotional chaos. If all he wants is a quickie, he can go and find some unscrupulous dolly who can handle the situation, not Granny Sarah. But if he can restrain himself and we can just have a 'bit of a carry on', remaining friends without being altogether more serious, then I don't see any harm in it.

He's a year off fifty, Irish, has a plate hip, is 5'2" with thick, white hair – but all that doesn't bother me. I like him as a person and enjoy the 'fooling around'. I like his good nature.

But I'm not going any further. It's wrong because of our ages and situation, because of the moral aspect and because the relationship has no future. I don't want to hurt or upset him, but I don't want to hurt or upset myself either.

I was bitterly upset this evening because of finding out his idea of me (largely my own fault for not refusing, I suppose) and his concept of marriage as a convention (oh, his poor wife).

'You know how to take precautions?'

Bloody hell, he is a Catholic! You bet he would retreat into his marriage or his religion if he felt I was getting too serious.

I wonder whether he *had* to get married?

26th – Friday

It's crazy. I went in early and found Frank and One-Eyed Jack chatting together about cars, Frank saying how expensive it is to repair them. I went up with him alone to the sixth floor. He was grinning away and asked if I would take him for a drive in my car one day. I refused, saying I knew what was in his mind and I wouldn't be able to concentrate. He asked what was in *my* mind.

'Sawdust.'

'Same as me then.'

In a somewhat broken fashion I confessed how confused I felt.

Frank:	Do you want it, then?
Me:	No.
Frank:	Are you sure?

Me: Yes, I'm not that kind of person.
Frank (with a haughty sniff):
        Well, *nayther* am I!

He said I should be careful because I have (apparently) a 'hot nature' (which I'm not so sure about). We agreed there was no harm in having fun, though.

Frank: So, where is it that you go home to this weekend?
Me: Chipstead.
Frank: Sheep's head? Where's that?

Much consoled, I did my duty at work, as Louise had left me drafts and queries to attend to.

I took some photocopying down to the Entresol and travelled back sitting on Frank's seat, with him leaning over me to drive the lift, jamming it once on purpose and then again by accident, which made me laugh, especially when he started singing, 'Dreams of love ...'

On the next trip, he complained of taking a 'bleedin' tablet, it stuck in me bleedin' throat'. I asked why he'd taken the tablet. 'For all sorts of things ... to keep me cool, calm and collected.'

Later on I had to go shopping in Wigmore Street for Louise so we went down to the basement. He left the doors closed and put the lights out so it looked as if the lift was out of action. When he kissed me, he slid his tongue in gently between my lips and teeth. I was so surprised I hardly noticed his hands moving all over me. In fact, I was pretty astonished by the whole thing and found myself holding him closer, gripping the rough serge of his jacket and breathing in a warm, clean, musky scent. Gosh, it felt good!

In a bit of a whirl I went off to the shops but managed to buy the right things for Louise. I came back in some trepidation to the basement and summoned the lift. Fortunately, Frank's came down first.

'Any complaints?' he asked as I got in.

'No,' I said, thinking he was talking about the shopping, and then realised he meant the kisses.

Fool!

But, thinking about it afterwards, it didn't matter.

We said a casual goodbye and I went into the Club, ate a sandwich and then went for a walk. I got lost in Bloomsbury. Walked back to Charing Cross Road and took the Tube back from there.

I think I shall go home on Sunday. I'm feeling very saint-like and swept along in a glorious halo of 'I'm only young, I love and trust too much.'

27th – Saturday

Some day; some ending to some week. I stayed in London today as I had agreed to meet Penny in the late afternoon and go to the theatre with her. After doing some shopping I walked through Kensington Gardens and Hyde Park, but was pursued by an inquisitive Kenyan-Asian, who appeared from nowhere and started talking to me. He thought I might be of mixed race because of my fuzzy hair. I managed to lose him eventually when we got to Marble Arch, having told him my name was Alison Brown, that I washed dishes at the Hilton Hotel, lived in Croydon and was going out with a friend tonight called Peregrine.

I was beginning to wonder whether Frank's challenge to my virtue had left me with a secret mark, invisible to me but obvious to all men, who were now invited to try their luck.

Walked down Oxford Street, had lunch at BH canteen, casting rueful looks at the Langham. Then on to the National Portrait Gallery for a couple of hours and met Penny for a quick eat. We tried getting into a few theatres and ended up with tickets for *The Winslow Boy* starring Kenneth More, which seemed a very safe bet. It was good actually, better than I had expected.

Certain I have strayed out of my depth with Frank.

28th – Sunday

Went home to Chipstead. Vera still miserable because of the old man. I tried to be good to Father but it was impossible. We argued about Enoch Powell's recent speech at Carshalton, and then he said he wanted to pay for me to have a holiday. But I want to pay for myself, so I can choose where I go.

I hate home. I dislike living in the hostel. I had nothing to do at work last week.

This Frank thing is just a bit of practice, giving me the chance to prove what I can do, convincing myself all is not yet lost.

March

1st – Monday

Got up at 6.30 for a bath and travelled up with Sue Moriarty. I found Frank already at the sixth floor, faffing about with the buzzer in his lift. He wanted to fix it so that it didn't make a loud noise, because it gives him a headache. Well, he did such a good job that it wouldn't sound at all above the third floor.

Worked all morning. Didn't see him again until about two or three.

Frank:	So, where have you been?
Me:	I've been hiding.
Frank:	Dat's what I t'ort.

I said I had had a lousy weekend and did nothing, at which he smiled enigmatically. We passed a bunch of men in grey suits on the fourth floor, whom he referred to as a 'pack of wolves'.

Louise has been to see a film with her psychoanalyst man friend. Called *The Music Lovers*, it's causing a bit of a stir. It's about the life of Tchaikovsky and stars Richard Chamberlain – improbable casting, if you ask me. She hated the film; said it's confused, degrading, corrupting and insulting. She reckons it has more to do with Ken Russell than with the composer.

Instead of chess, Gill and I went for a meal together in the canteen. We talked about my situation with Frank. She warned me that sleeping with a man changes the relationship, it crosses a line, and emphasised this by putting the green salt and pepper pots and the sugar bowl across the table.

'If you go to bed with Frank, you can never go back to what you were before. And you don't know how he will behave once it has happened, do you? You wouldn't want to be hanging around him if he had got what he wanted and then dropped you.'

It was a lot more interesting than playing chess.

2nd – Tuesday

Left eye closed up and painful. Went directly to Holborn Moorfields. The doctor took one look at me. He didn't say why but looked extremely concerned and said I was to go straight to their City Road branch that afternoon.

Back to the office. Frank very sympathetic. Discussed Irish accents, how those up north sound like Scots accents, and the southern Irish are more like Welsh. He has been mistaken for a Geordie in the past. As I left, he whispered, 'I'll see you soon ... in the dark.'

At the City Road branch I was seen by a very nice Canadian doctor, who examined my eye, photographed it and then took some samples. He gave me a bottle of eye drops and told me to come back again tomorrow at lunchtime. The tests were a bit painful and tiring, so I went back to the hostel and had a rest.

3rd – Wednesday

Father's birthday. Unable to go home because of the hospital appointment, and anyway, I didn't want him seeing my eyes like this. Hanging around in the hostel all morning would have been grim so I went into the office, not that I did much.

By lunchtime, when I went to Moorfields, my eye had swollen up like a fat plum. The nice Canadian, whose name is Dr Poirier, examined it and said it was healing. He told me to be at the Institute of Ophthalmology in Judd Street tomorrow.

Back to the office again. On the way I thought, well, I can't do my job with only one eye. The hostel is no place to be ill, and if I go home, Father will kick up a big fuss about me going back to London although I need to be there to be able to get to the doctors easily. So I worked out a crafty solution and appointed myself Departmental Dogsbody. I tried it out this afternoon. I ran errands for people, took copying to and from the Entresol and collected food and drink from the Club. It went very well, people were most appreciative and best of all, I got lots of trips in the lifts.

On arrival at work, Frank said I ought to cover up the bad eye, so I used the eye-patch the hospital had given me and ended up looking like a pirate.

Louise wasn't in because she had a sprained ankle. Miss Sharp didn't know what to say to me. Miss Malcolm, the Personnel Officer, called in and said, 'Oh, what a shame, you have such pretty eyes!'

Groan.

But they all seemed happy with my suggestion.

Frank was very attentive and sympathetic. In between errands I had plenty of time to chat to him. When I told him I would have to have some tests tomorrow, he was reduced to silence and went pink. Then he said cheerfully, 'Ah, they'll be havin' you on the table yet.' I asked if he would ever go back to Ireland to live. He said no, he didn't miss places or people.

'I'm a hard-hearted old bugger,' he said.

He asked me about Miss Sharp.

'She's not married, is she?'

'No, she's not that type.'

'Some marry and still manage,' he said.

Later on, 'Sharpy' (as Frank calls her) walked into his lift and as she passed him, he sighed quietly, 'Oh, me dahlin'!' She didn't hear him, though. I tried not to laugh.

At the end of the afternoon I was on the sixth floor, waiting for a lift. Carol came out on the landing as Jack's lift pulled up. She asked me if I was going to wait to go down 'with my friend' instead. I said yes. When Frank turned up, I told him. He asked me why she had said that and seemed quite cross.

I suppose I shouldn't have waited for him.

4th – Thursday

Right eye is now also a bit swollen. Went to the Institute of Ophthalmology in Judd Street, where I saw Dr Poirier again, and an older doctor called Dr Darougar. They took lots of photos, gave me some ointment and then consulted together for ages. They said I should come back tomorrow. Then they put nice round bandages over each eye and taped them down, which meant that I couldn't see anything unless I lifted up a corner and peeked out from underneath.

I blundered out on to Judd Street and made my mazy way up to King's Cross. Trying to read the directions for the Victoria Line was hazardous but finally I arrived at Oxford Circus, after an excursion to Seven Sisters.

Back at the office I disposed of the bandage over my not-so-bad eye and was greeted by the sight of a temp sitting at my desk, who had been drafted in to replace me.

Having brought him up to date with my medical situation,

I asked Frank what he would do with a million pounds. He thought for a while, and then said he would give 'some to me family, some to der haspitals and den I'd flaunt a little wid der rest. But I wouldn't go bloody mad and play der Great Oy Am widder cigars.'

He said that after he had The Fall in 1958, he was in Charing Cross Hospital with a brain injury – 'All der strange surjuns wit der bleedin' instruments, all der buggers came t'look at m'eyes.' I asked him how did the accident happen, and he told me he used to be a painter and decorator for Trusthouse Forte. He was working at Jew's Bar in Jermyn Street. Four of them were standing on a plank on some scaffolding, it tipped up and he fell down about eight feet, breaking his left hip and damaging his head.

He described the inlaid wood designs lining the walls inside of the lift as being 'alright for an outside lavatory' and pointed out that oil was coming in through the roof. He also showed me where there used to be light fittings round the back.

He teased me about getting the coffee and tea orders muddled up.

'Keep your hands to yourself,' said Frank as I left, 'See you tomorrow or Monday.'

5th – Friday

Went back to the Institute again and was seen very quickly. I have a severe and unusual form of keratitis, which only one other person has had since the 1930s.

Went home to Chipstead, bed at 5.30 p.m. Eye feeling sore and difficult; face swollen, ear, nose and throat painful.

6th – Saturday

Left eye opened in the afternoon. Up late, back to bed early.

7th – Sunday

Eye swellings down, so the medication is working. Feeling much better; washed hair.

Furious domestic dispute as to whether I should go back to the hostel or stay at home. Father adamant that I picked up the infection at the hostel and must stay in Chipstead for the time being. I think this is unlikely, because on the whole the place is kept clean and I spend as little time there as I can. Thinking back to the sneezing nurse, I reckon I got the infection at Moorfields, but I'm not going to tell him that or he will try to stop me from going there too. Anyway, I am needed at work – I have my Dogsbody duties to perform.

8th – Monday

Father insisted on travelling up to London with me as he wanted to inspect the hostel. I told him there was no point because he wouldn't be able to come any further than the entrance hall (men are forbidden beyond that point). And honestly, he wouldn't want to see the poor old ladies in their nylon dressing gowns and worn slippers creeping about the corridors. Nor would they want to see him. He didn't believe me, and so he came with me on the train.

We walked to the hostel and I pointed to the notice on the door that said only females could be admitted beyond the reception room. He wasn't having any of that; said he was sure I could 'get him in' to the place and he wanted to see my room. He was so impossible, in the end I left him on the doorstep – I had to get back to the Tube for the appointment at the Institute.

My eyes are less swollen now and feel a lot better. The two doctors spent some time scrutinising photographs and muttering together, and then I was taken into an office next door and introduced to a Professor Barrie Jones, who seemed to be the Head Honcho. He sat me down and inspected my eyes. For some reason they gave me drops to enlarge my pupils, and told me to report to Moorfields again tomorrow.

Back to the office. After solicitous enquiries about my eyes, Frank said his bloody hip was hurting him. I asked him what was wrong with it. He explained he has no hip joint – it has been removed and instead he has a plate holding his leg on. This explains the Byronic limp and the built-up shoe. I asked if that was why he had to do injections. He said no, he had to do those for his wife. She is diabetic and partly paralysed from a stroke so he gives her injections every day. She is also nearly blind.

That was a bit of a shock. So she must be heavily dependent on him, and his home life must be pretty restricted. He was chattering on about his family, and I was thinking this over, when I heard him mention that his daughter is twenty-eight years old. I looked up.

Frank:　So what's boddering you about dat?

Me:　Frank, do you know how old I am?

Frank:　No. And 'tis no matter to me.

Me:　I'm nineteen. I'm nearly ten years younger than your daughter.

Frank (Gets up from his seat, steps across the lift, puts his arm around me and gives me a hug):

You are too soft-hearted.

(Sits down again)

Anyway, 'tis nuttin'. I'm seventy-seven.

9th – Tuesday

Oh, no! Father has been on the phone to Louise, pestering her for information about me. She began by talking to him but now the novelty has worn off. This is so embarrassing.

I went to Moorfields again in the afternoon. I took a line-up of medical students. It was very uncomfortable as I had to have my eyelid rolled back and clipped so that it stayed put, but Dr Darougar kindly held my hand under the table. Then more photos. My eye felt so sore after that – the lights all seemed very, very bright.

More Dogsbodying. Is the world ready for my monograph: 'Life Has Its Ups and Downs: What It's Like To Be a BBC Lift Man'?

Frank calls the BBC the best holiday camp ever, because there is so much waste and so many people doing nothing all day. He said if he were younger (well, he wouldn't be in a lift in the first place, but …) he would cut down the number of staff, keep each department separate with only one or two supervisors. He thought about 12,000 BBC employees could be removed painlessly.

I asked him again about his hip, which creaks sometimes. 'I walk like Mother Goose,' he said, demonstrating along one of the landings. His left leg is shorter than his right and although his shoe is built up, it doesn't compensate enough.

We did star signs. I'm always embarrassed about being born under the sign of the scales, but it's worse for him. He is a Virgo (and that's a joke). He promptly asked again if I would go to bed with him. I said, 'No, you're married.' 'Well,' he said, 'circumstances alter cases.'

Huh.

10th – Wednesday

Frank was in a good mood, still working on that wretched buzzer; this time dismantling it by using the ash can from the Entresol. He hates it being so loud and in his ear all day.

He and I have been having some long chats lately, all hands off because I didn't want him to catch anything from my eyes. I like him more and more as a person. We've had some interesting and amusing chats. And I like his face and his hands. Is that dangerous?

I told him I liked the dark. ''Tis easier in the dark,' he said immediately, and then asked me how many different ways did I think there were of 'doing it'. I was at something of a loss here, and bluffed my way out, but I don't think he was fooled.

Now, I have learned an Irish word for people who are useless, which is 'Spalpeen' as in: 'There are too many spalpeen (or is it spalpeens?) in the School Broadcasting Council'.

Frank told me Jack once asked a man who got into his lift wearing a dog collar what he did for a living.

After work, Penny came to collect Gill and myself for supper. Frank saw us all and asked if he could come with us. 'Some other time,' we said cheerily.

He wished us goodnight.

11th – Thursday

Well, today Frank told me some riddles. The first few were pretty filthy: one was about a puppy, the next about 'the little hot water bottle,' and finally one about a teapot. These were followed by some cleaner ones.

Frank:	Wouldja be my lawful partner?
Me:	Wouldn't it be *un*lawful partner?
Frank:	Dat would depend on the parties concerned.

I asked him why he picked on me.

'I dunno why,' he said nonchalantly, 'why didja pick on me?'

'Well,' I said, 'if it's a choice between you and One-Eyed Jack, and he has about as much sex appeal as a tapioca pudding ...'

Frank says Jack spends a lot of his time counting his money. 'Perhaps he t'inks it's going to melt away or sometin'.'

12th – Friday

Frank told me about a time he played a croquet match with some woman who fancied him, or so he claims. On further enquiry, it turned out it was after The Fall when he was convalescing at Garston Manor, a Rehabilitation Centre at Watford. Then I heard all about his various scars, one from sawing his hand while up a tree and another from walking into a lamp-post when tipsy. More importantly, he is going to a hospital next Wednesday to find out about a hip replacement operation, which might happen quite soon.

He told me more about his wife, who is called Bridget. Each morning he gets up at 6.30 to dress her and do the injecting. They have a home help who goes in during the day.

'Consequently,' he said solemnly, 'I am nivver taking advantage of hor.'

At lunch in the BH canteen I had an argument with Gill and Adrienne about women working when they have children. Gill is against it. Then we got on to homosexuality and finished up with Irish republicanism. We were still on that topic when we got back to the Langham and spilled into the lift, where Frank's opinion was invited. He looked bemused and said wasn't it better to forget about it all? He seems to have adopted that solution because he didn't know much about Oliver Cromwell.

Went to Moorfields and the Deadly Duo were very pleased with my progress. Dr Poirier said, 'We're giving you some more medicine, Sarah. Whoopee!' While I was there, an elderly man came to sit next to me, having had some photos taken of his eye. When another doctor came to tell him the photos would be ready next week, he asked, 'And will you send them on to me when they are developed?'

Back to Chipstead.

13th – Saturday

Shopped with Vera. Saw the butcher, complete with false hairpiece.

Looked up keratitis in our medical dictionary. It said that one of the possible causes is syphilis. I wondered whether Father had read that.

Sat around listening to records. Even if I did decide to do it with Frank, I don't know how I would get hold of the equipment. I can't go to that awful doctor and ask her for the pill. Anyway, where would Frank and I go for the occasion? Surely not his bed, with his wife in it as well?

14th – Sunday

Bath, washed hair, listened to music. Had an enormous lunch. I found my mother's old copy of Mary McCarthy's *The Group* [a popular novel about women graduates in the US, published in 1963] and read the first few chapters. I remembered overhearing a conversation years ago in which someone said there was a sex scene in it, and I thought that might help to explain things a bit, which it did. Thought about Frank. He seems to know what he is doing, but he is so much older than me. And married. I'd be bound to get jealous if we went further. And upset. And how do I get on the pill?

Should I discuss this with Vera, or would she be angry with me?

15th – Monday

Overslept a bit and hurried up in the rain. Still being a Dutiful Dogsbody. Louise quite chummy – I do hope she is getting fed up with the temp who is replacing me.

Frank and I got along famously. Both in a warm mood.

Frank:	So, are you typing again today?
Me:	No, I will be in the lift with you, going up and down.
Frank:	Ah, I wish I was going up and down widja. (I punch him.) You must grin and bear it, me dahlin'. So, you'll come to bed wid me?
Me (with slightly less reluctance than last time):	No.

He told me more Gruesome Tales of Watford, of how some 'stoodent' attempted unsuccessfully to get a blood sample out of him, and about a woman in a black slip, who wandered round the place mourning a dead cock (snigger ... no, he meant of the feathered sort). He said he was worried about me but wouldn't say why, or rather he hedged.

He then showed me how to escape from the lift if it was stuck between two floors by flicking catches at the top of the concertina gate and the doors. I wasn't sure whether to trust him on that one, and couldn't imagine him climbing out through the roof.

Frank:	One morning, I'll wake up and find meself dead.

Supper with Gill – we've given up on chess.

16th – Tuesday

Institute again in the morning. Dr Darougar pronounced me much better.

Oh, Frank! We had some day. As I had the all-clear from Dr D, Frank put his arms around me and mumbled on about wanting me. We went down to the basement for a kiss, this time much more strong in a quiet way than before, and had a heated discussion about 'Was I sexy?'

I'm thinking I don't believe his boasts.

Jack appeared later in the afternoon with some brochures for coach trips, saying, 'Who wants to see the lakes at Killarney?' Frank reckons Jack has an inferiority complex. Says he spends his money on coach trips to places like 'Portsmutt' but doesn't do anything when he gets there.

Later on, Frank wasn't too well. Adrienne gave him a Redoxon, which did him no good. I gave him an aspirin. In the end he found some Panadol, which worked.

'It deadens everyt'ing,' he said slyly and suggested I gave some to Louise.

He mixed up 'prostate' with 'apostate', which was quite funny.

At the end of the day Vera called in at the Langham to see me. Frank was on the ground floor, closing the lift doors as she came by and they had a good look at each other. She said afterwards he looked pale and sweet and very short.

17th – Wednesday

Frank was off to the hospital in the morning. I managed all right without him. Just.

Louise remarked to me what a good-tempered man Frank is.

He came back at 2.30. I saw him downstairs and then met him at the Entresol. He said he is to go into hospital on

Sunday at 10.30 for the hip operation; he doesn't know how long he will be in for. Miss Handley came to my office in the afternoon to ask me for his address 'where to send the bottles', but I played dumb – anyway, I don't know his address.

Went down to the basement en route for the *Radio Times*. His not having been in that morning made a difference – I wanted him much more. I think he got an erection. I only found out what that was when I read *The Group* on Sunday, so it was a good thing I did – just in time!

It was odd, really because I wasn't expecting I could have that sort of effect on someone.

Me: They built lifts for people like you, didn't they?
Frank: And you.

Once he had calmed down a bit, he asked if I would miss him when he was away, and I said, 'Yes, I would. Louise thinks you're good-tempered, you know.' 'Not in bed!' he laughed and said we ought to take a room.

Anyway, I discovered he is one of fifteen children ('and I was in der latter half'). He hasn't seen his brother James since the First World War. He knows of eight of his siblings.

Terribly busy in the afternoon, and an older woman called Cynthia has now appeared to work as a temp for Louise. She has taken a fancy to My Chair and My Typewriter.

Frank still chuckling over the apostate/prostate thing. Threatened to alter the 'School Broadcasting Council' sign to read 'Skol Broadcasting ...' Oh, it's mad.

Gill and I decided that I only fancy him because there is no one else so I shouldn't make too big a thing about him. It will be interesting to see whether I miss him.

Went to the library and returned books. Was let off a fine as I had had the eye disease.

March

18th – Thursday

The weather turned wet. Cynthia is still in my office.

I told Frank I had not slept well because I'd been thinking about him, and he asked me something very odd. 'Have you been lyin' onya back?' he asked me. I said yes, sometimes. Afterwards I wondered what he meant, but I didn't want to ask. He said, 'Be careful, even der walls have ears,' and kissed me.

Frank: You know, somehow you have got it into your head that you fancy me.

Me: And you mean you haven't had anything to do with that? Honestly, I feel like throttling you sometimes. (Kicks door to lift and hurts toe)

Frank (laughing at me, hopping):

Look at you. You know, you let people do what they like wid you too easily. You need to step back from t'ings sometimes, Sarah. Don't worry about 'em. See, whatja doin' now is right. Maybe you'll be doing der wrong t'ing soon. 'Tis no bad thing for a man and a woman to be togedder, as long as he doesn't get her in der family way.

So, d'ye fancy any of der men at der SBC?

Me: Good heavens, no!

Frank: So, you'll miss me when I am away?

Me: Yes, I will.

Frank: And I'll be t'inkin' of you, how you are getting on, if you are in the Land of the Living.

Somehow we got on to God. Frank believes in a creator, because of the beauty of the moon, stars, planets, fish, and in reincarnation because he reckons there's not enough room for all the damned in the stoves. He talked about one small seed leading to a whole life ("'tis all a mystery'). He goes to church on Sundays and Saints' days (including yesterday).

He told me the Irish Gaelic for some phrases, such as 'Hello', 'How are you?', and one which turned out to mean 'Stop this gibberish' – unless of course he was making that one up.

I lent him my pen – he never seems to have one when he needs it.

He is going in to hospital on Sunday, and suddenly nothing else in my life matters to me.

19th – Friday

Little Frank's last fling.

Didn't see much of him in the morning, more around mid-afternoon and later on a little.

He asked how I slept and I said well; he said he did too because of his dreaming I was alongside him. He counselled me about not tying myself up in knots, saying sleeping with him would solve it, but I said no, it would make it worse and there was a difference between wanting something (and not getting it) and what is right. He said, 'Well, 'tis stealin', mutual stealin'.'

He told me a lift man at Bentinck House was sacked for making a pass at a secretary.

Why was he so sure that I wouldn't tell when he made the first move?

Then all the usual stuff about not being able to do anything with me in the lift.

Poor old Frank.

Late in the afternoon he managed very well, snatching every opportunity to kiss me on the Entresol, the ground floor and basement, and even down to the basement again for two very strong kisses. I think one of the cleaners saw us holding hands once and leaning against each other. Frank told me that while I was off somewhere the other day, Louise had had a chat with him. She told him she was quite worried about me. Frank just said how nice I was. I wonder if she was reassured?

Towards the end of the day I asked about visiting him in hospital. First, he agreed. Then he said no, because of other friends and family coming, and it getting back to his wife about a blonde floozie at the office. He said he'd phone the Langham Reception and let them know how he was, but I said I didn't want to ask them about him. Nor did he want to phone my office because Louise might answer. I said, 'OK, write to me.' 'I'm no good at it,' he told me. This last conversation was carried on despite being interrupted in succession by Miss Sheridan, Miss Handley, Cynthia and Gill.

He bought me a fruit juice and let me keep the change. I asked if he wanted me to go over to the Cashier's Office for him.

'No, darlin', I got all I need here,' he answered, 'and if you stay here any longer, I shall start swearing to God I love you.'

The last I saw of him, he was out of his uniform and wearing his suit, ready to go home. We laughed about the operation. He said he hoped it didn't remove the 'more dangerous parts' and did I approve of that? I said, 'Oh, get rid of everything from the waist down!'

I was a little sad at saying goodbye, and told him that I'd miss him. I offered to send him anything he wanted; he said to look after myself and not to mess around. I warned him too.

A quick kiss and a hug, and he was gone.

Had a drink with Gill, who had been praised by her boss.

Came back to the hostel, had a Chinese meal and then read this diary, remembering all that had happened between Frank and myself.

Six to eight weeks, he said. It's a long time but it could be worse. Perhaps it won't be too bad and by next Tuesday I will be over the worst of missing him. I hope he writes or does something. The last couple of weeks, because we were constantly seeing each other, we have become much closer. Perhaps it's just as well that he is gone awhile. Away from him I can say you've gone too far already, but when he's there it's difficult. Is Frank right about it being better after you've had sex? Once it was done, he might want nothing more to do with me.

Oh dear! When you want someone you don't get asked, and when you know you should refuse someone, he asks you.

I slept well, after a while of mixed crying, thinking, wanting and quiet.

I feel more strongly for him than I realised. Before it was just an attraction and didn't mean much, but thinking about everything that's happened, about what he's said, about us being courting in a way and his wanting me, I think I love him. I wonder if he will miss me more than he wanted to let on.

(Underneath is written 'What rubbish 13th April 1971')

20th – Saturday

Stayed in bed until 10.30 thinking of Frank nearly all, no, most of the time. Had a bath and decided my legs aren't as bad as all that ('You're firm'). I took Zelda, who has the room opposite mine, to the BBC canteen, ate lunch and we went hunting along Oxford Street for boots and other shopping. We went into British Home Stores and sprayed ourselves liberally with perfume testers.

Caught the bus back, ate supper at the hostel, then went to Penny's. All three of us went to see the film, *Ryan's Daughter*. So why would I be wanting to watch a film shot in the beautiful old Kingdom of Kerry? I thought the symbolism in the photography was terribly overdone and the story very contrived, but who cares when there's lots of Irish accents, heroic disfigurement and characters limping about dramatically? Robert Mitchum's voice reminded me a little of Frank, so in places I closed my eyes and dreamed.

Back at the hostel, Zelda and I wondered whether you wanted sex more once you have had it the first time, and what the emotional pitfalls might be if you did. If Frank had heard us he would have been chuckling. And the whole day was coloured by him and the fact that I miss him.

21st – Sunday

(Frank into hospital at 10.30)

Up about 9.30, put myself on a train home. (Home?) Miserable weather.

I needed to talk to Vera. I began by telling her Frank's story about the Bentinck House lift man. She said, and I agreed with her, that sleeping with Frank was out of the question. She could see why I was attracted to him, as he was kind, gentle, amusing and 'knew his onions', and she understood something is better than nothing, and it's good to have someone to 'warm your thoughts on'.

'There is no harm in having fun,' she said, 'but don't go too far.'

She explained that a lot of his reasons for why we should go ahead are typically male. Although the age/class/religious differences aren't problems at the moment, they would begin to count if things went on longer, or became more serious. She said it would be a blind alley.

'Anyway, the more you are involved with him, the more likely it is people will begin to notice. It would be hard to keep it from Father. And if Frank lost his job, how would you feel?'

Vera's right: I can see there is no future for me with Frank. It would be sad for both of us and worse for me than for him. The trouble is, I don't know where to draw the line. I'm not even really sure how 'far' we've gone in the sense of, how much further is there to go?

I said maybe we will feel differently about each other when he comes back from hospital.

'I doubt it,' Vera told me.

We talked about ideas for holidays, and she suggested I might like to go with a company called Active Holidays (A.H.) on a walking holiday on the Isle of Wight.

I miss Frank.

God help me now.

22nd – Monday

Back to work. No more Dogsbodying. Proper office work again and I was typing accurately without knowing how. Cynthia was still in the office but I rescued my chair and typewriter; she retreated to the other side of the desk with the old stuff.

Louise came in for a chat about the sex education report, which was nice of her. She explained how many children don't get sex education at home but primary school children were maturing earlier and there was so much more attention paid to sex in the media. She said the level of ignorance about sex among even teenagers was worrying. I agreed. So it is surprising how many people have objected and criticised us for making the programmes.

Lunch with Celia and Gill, discussing the report, God and moral attitudes. The morning went quickly but the afternoon took a bit of killing.

Went for supper with Gill, and I told her Louise had referred to Frank as 'such a nice little man' (little does she know). Gill agreed with what Vera had said to me yesterday.

Back at the hostel I was talking to Zelda about the idea of Vera's that I might go on a walking holiday on the Isle of Wight. Zelda immediately asked if she could come with me. I'm not quite sure I want to go on holiday with Zelda, but could hardly say no.

Yes, I did miss Frank, but not so much as I feared I would. It did seem odd that there was another man driving his lift. This bloke managed for an hour or so until he took the lift over the top at the sixth floor and jammed it, so it was out of action for several hours until an engineer came to fix it.

23rd – Tuesday

Miss Handley and Carol called in together during the afternoon. Handley said casually, 'Oh, the little white one is in hospital,' which I ignored, while Carol fixed me with a blazing stare. Then Carol asked if I was being secretive about anything ... Was I about to leave, or was I heartbroken?

I ignored both of them.

I missed him. At times I can forget him but I know something's gone and life feels poorer for it.

Met my cousin Sue after work. We ate at the Old Kentucky in the Haymarket and went to the Leicester Square Ritz to see *Country Dance*. At least Peter O'Toole enjoyed it. I told her I was involved with a married man, and she said, 'Oh no, don't do that!' Then the film started.

Louise said it was OK for me to go on holiday in August, and I can take another week plus time off at Christmas.

24th – Wednesday

Overslept in the morning, having had a weird dream about Frank which seemed to reconcile everything, but I can't remember how. Rushed to the office and was very busy with masses of phoning and typing.

As today was when Frank's operation was scheduled, I went to the Reception Desk in the afternoon and dutifully asked the woman there if she had heard anything. 'No, but we understand there is no cause for concern,' she replied loftily. She made it sound like I'd asked about a bomb threat.

Jack said he would find out which ward Frank is in.

Vera had been shopping in London and called in after work. We had a coffee together in the Club. She said she has been thinking about the Frank thing. 'You'll have to play it very cool with him when he gets back,' she said, 'and look for another job outside the Langham.' She reckoned he's been a bit cheeky, considering his age, and said his take-life-as-it-comes attitude is very Irish.

I walked back to the hostel and wrote a short letter to Frank, saying I was missing him and hoping he was OK, then a couple more to old school friends.

25th – Thursday

I went to Mowbrays first thing and bought a 'Get Well' card for Frank so I could enclose the letter in something. But it went no further because Jack announced to everyone that he was going to visit Frank tonight, and Adrienne suggested at lunch that we all signed a card for him, which met with general approval. Adrienne and I went down to Mowbrays and chose another card together, which we then took round the sixth floor and got everyone to sign. Miss Handley wrote an odd remark in it about not going down to the basement, which I endorsed. We gave the card to Jack.

I was riddled with jealousy that Jack was going to see him, but not worried about Handley's comment. I would be surprised if she has had the same experiences in the basement as I have had.

My challenge today was to find out the date for Good Friday in 1973. I first asked the BBC Reference Library and was referred on in turn to the Home Office, the Board of Trade, Civil Defence, Lambeth Palace and finally Westminster Cathedral.

Cynthia, who used to be a journalist, told me that she once interviewed Mick Jagger for a magazine and found him very evasive.

Went shopping in the evening and bought black sandals and a cucumber and onion sandwich at Selfridges.

26th – Friday

A report from Jack was eagerly anticipated, and indeed he saw Frank in hospital last night. Jack said Frank is getting lots of visitors. Our hero was well and cheerful, although he hadn't eaten for a day because he is having the operation *today* (not Tuesday or Wednesday, as planned, which explains why no word from him). He said to thank everyone and sent me a special message. With bated breath I waited for Jack to reveal this to me. It went: Have you ever seen a coloured man with two white legs? Turned out he meant a black man in the next bed, who had bandages on both his legs.

I had hoped for something a little more romantic.

Louise said a visit from Jack would be enough to put anyone off an operation.

Lunch with Adrienne, Gill and Cynthia: Cynthia finishes today and we parted on good terms, having a laugh about a strongly worded letter of complaint about the sex education programmes. It ran over five pages and was signed by a Mr N. E. Knight!

Went for a drink after work with Gill, her brother and his girlfriend. I played dumb and ate too many potato crisps.

Bought a beef curry with rice from the Chinese takeaway and had a long talk with Zelda.

Bed late.

27th – Saturday

Woke at nine but didn't feel much like getting up until about eleven. Got back to Chipstead at about 1.30 for lunch and a hearty row with Father. His sister, Auntie Phyl, is coming to stay next week. She is one of the world's most difficult women and needless to say has asked if I will be at home when she visits; in Auntie Phyl language this means she *expects* me to be there. Auntie P. has never gone out to work, so the importance of my having paid employment would escape her. Anyway, I am not making a special journey home during the week even for her, and Father was not pleased.

Saw a football match between Everton and Liverpool. Pretty rough game, most enjoyable.

28th – Sunday

Considering the ideal friend, you always come up with someone who is like yourself. Which suggests that we ought to be our own best friend. Perhaps we are, without realising it? Or is this in theory, and in reality we prefer someone who is a bit different to ourselves?

Father, still cross with me about Auntie Phyl, accused me of being 'half-formed'. This is ridiculous! We are all perfectly formed as we are in the present, although we may be a different person in twenty years, or even one day's time. Some children are more knowledgeable and wiser than some adults. Then Father announced he is coming with me to see Dr Darougar tomorrow. Told him no, it was my business, not his.

29th – Monday

Father backed off so I went to the Institute on my own. Dr Poirier said I was much better – I had had a 'rough infection' quite badly, but it was now gone. I look forward to a starring role in his PhD thesis.

Back to the office, on my own again. Louise was in a good mood until she was asked to check some work for Miss Sharp.

'It isn't as if some people haven't enough to do,' she said.

Gill was upset because Kaz's friend, Simon, was rude to her on Friday, saying all she cared about was money, and that Kaz should be allowed to spend his time painting rather than looking for a job. Gill was annoyed and had taken it to heart, which is understandable.

We decided we both liked older friends (because we both have older parents?) and were overheard in the loo discussing the SBC by a foreign (Czech?) woman. She instantly asked how much we both earned! At least Miss Sharp didn't come in and start trying to dictate an 'aide memoire' while we were there.

The loos in the Langham haven't been updated since the 1920s. They are very basic, with white tiles, sinks and pedestals and heavy wooden doors – you don't want to linger in there. Worst of all is the toilet paper, which is terrible: rough on one side, shiny on the other and completely unabsorbent. It even has 'Property of the BBC' stamped on each sheet so you wonder if you ought to hand it back to someone after you've used it!

Saw Carol's fiancé at a distance. He was a bit of a let-down.

30th – Tuesday

Office in a rush because the sex education programmes are to be discussed on *Talkback*, a Radio 4 programme, this Sunday.

But they are putting on the Head of Educational Broadcasting, Mr Postgate! They should have had Mr Roberts or Miss Sharp, or even Louise, who know more about it, not these memo-scribbling idiots who never see the follow-up work or speak to complainants on the phone.

Adrienne has handed in her notice, which is a shame because we are just getting to know and like her.

Still nothing about Frank. I gave Jack my own card with the note in it and asked if he could take it with him on his next visit.

Went to Peter Robinson with Gill at lunchtime and decided it was all rubbish at stupid prices.

Went to the City Literary Institute after work and enrolled on a course called *Pop is the greatest!* At least at 95p it is cheap, and most of the people there looked OK.

Bought another takeaway curry and came back to discuss education with Zelda.

31st – Wednesday

Woke up from a nightmare about returning to school and finding there was an English A-level exam for which I had done no revision.

Jack went to see Frank last night. He's had the operation and was in absolute agony for two days, but is more comfortable and feeling much better now. Poor man! I missed him today, about as much as I have ever done. I really want his sexy humour back again. I keep on hoping for a letter, but rationally, I shouldn't expect one.

The office was busy, though. Louise went to the Education Officers' meeting and was lumbered with taking the minutes.

It was hectic about *Talkback*. Some woman, I don't know where from, came to look at the filmstrip and publications for the primary sex ed programmes, and a woman from the

DES [Department of Education and Science] rang about the sex ed report, which was terrifying as everyone was in the meeting. Anyway, Gill helped me sort it out.

Had supper at BH (salad and milk).

Here is my *Desert Island Discs* choice of eight records:

Britten – Down By the Salley Gardens
Gershwin – Second Prelude
Bach – St Matthew Passion opening bit
Beatles – 'A Day In The Life'
Mozart – Clarinet Concerto
Alec Guinness reading T. S. Eliot's *Four Quartets*
Glenn Miller – 'Sunrise Serenade'
Bernstein – Overture to Candide

April

1st – Thursday

Louise had gone out and left me some stuff recorded on a Dictaphone, which I HATE! When you start transcribing from it, you don't know how long the letter is going to be and where to begin typing on the page and, because you're hearing a voice instead of reading back shorthand, you spell words as they are said rather than as they are written. Also, I really dislike having those little insect-like things in my ears. Ugh!

Masses of work, kept myself busy anyway.

Gill told me Miss Handley had been asking whether I had heard from Frank. Sounded suspicious. I mean, I haven't heard anything more than anyone else has, apart from the crack about the man in the bandages.

Another panic. The printers of the sex education report phoned Miss Sharp to say they couldn't use purple ink for the cover because it was the same colour as the one used on packets of condoms. Miss Sharp asked Mr Jones if that was the case. He said, 'So it seems' (i.e. he probably didn't know). So Miss Sharp went round the offices asking other men if this was true, but apparently she only got evasive answers.

2nd – Friday

Spent a happy, if busy, day at work, filing pamphlets and being given masses of stuff to do in the afternoon.

Louise found an article about Siamese twins, in which a small boy said, 'It's a pity; they can't give each other unexpected Christmas presents.'

Gill said she'd forgotten about Frank. Lucky her.

Came home to find Vera with a dreadfully sore throat, eye trouble, tired and depressed. She seemed exhausted. Diagnosed Auntie Phyl. The wretched woman dotes on Father, always has done. She created a lot of extra work, sided with Father over everything and treated Vera like a paid help. As for me, Auntie P told Father, 'In stories, nice nieces always come home to see their Aunties.'

Bloody hell! She's enough to make me a communist.

Saw an interview with Doris Lessing, who gives our civilisation ten more years and didn't seem too concerned about it. That was enough to turn me into a Conservative.

3rd – Saturday

Can't understand the money situation. It seems either I have £66 or £127 in the bank, but I'm not sure which. Anyway, spent £4 on a pair of shoes. Vera's throat not good, Father now down with a cold as well. Bravo, Auntie, you've done for them both in one visit.

Puzzled over the chequebook; played guitar. Saw the Grand National and the Eurovision Song Contest (won by Monaco). Took Father on a fruitless hunt for the last post, having missed it at both Coulsdon and Purley. He suggested I 'got my hooks' into Gill's brother.

My God! I'll fry my own fish, thanks. Besides, I don't fancy him – well, I hardly know him. And Little Frank is languishing in hospital.

4th – Sunday

Spent the whole afternoon on two and a half verses of a not very melodious tune and unsatisfactory words. No prizes for guessing the subject.

*I dreamed of loving, but this time it's real, and the
    waking is deeper than wishing,
The have has been given, the sharing is we, and though
    the miseries in life seldom die,
I'm hung on you, so hung on you I let you break the
    rules for the game was so new,
We took the moment life gave us for using like anybody
    losing a lonesome tune;
There were misunderstandings, some came by surprise,
    both living a present the past had denied;
And silently you took your prize, and the only man I
    care about is you.*

*Your past is filled and my future is free, and I don't
    want to be disadvantaged,
And if she owns your loyalty that, I agree, is more
    precious than your sad fantasy,
But I'm hung on you, so hung on you, that every little
    dream is a dream made of you,
You came, you wrote your name across my living, and
    just the same I'm giving all I have to you,
And since you've been gone I have never once declared
    all the mad, sad delighting that we have shared,
And I miss you, oh, I need you to know that the only
    man I care about is you.
And if you leave me, and you don't want to see me again,
Then you'll break me, make me lonely like I was if I
    don't know why so I'll only try to smile because
It wasn't your laughter, nor your satisfied eyes that in
    kindness confused all my half-made lies,*

*It was knowing you would be coming back to me, and
the only man I care about is you.*

I didn't want to include 'disadvantaged' – it sounds like an educationalist leaflet, but it was the only word that fitted.

Not much else to report. Test card weather (grey sky). Father subdued because he has a mild cold, mild because he smothered himself in eucalyptus. Feels like Frank's been gone for months, not two weeks. Something tells me it will be eleven weeks before he is back.

5th – Monday

Bank says I have £130!!

The trains weren't bad, even though a Go Slow has begun [it lasted ten days]. I left early just in case, and caught a fast one to Victoria, but it still arrived late and I had time to do battle with an overcrowded Underground. There was only one platform operating on the Victoria Line.

Louise and I discussed the *Talkback* programme and agreed the SBC case for the programmes had been well put. She is pro both prison and abortion, which confuses her anarchist friends, and calls herself a Liberal Fascist ... or a Fascist Liberal. She agreed that it already seems like Frank's been gone for at least a month. Miss Handley asked me about him, with a funny look.

Louise and I had a laugh about a postcard enquiry from Ireland with 'Guinness for strength' on the picture side.
Supper with Gill. Carol has been in her office, asking pointed questions like, 'Is Sarah missing Frank? She is looking rather miserable.' Gill answered, 'Yes, her eye is clearing up, isn't it?'

Jack is going to see Frank tonight, so I quickly wrote out a note and gave it to him to deliver. Sealed.

6th – Tuesday

Dreadful night. I woke up at 12.45 and lay in bed listening to Big Ben chiming out the quarters, reminding myself what a privilege it was to hear the passing of time marked by the most famous bell in the world. Sleep was elusive, so I got up and wrote a bit, went to the loo, sat in my chair and looked out of the window. It felt as though I had to keep watch through the night in the form of a vigil. For what? Of course I was thinking about nothing but Frank, and it wasn't until I began thinking about writing a song that I fell asleep, by which time it was around half past five.

Even so, when I woke again I had time to spare, so when I got to the Langham I went on an expedition. Frank travels to Great Portland Street Tube station every morning and walks from there to the Langham, so I went to look at what he sees, but it wasn't much to look at.

Ate little, felt a bit sick. Letrasetted an 'O' onto the office window to look like a Polo mint, to remind me of Frank.

Lunch with Adrienne; discussed Women's Lib. She says the movement isn't so radical and left-wing in the UK as it is in America, and in the Middle East to argue with a man is to imply you are a prostitute (i.e. an aggressive woman).

Gill told me she had a furious argument with a friend of hers about Women's Lib. This friend was married when she was nineteen to a man who turned out to be impotent. Since then her friend has had various men and an illegitimate child. Now she advocates communal living, saying most marriages are unhappy and we should abolish the whole system. Gill said she shouldn't use her own circumstances to say that marriage was out-dated when it has lasted for so long.

Jack told me Frank was OK and that he had given him my note. I'm not sure Jack understands what is going on, or he takes it in a funny way. Maybe Frank said something off-hand to him.

Anyway, after work I walked down Jermyn Street, looking out for 'Jew's Bar', i.e. the place where The Fall took place, and there it was … 'Jules' Bar'!

There were no lights on; not even the neon sign above the door. I peered inside but it was too dark to see anything. Too early for the party types, I suppose. I wondered how many people who frolic around in there would be aware that someone wrecked himself painting a wall for them? Then I thought I was being a bit melodramatic and anyway it must have been repainted several times since 1958.

As I write this, the slow movement of Beethoven's 7th Symphony is on the radio. It always destroys me.

7th – Wednesday

Luckily I slept well, although I had a splitting headache most of the day.

Gill was suffering from a hangover. Louise was very happy and speaking in a far more friendly and 'revealing' way – almost embarrassingly, to be honest.

Went for an expensive-for-what-it-was meal at the Old Kentucky and a chat with Penny. We discussed tape recordings of Voices of the Dead, and whether they were fake or not, and other psychic matters like astral projection and psychic drawings.

Leah, who is a new secretary working for Miss Handley, keeps trotting around after Gill and me. She is dark-haired and quite pretty, but says nothing at all. Is she shy, or dumb?

Miss Handley is still asking me questions about Frank, but I'm not saying anything.

8th – Thursday

Had a busy day at the office, folks. Finished the analysis figures and got masses of work done, letters mostly.

Lunch with Adrienne and Carol, and also Marion, the latest victim despatched from the security of the secretarial reserve into the jaws of Miss Sharp. Marion quickly summed up the situation and asked Miss Malcolm if there was anywhere else she could work, but was told the BBC has no other vacancies. I'm sure that is not true, in fact it is a flagrant lie. Miss Malcolm is probably fed up with trying to find secretaries who can cope with Miss Sharp, and vice versa. Carol reckons Miss Sharp doesn't want any secretary to stay for long because she would want to take on some responsibility.

Louise and I discussed Renaissance sculpture (she likes Botticelli).

Gill told me Kaz has suggested he goes off travelling with Simon for a month. She was quite upset and said it was a rubbish idea.

She's right.

Home to Chipstead for Easter.

9th – Friday (Good Friday)

Drove over to Reigate to see Uncle Rupert, who was busy rebuilding a tape recorder in his pyjamas (if you see what I mean). Talked to him about records, cars, the Isle of Wight and so on.

Home for lunch. Wrote letters, played guitar and saw Verdi's Requiem on TV, conducted by Bernstein.

10th – Saturday

A discussion over lunch about what we would do if we won the Premium Bonds. Vera said she would buy a cottage and give some money to two of her close friends, Grace and Phyl.

'Grace who?' asked Father, knowing full well who she means. Vera glared at him. Then Father said hers was a stupid idea because the fastest way to lose a friend is by giving them something. 'Most people,' he went on, 'are very ungrateful. Look at Charles de Gaulle, we did everything for him in the war and he has hated us ever since.'

From memory, I thought it unlikely that either of Vera's friends behaved like General de Gaulle, so I said, 'Maybe only *some* people are ungrateful when you help them.'

Father said, 'You don't know what you are talking about.'

'Perhaps,' I said, 'you have mixed with some very strange people?'

We ended up shouting at each other.

Unable to stick it in the house any longer, I went out for a walk. Halfway round the village, I realised, with brutal clarity, what it is that Frank wants to do with me. I wondered what it might feel like for two people to be that close, and whether it was what I wanted to do with him, or even with anyone else, ever.

I have been thinking about it all as it being Frank's responsibility – he was the one who started it, he came after me, and so on. However, that's not the whole story. I am involved in this too. I could have reported him, but I didn't. When he gets back to work, I could avoid him – I could use the stairs or go with Jack. Frank would just have to sit in his lift, as he does, like a bird in a cage. I'd have to put up with people asking me why I was avoiding him, though. To be honest, it feels as if I have gone past the stage when I could avoid him. It's as if that's not an option anymore.

I started this because I was curious; because it was fun and flattering to be kissed, and so on. I never foresaw that it would go this far, or that I would feel as much for him as I do.

Vera is right: I must be sensible and try to simmer things down a bit when he gets back to work.

Oddly enough, she told me that recently an Irishman tried to pick her up in the park.

11th – Sunday (Easter Sunday)

Weather has turned sunny and it's quite pleasant, apart from a rather chilly breeze. Had a bath, washed hair and did the ironing for Vera, listening to *Options* [BBC Radio 4 arts programme]. Am reading a book about the Holy Grail. Decided I'd hate to have a churchy, full-blown wedding.

Both fingers bandaged up again; it feels as if I am riddled with poison.

12th – Monday (Easter Monday)

Up late, pottered around. Read *Room at the Top*.

13th – Tuesday

Clasping my mighty M&S tartan bag, I trotted to Coulsdon South and, courtesy of the current ASLEF dispute, arrived back at Victoria after a tedious train journey. The Underground was very crowded.

Busy at work. Louise revealed that at a recent meeting someone said that BBC schools programmes were too 'middle-class' but, when asked, no one could actually define what they meant by the term. I wonder what would happen if the programmes were described as being too 'working class'? I don't think sneering at the middle classes is a good start to a classless society.

Gill suffering from a row with Kaz, and more trouble from that Simon.

Jack said no news of Frank. I wonder whether he is out of hospital yet. So much of our conversation was virtually a send-up of a romance anyway, and then I go and take him seriously about sleeping with me ... Maybe he was just playing about, or he thought that I was the one who was only out for one thing? And here's me wishing him only good.

Had a lousy omelette from the Chinese takeaway.

14th – Wednesday

Overslept, having dreamt about Miss Handley playing the piano.

Louise overheard an item on the *Today* programme about the Finger Dancers of Tunbridge Wells.

Lunch with Marion and Valerie, the new permanent secretary to Miss Sharp. She comes from New Zealand and is very pleasant.

Saw Miss Handley and mentioned my funny dream. She said she did once play a piano or two.

Terribly busy still but eased off towards the end of the afternoon.

Back from the library, where I browsed through a book on Catholicism. I'd feel terrible if Frank and his wife fell out because of me. I can see in his eyes his frustration with the situation, but it is still wrong of him to want me. There is so much I want to say to him now.

Still no further news of him.

Listened to Beethoven's Piano Concerto No. 4.

15th – Thursday

Went up quite early; office less busy. Louise and I had a laugh about 'Pers. and A.A.' (the Personnel and Administration Assistant), which to me always sounds like a music hall double act. Miss Handley called in and continued our conversation, explaining that she nearly became a pianist once, but 'there was a war on'.

Gill and I went for a coffee at Fortes and ended up discussing Frank. Gill suggested that I should avoid him when he gets back, but I said that was not the answer. She was ever so sympathetic; she said I shouldn't brood about him.

Talked to Zelda at the hostel about the A.H. holiday and her evasive German.

16th – Friday

Weather turned a bit chilly. I have booked a holiday for Zelda and myself on the Isle of Wight in August.

Amusing lunch with Carol, Marion, Gill and Adrienne discussing names. We saw Kenneth More in the canteen, but only Carol found that exciting.

Louise spent most of the day checking the sex education report with one of the officers until he vanished, pleading a migraine, so I helped her finish it. We were pleased to note that the Chairman of Educational Broadcasting has an appendix.

Talking to Marion about Chipstead, she asked me, 'Do you have skinheads?' I thought she was talking about something personal, like blackheads, but she meant thugs. When I told Louise, she wondered whether skinheads could be classed as a public amenity.

Then we got on to Women's Lib. Feminists pride themselves on campaigning for underprivileged women. Right, so are those of us who have had a strict, inhibited upbringing denied the chance to get married and stay at home?

17th – Saturday

Went up to Southwark to meet Penny for a performance of The Messiah. They went all the way through to the Hallelujah Chorus without an interval so we were glad when we could stand up. Penny was in agony! The singers were from Holland, I think. Orchestra was good. Penny and I got the giggles about 'They shoot out their lips – Gazoooom!'

I had to leave before the end to catch the train back.

18th – Sunday

Usual sort of Sunday. Discussed the Holy Grail and Hengistbury Head with Father, so we were on uncontroversial ground there. Saw Britten's *The Burning Fiery Furnace* – whole opera infused with a religious spirit and oddly moving.

19th – Monday

Went up with Sue Moriarty, discussing secretarial matters, e.g. how much responsibility we were allowed to take in our jobs.

Louise was annoyed with Mr Jones – he is so blithely impractical. He wanted to use Room 661 as a Viewing Room. 'What colour is English?' Louise asked me and then muttered, 'A McLuhan thought.'

Gill was upset because at dinner on Friday night Kaz threw some wine at her brother and walked out.

After lunch, fantastic news! Carol burst into my office to tell me that One-Eyed Jack had told her Frank had been on the phone to him, and that he sent his regards. Heroically putting aside my insane jealousy that Jack had passed this news first to Carol and not to me, I dropped what I was doing, rushed out to the lifts and practically throttled him for the full story.

He said Frank is out of hospital, has been out for a week, but will not be back at work for 'a few weeks'. However, he sent his 'very special regards' to me, personally. 'You know what I mean,' said Jack with a less-than-attractive leer.

So, as Carol said, he sent his regards. Very special ones. To me. Personally.

I know it's silly, but I felt so happy.

20th – Tuesday

A bloody awful night. 'Very special regards'. Oh, Frankie!

Woke up again at quarter to six, finally got up at 7.30. Ran a bath quickly before any of the old ladies could get in before me and deposit long grey hairs, and then walked up to the office.

Jack, as usual, was moaning. The Langham felt strangely empty and its Frank-shaped space was more evident than usual. Anyway, I settled down to typing up the programme correspondence analysis for Louise, and at lunchtime I bought her a copy of *How to Pronounce Names*. Her maiden name was Simmons, as in Simmons Yat, whatever that is.

21st – Wednesday

Slept much better and was reluctant to get up. Louise was smoking in the office again.

Miss Handley asked me about my fingers. 'Are you worrying about something?' she wanted to know. I thought I detected an underlying menace in the question so I said I wasn't, unless I was worrying about her thinking I might be worrying about something.

One-Eyed Jack said he used to be a comedian for fifteen years, part of which was spent with a touring company. He added he hasn't got the breath for it now and that people on the street are funnier than he was.

Louise said she'd never seen a man so happy being miserable.

Oh God, what a fool I've been with Frank! I wouldn't have done any of it if I hadn't been so ignorant, innocent, trusting, inferior and curious.

Supper with Vera and Penny. Came back to fill in the Census form.

22nd – Thursday

Weather a bit cooler. Louise in a brown-patterned floral trouser suit.

Jack still moaning. Haven't bothered to ask him about Frank because he will tell me if he knows anything.

Dashed into the library at lunchtime and borrowed a few books, one of which is a book of seventeenth-century erotic poems. It looked like there might be some useful stuff in it.

In the evening I went late-night shopping with Gill, and she finally bought a very pretty dress at Peter Robinson. We had milk shakes at Fortes. Gill is still worried about Kaz.

Came back and got a fabulous beef curry from the Chinese takeaway. Read the book of poems, which are incredibly rude and sexy, and listened to Harold MacMillan on the radio.

23rd – Friday

Woke up feeling really tired. Gill and I agreed some of the people who go to lunch with us are not easy to talk to because they are always on their Best Behaviour. Sometimes this can be as off-putting as bad manners. Gill is off to Rye for the weekend.

Back home. Saw Harold MacMillan on the TV. He appeared to be so modest and diplomatic and played the part of a dignified elder statesman to perfection. His comments on Europe, de Gaulle and Germany's alliance with Russia were interesting.

Missing Frank again. I'm tired of treading water, I want to swim.

24th – Saturday

Father in excellent humour, having made a well-received speech at the Whitefriars Club on Thursday (he wouldn't say what it was about). Anyway, he was much more convivial than he has been for a long time.

Thinking about the Isle of Wight, I realised I hadn't worked out how I was going to get there. Must look up trains or something.

Is it really five weeks now since Frank went to hospital?

25th – Sunday

It's 4.15 on a Sunday afternoon, and here am I, feeling like an animal undergoing psychological examination. Bored and aggressive. Refused to help Father in the garden on the grounds (!) that I wasn't interested in it and wanted no part in perpetuating it.

Vera has updated her Plan. In Version Two we sell the house and move to a flat in London. That would be a great idea, apart from the fact that I wouldn't be rid of the parents.

Frank isn't God or a hero. I don't love him, I don't know him. The whole thing is a misunderstanding and a mistake.

26th – Monday

Weather cold and rainy. Louise huddled to the radiator (I thought at first there was a spider under her desk). She was staring away out of the window. Gill wasn't in (nor Frank, of course) and I missed her. Saw Jack, who was gasping for a fag, at the end of the day but he didn't volunteer any further news. I'm not surprised.

Adrienne to go into hospital for birth-uncontrol reasons.

Supper at the hostel. Paid out a great deal (£48) for two months' rent and now I'm broke. Zelda came in to read my book of dirty poems. She was shocked by some of them, which cheered me up no end.

27th – Tuesday

Walked up to the Langham, taking with me the small file of poems, which Gill said she would take a look at with me.

Louise and I talked about *Lord of the Flies*. I told her I had started reading it when I was at school, but my father had taken it away and hidden it because he said it was an awful book that was having a bad effect on me. She said I ought to read it again now. Writers write because they want to make a point, and books will only change your way of thinking if you are already heading in that direction anyway.

I kept quiet about the erotic poems book.

Mr Jones gave Carol some daffodils.

Gill was back. She and I had supper in the canteen and looked at some poems I had written. She struggled through them and said they had some good stuff and to keep going. She preferred the less personal ones, which is understandable, but said I should keep them as souvenirs so I could remember how I felt about things later on. We talked about the limits of the individual in society, how much one could or should conform. Perhaps my youthful rebellion is against the permissive society.

Gill said, 'You haven't yet had an ordinary love affair.' She tried to assess its importance to me and the poems.

Kind of her and a great relief that someone was interested.

28th – Wednesday

Lunch with Gill only today, which we both enjoyed, discussing respective parents' houses and illnesses and societies in which we were brought up.

Louise and I discussed fascism. Mr Jones was in her office for ages.

I said to Jack, 'You'll be glad when Frank gets back.' He replied, 'Yes, it's been bleedin' awful since he's been gone.'

Marion had an argument with the other secretary in her office and instead of making them patch it up, Miss Malcolm gave in and separated them. Marion was moved into Carol and Valerie's office, and this led to a bunch of the others ganging up on them. War was declared between Two Sides of the Building.

Oh dear!

In the evening hurried to John Bell & Croyden and Hatchards for Louise (that's devotion to duty for you!), then bought a curry and went back to the hostel. Zelda and I discussed God.

29th – Thursday

Walked to work – chilly, sunny, pleasant.

Louise chatty and cheerful; pointing out the irony of the SBC selling black and white films to South Africa.

Adrienne's farewell lunch today. A long discussion on the aftermath of the Marion episode.

BIG NEWS OF THE DAY ... FRANK CAME IN!

Carol came into my office in the afternoon with a smirk and said, 'There is someone downstairs who wants to see you', but she didn't say who it was so I carried on working. I thought it might be Vera or, even worse, Father. After about ten or fifteen minutes I took the lift down to get a coffee for Louise from the Club.

But it was Frank, standing by the lifts. He was in a fabulous wide-brimmed, brown trilby, a grey suit and a brown tie, leaning on a walking stick. Gill and Carol said later on they thought he looked quite ill, but I thought he looked OK. At least, his eyes were good but he was a bit shaky. He was biting his nails and tearing apart a plastic teaspoon.

He said hello, and I asked him how he was and how the operation had been. It had lasted four hours and he had been in a lot of pain afterwards, he told me. Still, he said, he has had his leg 'put right' and won't need a built-up shoe anymore. He came out of hospital on Good Friday. This week he has seen the surgeon and was told it will be four or five weeks before he is back at work. He'd been over to see his boss in 16 Langham Street to let him know the situation.

'So,' he asked me, 'how are you? Have you been misbehaving?'

'What?' I said, rather taken aback, 'No!'

'I'll kiss you later … I'm sorry I didn't write to you, but I lost the paper with your address.'

'It's OK,' I said.

And at that moment, looking into his blue eyes, everything was indeed very much OK.

'You could come and see me, you know,' he said in his low voice, 'Just take the t'irty six boos.'

I said no, I couldn't visit him in his home. I would rather wait until he was back at work.

He said, 'Don't worry, it will be a long wait, but it will be worth waiting for.'

He thanked me for the cards and notes and said the tea from the Club was lousy.

And with that, we said goodbye. As I watched him go, he was hobbling slowly and with some difficulty. Then I went into the Club for Louise's coffee.

After work, Gill said that shows he still wants me, even that the poor guy may be scared of losing me. After all, he couldn't phone or write but called in to see me, even though he wasn't very well. Which is flattering, but also a bit … worrying.

30th – Friday

I guessed it would be eleven weeks from the start, and it looks like I may well have been right. Had to work through lunch today, and then found out that from Monday I will be sharing the office with someone else.

Blast!

I had supper with Vera and told her all about Frank's visit. She said it was a shame I was tied up with him because there was no future in the relationship. He might be out for what he can get, she thinks.

After yesterday, I am not so sure.

May

1st – Saturday

Sunny. The new oven, which uses North Sea gas, burns very fiercely and incinerated the steak we were going to have for lunch. That was very sad.

Cleaned the car.

2nd – Sunday

Another fine day. Had a bath, washed hair; read the papers. Went to see old school friends after lunch, one of whom is having an affair with her physics lecturer.

3rd – Monday

Walked to the station with Sue Moriarty. She said there are no attractive young men in Chipstead, they are all 'weedy'.

The new temp working for Miss Sharp is called Wendy, and she is sharing my office. She has worked in various BBC departments, including the House Services Personnel, which is in Bentinck House. So that's where I'll have to go if I want to read Frank's file.

Took Wendy to lunch with Gill and a couple of the others. Louise was out for most of the day, but when I did see her, seemed cheerful, probably because she is going on holiday soon.

After work, Gill and I had a drink and a chat about men. She reckons Frank is a bit of a Walter Mitty fantasist.

4th – Tuesday

Good day, but missed Frank as much or more than I did before. Really want him back.

Louise in blue trousers and a cream shirt, which looked rather odd for some reason. She complained about having so much work to do before going on holiday. I was glad she has stalled my going on a pointless training course; even Miss Malcolm [Personnel] thought it would be useless.

Lunch with Celia, Carol and Marion. Bit jealous of Celia working for Mr Roberts as he is quite attractive, but that's nothing compared to how I'd feel about another secretary messing about with Frank, so she may as well have him.

In the afternoon there was big panic – slamming doors, feet running up the corridor. One of the *Science* TV programmes included a sequence showing how to make ginger beer. However, the pamphlet accompanying the programme had one of the ingredients listed incorrectly so anyone using the recipe would blow themselves up, suffering horrible injuries in the process. So Miss Sharp decided that the SBC must write to every school and every teacher-training college in the country to correct the mistake. Now, the programme is aimed at 9–11s, so that means we must cover junior, middle and senior schools, and not only those who bought the pamphlet because apparently schools copy and share it. Miss Handley's girls are doing most of the typing, but there are still another 168 schools on her list.

I said I would help out.

5th – Wednesday

Louise went off on leave, bestowing on me piles of work to do, along with the Great Exploding Ginger Beer letters. Miss Handley said they are spending £14,000 putting right that mistake, and it annoys her.

In the afternoon Miss Sharp called in and congratulated me on my efficient office (she must be joking!).

Had a nice salad and a yoghurt for supper in the BH canteen.

I met Adrienne on the Tube. She didn't realise I am only nineteen.

'Gad, you're young!' she said.

Still haven't found any nice shirts or dresses anywhere.

6th – Thursday

Chatted to Miss Handley about moths. Miss Sharp popped in and out to make sure we all knew she was busy, and Wendy went off for a couple of job interviews with the ILEA [Inner London Education Authority]. The lunchtime discussion was on insanity and spiritualism. Carol said she hoped we were all going to see Louise's holiday photos when she got back.

Back to the hostel. Thunderstorm in the evening.

7th – Friday

Poured with rain. Gill upset, she has had a row with Kaz.

Wendy working like crazy for Miss Sharp, but squeezing in phone calls to her boyfriend. She has to do this from work because her mother doesn't approve of him: he is an Arab.

Back to Chipstead.

8th – Saturday

Watched the Cup Final. Arsenal did the double.

Uncle Ron has gone into Dorking Hospital to have a hip operation, so I took Father over in the car to see him. He seemed quite cheerful. On the way back, Father complained that Ron could only talk about the hospital (Father wanted to talk about Lady Henry Somerset or something).

Vera and I watched *The Two Ronnies* on TV – think they will do well if they stick together.

9th – Sunday

Gah! Why is having 'a young man' such a social necessity, like it's a passport to the adult world? Vera overheard a phone call between Father and Mr Holmes. We were all invited to theirs for lunch, and he said I could 'bring my young man' if I wanted to. Father said, very firmly, that I didn't have a young man and wasn't likely to for the time being. He was so certain about this he annoyed Vera, and I was none too happy about it either when she told me.

Another argument. Father thinks I'm crazy.

Not having a boyfriend is a misery, all the time you feel like you are a failure. And nice boys don't fall down chimneys.

10th – Monday

Travelled up with Sue Moriarty. This time we were joined by a bloke she referred to previously as 'Little Weed', whose name, I think, is Richard.

Office dreadfully busy. All the Knitts had written in, not to mention all the Cranks. Wendy still staggering under the load of Miss Sharp's work and is considering absconding. She met her forbidden Arab boyfriend yesterday. I imagine him as something out of *The Son of the Sheikh*.

Had a chat with Miss Handley as I reached the end of the wretched Ginger Beer letters. She said she thought I was not eating enough so I went over to the BH canteen after work and piled into a mincemeat à la Grecque before going back to the hostel.

11th – Tuesday

I wanted to walk to work but was too late getting up. It was busy, but I was pleased with what I got done, especially some efficient-sounding letters. Miss Handley asked me what I was doing tonight! She also inspected my dead plant and offered to give me one of her African violets.

Was nabbed by Miss Sharp for some dictation. She told me that someone had written in to complain about the use of the phrase 'shagged out' in a schools programme. Sharpy wasn't sure what that meant, so she phoned the BBC Reference Library. 'And do you know,' she told me very seriously, 'it means "exhausted after physical intercourse"!'

I wasn't sure why she told me this, and I can't help wondering how she carries on while being so unaware that all her secretaries hate her guts.

Supper with Gill. Discussed how little things happen that can change your life, and was this due to predestination or coincidence?

12th – Wednesday

Walked to work in my new sandals. First day of No Coat.

Lunch with Wendy and Carol. Wendy has had enough of Sharp, who today pursued her into the Ladies while still dictating. Carol is thinking of leaving in September.

I am keeping up the habit of going to the basement to collect the *Radio Times* on a special after-lunch trip. Of course I could get it anytime on a Wednesday, but if I stick to this routine then I can continue it when Frank is back without arousing suspicion. Which means he and I can ...

But is this wise?

13th – Thursday

Miss Handley came round with some booklets that needed stamping. She asked me how does Louise get on with Miss Sharp? I said I thought they got on OK. Handley said she liked Louise, and then gave me a Twix bar as a thank you for doing the stamping.

Gill reckons Miss Handley is a lesbian.

After work, I was walking down Carlisle Place to the hostel when a young man shouted and ran up behind me. He said he was a banking student. Then he asked me my name and where did I live, so I gave him a false name and quickly tried to think of a road I could take to avoid him following me to Francis Street. After a bit of a detour he realised I wasn't interested and I reached the hostel unscathed.

I don't think he qualified as one of the nice young men that might fall down a chimney. Also, he was black, so I couldn't imagine Father taking to him.

Instantly wanted Frank back.

14th – Friday

Work dwindled down to not much. Miss Handley had nothing for me today, apart from a story about being stopped by the police for carrying a liver pâté in Oxford Circus.

Had lunch with Carol (who dislikes Wendy), Wendy (who maintained a stony silence), Leah (who never says anything, anyway) and Gill.

Gill and I went shopping in John Lewis and Etams afterwards. Clothes all foul – it's a communist plot to degrade the national morale (if there is any left).

Wendy finished today.

Came home.

I could really do with having Frank back.

15th – Saturday

Vera has done my washing again. Kind, but I wish she wouldn't. Father had complained that he didn't like the meat Vera bought from the butcher, so for lunch she cooked fish. He wasn't amused. Nor was he keen to visit Uncle Ron again, but we set off in the early afternoon. As we drove into Dorking, Father suddenly spotted a greengrocer's and remembered he had to buy potatoes but by that time we had passed the shop and were going up a narrow road to the hospital.

'Stop the car!' he said, but I couldn't stop there. He lost his temper, started shouting and hitting me, and swearing. Then he grabbed the keys, switched off the ignition, got out and began walking back to the shop.

I started the car again carefully, drove on and then did a circuit of Dorking, ending up in the hospital car park, where he was waiting for me. Leaving the engine running, I wound down the window, handed him the shoes and the grapes we had brought for Uncle Ron and said I was going home. 'Don't leave me here!' he yelled, but I drove off.

I did the Dorking circuit again, by which time I thought I had probably done enough to give him a fright and I couldn't really drive home without him. When I got back to the car park he was making a call in a phone box. He came over. I asked him to apologise for switching off the engine and shouting at me, but he wouldn't – he just stood there.

So we went in to see Uncle Ron, and then Father and I came home again in silence.

16th – Sunday

Weather cold. Furious argument with Father at lunch. I'd been listening to some Benjamin Britten records yesterday evening, and wanted to see *Owen Wingrave*, his new opera, on TV this evening. Father insisted that Britten is not a genius. I said he didn't know enough about the composer to make a judgement. Retired to my bedroom to console myself by reading about the Irish Potato Famine. There were no heroes in it called Browne, but I found the original 'spalpeen'.

Saw *Owen Wingrave*. It was OK, but not brilliant.

Father sneaked in to watch some of it.

17th – Monday

Gill's birthday. I gave her a card and presents from Vera and myself. Unfortunately, she had difficulty in seeing, possibly after drinking some bad wine yesterday. Then she said it might be the result of Kaz bashing her up last week.

Office very busy: we have had a flood of letters, some of which were tricky to deal with as Louise is still on leave. I took some shorthand from an hysterically funny Miss Handley ('Well, Sarah, isn't this exciting!') and dealt with the mundane stuff myself. We were interrupted once by Mr Roberts – it struck me that those two would make a good couple.

One-Eyed Jack was on Frank's lift today.

Curried beef again. Chatted with Zelda – I do wish I could really do something for her, but you can't run other people's lives for them.

18th – Tuesday

Very busy, lots of letters. Marion seems a bit off with me at the moment. However, Carol is very chummy and keen to talk about her forthcoming wedding.

'There are lots of right men around,' she said, 'and you can wait forever for perfection. I thought, it's now or never.'

She told me she is thinking of having Morris dancers at the reception. I doubt whether her heart runs her head often.

Miss Handley was also very chatty, flinging her arm around me in an unnecessary fashion. Perhaps it was because I had typed all those letters for her.

Miss Malcolm told Gill she ought to get pregnant.

Apparently it's in the wind that they might mechanise the manned lifts. If they do, I suppose the BBC would find Frank another job. Maybe I will have left by then.

Met my old school friend Georgina Fox for supper and we talked about the possibility of sharing a flat next year, which would be great and something to look forward to.

In fear of Louise's return tomorrow – we will be so busy.

19th – Wednesday

Expected Louise back today but in fact she isn't back until tomorrow.

A letter arrived this morning, complaining that the Radio One Club had caused truancy in Monmouth.

Carol kept asking me about Frank.

Saw Steve Race [musician and broadcaster best-known for chairing *My Music*] outside BH at lunchtime.

Went to Charing Cross Library, got out a book on the Battle of Bosworth and renewed the Irish potatoes book so Gill could read it. Went to bed early at 9.30.

Have semi-decided to call it all off with Frank. Easy to say that after nine and a half weeks without him, but surely, he can't expect me to take it all seriously?

20th – Thursday

Louise back – she said the sight of all the bulging files on her desk made her want to go straight back to Corsica.

Lunch with Carol, Gill and Leah, discussing what Carol should cook for supper.

Miss Handley called round to my office and gave me a wink, which was a bit saucy. She also appeared when I went round to her office to check with one of her girls on the address of a school in Bude.

Oh Jesus, if she is a lesbian, is she after me? I know one shouldn't assume she is. Anyway, is it wrong to be attracted to the same sex …?

I've decided I can do without Frank. Gill's been against it for ages, so has Vera. Of course they are both right. Maybe I just had to go through it all to understand what was wrong about it.

Came back to hear from Zelda about her child study project – amused by her candour at not knowing the child at all.

21st – Friday

Telephoned Vera as it is her birthday today.

Lunch, a hurried fish pie, with Gill and bought a purple dress at M&S.

There was a fire drill. A very loud panic-inducing bell went off and we had to WALK down the six floors and gather outside the front of the Langham. We waited for fifteen minutes – I was feeling very uneasy as I was being looked over by Miss Handley.

One-Eyed Jack calls Paddington 'Wog-land'.

Louise has adopted both the plants Miss Handley brought round for me.

Back home. Vera annoyed that Father ordered 50 cwt of phurnacite [smokeless fuel] and wasn't taking her out on her birthday. Father in a bloody mood too.

Cross about Frank. It's not a lasting relationship and I don't see why I should be involved in it.

22nd – Saturday

Shopping in Purley with Vera, and then Coulsdon with Father.

Shortened hem of new purple dress.

Vera and I concluded that Miss Handley is probably not a lesbian, just one of those ultra-tactile people.

Saw the England v Scotland football match. England won by virtue of a goal which should have been disallowed. Mind you, Scotland's goal was from a mistake – a Banks' own goal.

23rd – Sunday

Father attempted to shoot a squirrel in the garden but only succeeded in hitting it in the leg. Vera had to suffer the sight of it scrambling away while Father denied having anything to do with it. Eventually the poor thing expired by the dustbins. Vera was so upset. Then they argued at lunchtime – Vera accused Father of telling her 'fairy-stories'.

Frank may be back tomorrow.

To tell the truth, I am weary of that whole business now.

24th – Monday

Went up with Sue Moriarty, who asked if Uncle Rupert [my dentist uncle] could take her on as a patient.

Frank not back this week. Nor did Penny phone, and Gill has a cold so she didn't stay on after work.

Louise and I had a fabulous day, though – hard work, but we laughed a lot. Mr Jones is sceptical of One-Eyed Jack's claim that he was ever a stage comedian.

Lunch was a disaster in that Leah tagged along, said nothing and did nothing but restricted our conversation. We tried, but failed.

Gill and I had a chat about The Pill.

I had to go round to Miss Handley's office for some information. Seeing Leah sitting there, I asked her the question but she didn't reply. Miss Handley must have overheard and called me into her office. She told me to shut the door. I repeated the question and explained that I thought Leah might have been able to answer it, and Miss Handley sighed, 'Didn't you know by now?'

Later on, Miss Handley met me in the Club when I went down for Louise's coffee. Apparently, Leah had a twin who died at birth. Miss Handley took her on because the Training Department told her that Leah had potential, but she has yet to see any of it.

'Don't get lumbered with her,' Handley told me.

Chicken curry, Brandenburg Concertos.

25th – Tuesday

Oh my goodness, what a day!

Up late, raining and cold, so I took the Tube to work. Madly busy in the office. Valerie doing masses of super-efficient typing.

Well ... Went to the Recordings Library and was ushered into the demo room by Miss Handley. We had a very odd, superficial discussion about some programme pamphlets, which didn't appear to have much bearing on anything. Miss

Handley told me she joined the BBC in 1943 and worked at the BBC Club for a while. She gave me a most extraordinary stare at one point, which really unnerved me. When I told her I was thinking about moving on to another job soon, she said she hoped I wouldn't leave for a while, and that the thought of my leaving quite put her off her lunch. I suddenly remembered something important I had to do, and made a quick exit.

Over lunch, Gill and I discussed that episode and she pointed out the root of my problems was the lack of a man. I said I was through with Frank because we had done everything we were going to do, but I was worried now about how to break it to him. Gill suggested treating it all as a joke, but I don't know if that would be true, either to myself or the way in which things had developed between him and me.

I went back to the office, and after a while Reception phoned up to say there was a parcel for Louise waiting downstairs. Down I went and …

Oh blimey, there was Frank, large as life, in his grey suit, a blue tie and a soft grey hat, looking very swish, sitting on a chair by the lifts! My first thought was to wonder how on earth I had done what I had done with him.

'Hello,' I said, and darted off to Reception to give me time to collect my thoughts as well as the parcel. I returned and sat down next to him.

He seemed a bit nervous to begin with, finishing every sentence with 'Unnerstand?', which was familiar, but I hadn't really noticed him saying that before.

His leg has recovered well. He hasn't had the same operation as Uncle Ron, he has had an E-plate replaced by a proper ball joint, and he showed me his new shoes. They are just ordinary ones, he doesn't need a built-up one anymore. He's going for a check-up next week, and may be back at work on 7 June.

He asked if I would go into the Commissionaires' room and check his locker to see if he had any pills in there, but I wasn't happy about doing that. I said maybe he wouldn't need pills anymore but he said, 'Oh oy'm still takin' some, y'know.'

I asked what he was doing all day now, and he said he was helping his wife to walk (she has special boots, which he has to put on for her) – 'See, she has two disabilities, the diabetes and the paralysis'. One Monday morning, she woke up with the paralysis, and the diabetes has been so bad that four times she has had to be taken to hospital on a stretcher. To have two things like that, he reckons, is bad. I asked him how she was in herself. He looked glum and shook his head.

He had planned to see his daughter and her family at Whitsun, but they are having 'the other side', so he isn't sure what they will do.

I told him I had read a book about the Potato Famine.

'We were rotten to the Irish,' I said.

He laughed.

'May I apologise on behalf of the English?'

'Potatoes!' he snorted.

Me: Well, life is short ...
Frank: Yes.
Me: And so are you!
  (He threatens me with his umbrella)
Frank: No, I'll not hit you with this – it cost me two pounds and ten shillings.

He told me he comes from Kerry, near Killarney. There are lots of islands around there, which are now very touristy. I asked if he would recognise his relatives if he went back and he thought so. He said he had won five bob on the football pools.

'This tea,' he said gloomily, staring into the cup, ''tis not much cop.'

A woman I didn't know came by and said, 'Hello Frank, how is your foot?' 'Oh, 'tis very well,' he replied. After she had walked off, he turned to me and chuckled, "Tis not me bleedin' foot what's wrong, 'tis me leg!'

He was looking at me with an amused smile and suddenly it felt as if the space around us had become fixed in an invisible circle, holding us together. Suddenly nothing else mattered or even belonged in our world; not the people going past us into the Club, the lift doors opening and closing, or the phone ringing in the distant foyer. I had never understood how people could say that time stood still, but at that moment it did, and it was deliciously scary but exciting.

Did he feel the same?

Frank (quietly):   So, are you still in love then?

Me (worried this was all getting a bit serious):
>No.

(Frank looks down at the cup again)

Frank: You'll be askin' me how I'm feeling about you then.

Me (with mock surprise):
>How did you guess that?

Frank (looking straight at me):
>Just the same.

He asked after my fingers, eyes, holidays ... The atmosphere relaxed. I told him Adrienne had left. He used to laugh at her because he said she had a big bum.

Then a surprise. I got up to go back to the office and as I stepped into Jack's lift, Frank followed me. We stood behind Jack, and Frank leaned against me as we travelled up, which I didn't much like. Some men got on at the third floor so he moved away and began examining the wood panelling

– which was funny because it's the same as that in his own lift and he must have seen it a thousand times before.

When we reached the sixth floor, he followed me out of the lift. I said it was good to see how well he was walking, but I had to go and get on with my typing now. Then, at the top of the staircase, where Jack couldn't see us, we kissed in a funny sort of halfway fashion.

He held my hand and said, 'God bless you.' I told him to please, look after himself.

Couldn't type a bloody thing after that.

Two more weeks, he says, and he will be back.

26th – Wednesday

After yesterday, I was on cloud nine most of the morning.

Can't think of anything but Frank.

Louise sent me off to MultiCopy in Regent Street to have them reproduce a letter about the seventy-fifth birthday of her psychiatrist friend. She is organising a special event for this.

It was a typical Louise letter.

Astonishingly, there is news that Leah spoke yesterday when the technician, Graham, went into the Publications office.

Louise and I had a laugh about a sex education letter in which someone had complained about something being a 'phallacy' and a 'misconception'. Miss Handley came in for a fag and a chat with us both.

Frank and I had a really good talk yesterday, a lot of laughs and got on well, if not better, than before. I missed him today.

Went down to the library and borrowed a record of Irish folk songs.

Back at the hostel poor Zelda's being destroyed by herself and her German. She's screwing herself up and it's terrible to witness. He's not responded to her letters and phone calls so I think he's not interested.

Perhaps she should finish it.

27th – Thursday

Made a bit of a hash of the typing today and apologised to Louise. It evened up later on when she opened my pay envelope by mistake.

Gill and I went to the Scholls shoe shop in the rain – I bought some sandals, she had some foot treatment. I came back and interrupted Louise in her office with her feet up on the desk, eating sausages.

Later, Miss Handley told Gill and me how she was looking forward to seeing the film *Jesse James* on TV on Saturday, having had to miss it in 1939 due to being evacuated out of London.

Marion invited me to her leaving drinks do tomorrow. Silly, but I felt quite flattered.

Gill invited me to go to the cinema with her and Kaz after work, but when he arrived, he was pointedly polite to me and bolshy to Gill, so I made an excuse and left them to it.

Curry again. Tired.

No sign of Zelda in the room opposite. She was so low last night – I hope she hasn't done anything drastic.

Tuesday went so well – I don't think it can ever be so good again.

28th – Friday

It was Marion's leaving do at lunchtime. Leah, who hadn't been invited, rang just as it was due to begin and asked if she could come to lunch with me. Awkward. Anyway, in the end she came to the drinks do, much to the amusement of Miss Handley, who had overheard the phone call.

Of course, Leah had nothing to say to anyone when she got there.

Miss Handley was teasing me about my John Lennon leather cap, from which I shall not be parted.

Came back home to Chipstead. Uncle Rupert was already there on a visit, armed with a glass of sherry and the cat. Father bloody, laying down the law about things he knows nothing about.

Vera and I discussed Frank, love, sex and North Sea gas (which Vera still hates). Saw *Bel Ami* (young man, older woman).

Now I'm confused and muddled about Frank.

29th – Saturday

Vera had invited Uncle Ron to stay and convalesce after his hip operation. As soon as he arrived, Father dropped hints about wanting to be left alone.

'It's very quiet here, Ron. We work a lot.'

And then he vanished into the garden.

I listened to some more Britten and then talked with Vera and Uncle Ron. Ron said he was shaky after the operation and the anaesthetic was depressing. He has to do exercises every day.

I wonder if that's why Frank stood all the time on the first visit.

30th – Sunday

Uncle John, who is Father's youngest brother, and his wife, Aunt Marjorie, came over to see us and Uncle Ron. There was a lot of talk about golfing and shares. Then they got on to the MRA movement and the Holmeses, and Father was embarrassing – he was so childish, giggling about them. Uncle

Ron potters about quite cheerfully but I'm afraid he will find it awfully dull in our house. At least he doesn't seem to be bothered by all the arguing – I think that's a kind of family tradition with us.

Finished reading A. L. Rowse's *Bosworth Field*.

Waiting for Frank to return with a mixture of longing and dread. I know we can't go on as we did before, but it feels as if he is impossible to resist.

It's a terribly sad situation to be so happy in.

31st – Monday (Whitsun Bank Holiday)

What a dull diary! It might have been written by E. L. Wisty [character invented by the comedian and writer Peter Cook].

Got up. Ate breakfast. Played the guitar. Washed tights. Played guitar again. Played a record. Wrote a letter to Auntie Phyl. Posted the letter. Sat in the kitchen and watched Vera. Played the guitar again. Ate lunch. Wrote a poem. Listened to a record. Pulled eyebrows and bathed a stye in my eye. Read W. B. Yeats and Matthew Arnold. Wrote diary. Have also been to loo and brushed my teeth.

Father bolshy, Vera silent; Uncle Ron keeping to himself.

My feet are cold.

June

1st – Tuesday

Caught an early train as I had planned to buy rail tickets for the Isle of Wight. Instead I ended up buying them at lunchtime. I hope I lost some weight because it involved a fair bit of walking.

Just as Gill and I were about to go to lunch, Leah rang. I had dropped a hint to her about not coming with us, but she didn't take it. Gill wasn't pleased about her tagging along, it meant the two of us had a very strained conversation while Leah sat there in silence. I mentioned it to Louise afterwards, who listened attentively, and the next thing I knew Miss Handley was in my office, promising that tomorrow she would keep Leah at her desk until Gill and I had gone for lunch, and then suggest to her that she go with someone else. However, another temp (replacing Wendy) will be sharing my office from tomorrow. BLAST! HELL!

After a supper at the BH canteen I went for a walk. Sitting on an iron railing was a single glove, its finger pointing up sinisterly at the sky. I found a corner called 'Cockpit Steps', and outside Westminster Abbey there was a sign saying, 'Danger: Men working overhead', which was funny. I hadn't realised that around the Abbey are the Methodist Hall, Westminster Cathedral and the Christian Science Reading Room.

Penny rang. She is off to study Ancient Hebrew mystics on Thursday in some remote countryside mansion, which sounds very Gothic.

2nd – Wednesday

The new temp has arrived. She is called Monica and is quite a bit older than me. I found it very hard to suffer her conversation gladly. It is very intolerant of me, but my feathers were ruffled.

The lunch plan worked, though.

I am thinking more and more about leaving the BBC, but maybe I should give them a fair chance and look for another job in the organisation first.

Came back to the hostel with sore and blistered feet, and sewed up my tights with the last of my nylon thread.

Cross that I even contemplated getting involved with Frank. I don't regret it but can do without it now. I must start again from new on his return.

3rd – Thursday

GROAN. Well. Got on better today. Louise gave Monica longer pieces of work to do in an attempt to shut her up. Monica did, verbally, a little, but also she shut up the office window, which turned me puce with claustrophobia.

Monica has taken a quick dislike to Louise, and I am ashamed to say I approve of that because I don't want her getting between us.

I had lunch with Gill in a pub in Mortimer Street, the BBC one. The food was good (I had a salad) and I got mildly merry on a couple of shandies.

Miss Handley being very friendly, as usual, although she has stopped squeezing me. Hoorah!

After work I went to the 'Book Bang' exhibition in Bedford Square. I didn't think much of it. The National Book League organised it as a 'book circus', and it seemed to fall between two stools, neither circus nor book, and both the quantity and quality of what was on display fell short of, say, the book department of Bourne & Hollingsworth, where I went afterwards. The 50p entrance fee was robbery. There was some underground trash, which I browsed through out of interest, but it was pretty conventionally 'radical'. Shakespeare was noticeable by his absence, as were many other famous writers.

Where were they?

I am really hoping Frank never comes back. I don't ever want to see him again. To be honest, I feel a fool for having taken him seriously and for having bothered Gill and Vera so much.

4th – Friday

Up late. No time for breakfast. Bought some more Girl Guide badges for Carol.

Monica still complaining about Louise, but the good news is that she is not coming back next week, so that's a relief. The window was still shut (of course), which made me sleepy.

Miss Handley went to see the Beating Retreat and was very impressed by the Queen.

Did the catalogue entries for the music programmes, alone and more or less unaided.

Mrs Chambers of the Photocopying Service on the Entresol is off to Marbella – she says she is going to see Cary Grant.

Jack says he is writing a story, *Murder at the Langham*, with himself as the murderer, who gives himself away when an Inspector of Lifts finds the bodies down the lift shaft. I suggested this would make an ideal basis for a schools programme. He says Paddington is such a slum that the authorities don't believe how bad it is, e.g. garbage in the gutters.

Came home to find Uncle Ron recovering well.

5th – Saturday

The outside tap sprang a leak, so consternation and deluge until at 2 p.m. we acquired a plumber. By this time I was tired of hearing Father sounding off about the inherent laziness of the working classes.

Vera and I went shopping in Croydon – I haven't been there for ages.

I began to wonder if there might be a case for carrying on with Frank in that it would be easier in the short term, even pleasurable. But then I remembered all the reasons why I shouldn't.

6th – Sunday

Rang Georgina Fox and we decided we would try to get tickets to see the play *Kean* on Tuesday. Dull and overcast. We are wearing pullovers in June.

7th – Monday

Two months and two weeks later ... and ...

FRANK BACK.

Oh, frabjous day!

I turned up in hope, rather early, having dumped Moriarty at Victoria.

It seemed at first he wasn't around, but then he appeared from the basement. I travelled up in his lift with Old Misery and a girl. They got off at the third floor, and we went up to the sixth together, alone.

He took my hand and said, 'How's Sarah?' I said OK and, before anything else could be said or done, launched into my brief, polite and well-prepared speech about how I was sorry but there wasn't a foreseeable future for us, and therefore I didn't want to go to bed with him and I hoped he would understand that.

Frank (looking at me quizzically):
        Well, it's up to you.
Me: It wouldn't be fair on me, you or your wife.
Frank: I just want a little fun ...
Me: OK.
Frank: . . . although I might be needing a bodyguard.
        So, we'll have a little fun?
Me: Yes.
Frank: And then all the way.
Me: No!

Then we had a couple or three not very exciting but at least human kisses (more fool me!) and off I went into my office.

Louise came in shortly afterwards and said, 'Did you see the little Irishman's back?' I said, 'Yes, I had' and carried on typing. Gill said he seemed glad to be back and was very chatty with everyone this morning. It was nice to hear his singing echoing around the stairwell again.

We had a super-nice temp in called Janice. I took to her right away. Leah came round, asking to go to lunch with us, but I said no. She ended up with Carol instead, who hated it.

I didn't see Frank again until we went to lunch. In the afternoon he asked how I was, saying he thought I had lost some weight (he called it 'thinning') and that I have a good complexion. He wanted to take me down to the basement. I said no.

Feeling very happy today.

8th – Tuesday

Oh, Christ! I am into it again with both feet.

I couldn't sleep much last night and couldn't eat a thing. Walked up to work.

I went with Frank to the sixth floor. I asked him if Jack suspected anything about us, and he said Jack didn't know anything, apart from my having sent him the cards. Then, as no one else was around, we hugged and kissed and explored each other, and I didn't want him to stop – I was definitely all there this time.

'I've never felt like that before,' I said.

'Aye, dere's many t'ings you've not done before.'

I complained he hadn't shaved. He said, 'Don't get lipstick on me collar,' but it was OK because I hardly wear any make-up. I said his hair smelt good, he laughed and said, 'It's the Loxene.'

He took my hand and led me out of the lift into my office. It was still early and there was no one else around. We became very passionate; he was all over me and wanted me to touch his thing but I refused because I thought he might get the wrong idea. (Also, I wasn't entirely sure what I was supposed to do with it – even the seventeenth-century poems hadn't been too clear on that.) By this time we were laughing about my tights. He said, 'You're well covered,' and I replied, 'Well, I didn't dress for the occasion.' I said he was doing well anyway, and he said he had all he wanted, he wouldn't want 'to do you' (ugh!) until we were in the right place at the right time.

Finally I showed him out, threatening to douse him with the fire extinguisher. He bowed, kissed my hand and off he went.

It had felt so good when we had been in the lift, but once we were in the office I became worried about what we were doing, so I was glad when he stopped. He doesn't see it all the same way as I do. He enjoyed it, but it should have been with his wife, not with me, shouldn't it?

He's got very hairy arms.

I didn't see him again until I came back from lunch and we kissed again several times, by which time my lips were looking a bit sore. Needless to say, Carol spotted that when she delivered some papers to the office.

'Who have you been kissing then?' she asked.

'Who do you think?' I replied, 'Frank?'

That shut her up because she wouldn't dare say anything outright.

Gill was cold and unsympathetic.

Later, I showed Frank the draft description of the *Going Steady* programme which I'd written, and he suggested I should type it out again with additions. I said I didn't know about that, he'd have to show me what to put in, which of course he jumped at, but I just laughed it off.

Frank complained of a headache and asked if I had any tablets but I hadn't. Miss Handley found some for him.

In the end, around 5 p.m., I went down for some copying and told him they had been on at me. He snorted about it being just women talking. He said Carol had been on several lift journeys with him today, asking him questions and trying to find out where he came from. In the end he'd admitted it was Kerry, the Kingdom.

'She chatters,' he said, 'You and me, we're secretive.'

That made me pretty sure Carol and Miss Handley had been talking about us. I was worried that word would spread and he might lose his job; and maybe after this morning we were going too far again. So I told him I thought we should stop altogether. I held out my hand, he semi-shook it, and looked at me as if to say, 'Do you really mean it?'

When I finished work, I avoided Frank and went down in Jack's lift instead, but he kept going on at me about Miss

Sharp being a sex maniac. I suppose they overhear the conversations about the sex education programmes and wonder what on earth the people on the sixth floor are up to. I felt awful then, ashamed of the SBC and of myself too.

Met Georgina Fox in Leicester Square, and we went to see *Kean*, which was fantastic and cheered me up. Alan Badel was really enjoying himself and it was so funny.

Bed about midnight.

Yesterday evening I had been so happy.

9th – Wednesday

Bought Frank some codeine as a present, and went up with him in the lift. He kissed me, but I broke away and said I didn't want to carry on anymore. He then went on about what he needed, how it was all play, he wouldn't force me to do anything I didn't want to do, he just wanted me to equate his actions. When I mentioned his wife he went on about how he 'wasn't ever touching' her, and how her being disabled meant his situation was different. I do feel sorry for her. He said he was in a state last night and had to get up at five in the morning. We kissed a couple of times then he said he didn't want to lose me, and was concerned that he had frightened me yesterday.

I collected the *Radio Times* in the afternoon, via the basement route, but didn't do anything with Frank. I can't get used to the luxury of seeing him every day and it makes me feel so contented and happy that somebody thinks so much of me and cares about me. Was I unfair to him yesterday morning?

I found a book in the library this evening that mentioned how a younger partner can rejuvenate an older man (Frank saying, 'It's what keeps you young') but that it only lasts for between a month and two years, not longer. So, another reason not to lie with him.

I needn't let him get to me.

10th – Thursday

Woke up in the strange state of having absolutely no desire for Frank. I strolled up to work, only hurrying at the end as it began to rain. He took me up to the sixth floor, where we had a couple of kisses and then he took my head very gently in his hands and said, 'Give me your tongue.'

I felt differently after the next kiss.

It rained all day and was very cold. There was masses of work.

Waiting for the others to join me for lunch, I chatted to Frank on the sixth floor, getting lots of fruity looks. He promised to buy me a new pair of tights (bet he doesn't). He tried on my leather cap – it was several sizes too big for him so I told him he was undersized and oversexed. He told me I was a big girl. He also mentioned he had been very startled by a photo in the *Sun* this morning of a naked couple.

Gill and I went for a drink in the evening.

'Things are going well,' I told her, 'I have drawn the line with Frank.'

11th – Friday

Such a strange day! Louise was in a good mood. I typed a couple of letters for her and, as usual, couldn't read back all my shorthand, so I substituted my own wording in some sentences. As she handed back the file to me, she said, 'You may be careless but you are not unintelligent.'

Frank was difficult. He took me down to the basement in the morning and we had a very long kiss, followed by another two. He wanted more; I refused. I told him he was out of favour for suggesting it.

I lent him a pen, and I told him about the Beatrix Potter story – Squirrel Nutkin dancing up and down in front of Old Brown (!), and how he lost his tail. That amused him.

In the afternoon I took some papers for copying down to the Entresol, and instead of us going straight back to the sixth floor, we descended to the basement, where he turned off the lights. He was taking things very slowly, when Jack's lift suddenly dropped down next door and its lights were switched off as well. Frank paused and looked at me.

'What's he doing?' I whispered.

'Der booger! Wait.' He put his finger to his lips.

We stepped back from each other and stood there, listening. I heard Jack cough and shuffle. Frank and I stared at each other in mild alarm, frightened that Jack would come round and peer into our lift. However, after what felt like ages, the light went on next door, the cables clanked and whirred and off he went.

Frank kissed me and laughed it off, but it felt like a close thing.

Later on, when I went down to the Entresol to collect the copying, Frank jammed his lift so that he could wait there for me, thereby forcing Jack to take all the other calls. He gave me a wink and said, 'Dat'll teach him.'

Frank has a good record, but he said nobody would stop to ask questions if we were caught together – he would be instantly dismissed. Then he gave me another warm kiss, and asked me again to sleep with him. Furious, I said it was quite out of the question – I wasn't even in love with him.

He asked if I would, if he were free. I said no. He didn't believe me, or didn't want to.

He had gone home by the time I left work.

I came back feeling sick at heart about him. Gill said he was trying to hold a girl's hand in the lift this morning.

I am very upset. I am so fond of him, but he destroys it all by being so bloody pushy.

This is a poisonous situation.

12th – Saturday

Went to Purley and Coulsdon. Talked incessantly about Frank.

Is this an 'I can't live with/without you' situation?

Played some of my songs to Father and Vera. Father said he thought one of them sounded like a first millennium Anglo-Saxon chant.

Vera said she is depressed at the lack of laughter in our house. She needs a break, so she has arranged to spend a few days with her friend in Dorset.

13th – Sunday

The morning was spent preparing for the 11.30 a.m. arrival of Uncle Rupert with his daughter and her three children. We had a cold lunch and sat in the garden.

I've got Frank on the brain, and I'm sure he is not one jot concerned about me really. If only he would stay put and not spirit me away to the basement; it's too dangerous. And I am definitely not sleeping with him, as we all know by now. It's not going any further than a friendship.

14th – Monday

Weather reverted to rain. Went on the train with Richard, who is a bit of a drip himself.

Frank was surprised I had had such a dull weekend and asked why I didn't take a donkey and cart to the railway station. We talked Friday over. We are sure Louise knows about us, probably Miss Handley and Carol too, but he said Jack was no threat.

Frank didn't hang about the sixth floor today, which was good, but I think we were observed by a girl on the fourth floor as he was kissing me.

I lent him my comb and watched as he combed his hair like a Teddy Boy, patting it down with his left hand, using the brass buzzer case as a mirror. When he passed it back to me I thought, how strangely intimate we are already.

Madly busy, especially on a table of estimates for Miss Sharp, which I typed beautifully and then dropped into a puddle outside the Langham. I dashed back inside, dried off the pages and only had to retype a couple of them.

Richard Baker [broadcaster and BBC newsreader] was sighted in the BH canteen.

Cider and a Wimpy cheeseburger for supper – La Dolce Vita!

15th – Tuesday

(Vera is away to Beaminster.)

Walked up to work through Green Park. Every time I pass Buckingham Palace it reminds me of the newsreels of VE Day, when crowds stood around the gates, across the road and on the Victoria Memorial. Somehow you expect they will still be there.

That reminded me of the man who had tried to pick me up in Hyde Park some weeks ago, and I told Frank about him.

Frank:	You're an attractive girl, you should be careful wid yourself.
Me:	I thought I was. Or do you mean I should be more careful than I am?
Frank:	Yes, but not wid me!

I bought him some Murray Mints in the lunch hour. He's convinced his breath smells of onions, but I've never noticed.

It was so cold in the offices. I could hardly type, and Sharpy complained to the powers that be, threatening to have us all out. There were only three secretaries in to cover five phones.

I went to the City Lit for my first evening class: *Pop is the greatest*! It was given by the film director Tony Palmer. He was very good and not at all trendy, but mostly covered ground that I was familiar with, such as Elvis and the Beatles. He was very scathing about the commercialisation of music.

Intelligent man; looks a bit like Denis Norden [TV presenter and comedy writer].

16th – Wednesday

Still cold, but not as bad as yesterday.

Went up with Frank. A little kiss and then I was working hard. I had lunch alone.

In the afternoon I bought Frank a 'coppatay'. He told me a man got into his lift and asked for the SBC.

'Oy'm t'inkin' to meself, What's he wantin' der NSPCC for? That cruelty to children thing?'

Me:	You're a nut.
Frank:	A tough nut to crack?
Me:	No, a lovable nut.

I said I had noticed there were lots of Irishmen in the Victoria area. Frank said, 'I know that, I used to go there before I was married, for the girls.'

We had a discussion about human nature, which, he informed me, takes its own course.

'You and I are human,' he said, 'and when we get together, that's human nature. I'm only a human t'ing, Sarah.'

But actually I wasn't so anxious about him today and felt a lot more relaxed. Beds weren't mentioned and he hasn't tried any real sex for ages.

Good!

Gill was back – I was so pleased to see her. Carol botched up a stencil.

Supper with Penny, we got on extremely well. She told me all about the Kabbalah, how she had been painting her room and Percy the murderer at the Badminton Club. I suggested we could go to Chanctonbury Ring on the South Downs one day soon.

All good fun.

17th – Thursday

This morning's nugget of information: Frank has a green budgie called Marty. His daughter, Betty, brought it back from her convent school in Holloway in a matchbox. It is now eleven years old and says all the usual stuff like 'Who's a pretty boy?' – but in an Irish accent.

Frank was friendly enough, the best this week. He helped get the rain off me in the morning. I showed him my book of poems by W. B. Yeats and he read one out loud very solemnly and almost well ('The heaviest arm under the sky'). That certainly sounded better in an Irish accent.

Also, we had a chat with the other Irish lift man, the one who drives the goods van. He is a nice fellah, too. Frank said he comes from 'Wahterrfahd' and has four children.

Gill and I went for a Dubonnet after work.

18th – Friday

I have had too much to drink so this may be incoherent.

First, I woke up at 5 a.m. with a swelling in my left eye. I went up to the Langham at nine, ditched my things, wrote a note for Louise, spoke to a very sympathetic Frank and headed for the Institute of Ophthalmology, where I was told I was unlucky enough to have keratitis twice.

Oh, Christ, not all this again!

Back to the Langham. I told Frank it was keratitis again, and added that one of the possible causes is syphilis. He laughed and said, 'Well, it can't be that, can it?' 'No,' I said, 'I reckon it's God's judgement on me for messing about with a married Catholic.' He said he has painful spasms in his leg, and frequent headaches.

'Conclusive proof then,' said I.

'Think of me,' he said, 'before you go to sleep.'

Lunch in the Salad Bar.

Busy in the office. Louise lost a stopwatch.

Home, ate steak, retired sloshed.

19th – Saturday

Vera is still away in Dorset, so Father and I went shopping. He was in a bloody mood over the tomatoes. We had soup and cheese for lunch. Wrote a long letter to Vera, telling her all the week's news.

20th – Sunday

I cooked lunch – roast chicken (underdone), cauliflower (unsalted), carrots, potatoes, burnt bacon and sausages. Father will appreciate Vera when she is back.

Love is like a guitar: you can hear what it produces, but can't see what makes it.

21st – Monday

Frank was glad to see me. He said he had been having rotten mornings about me. We had a long discussion about abortion (there is a story in the news about a twelve-year-old girl having an abortion). Of course he is opposed to it because it is against the Catholic doctrine and against 'der course of t'ings'. He said, delightfully, that after all there were plenty of ways of enjoying yourself 'while keepin' der legs togedder'.

After work, I went to see Miss Fenn, who is the head person at the hostel, to ask whether I might be excused from paying for breakfast and evening meals as I never take them. Hostel food is inedible and the portions very small. She said there was only one option: you pay for bed, breakfast and evening meal, no reductions. She pointed out that I was in paid employment, and that there were a number of elderly women in the hostel living in very reduced circumstances. Eventually I realised she thought it was a bit of a cheek of me to make the request, so I accepted what she said and went up to my room.

22nd – Tuesday

Vera sent me a card from Dorset with a fish on it and a little ring inside. I showed it to Frank, who immediately took my hand, and we performed an impromptu marriage service. We got most of the words wrong and back to front, but said the 'I do' bits and 'Till death us do part'. I went to kiss him in the usual way, but he said, 'No, not like that, Sarah, do it politely.'

He pointed at the empty landing outside the lift. 'Look, there is all the congregation watching us, your family and mine!' and kissed me very lightly.

Then he took the ring and tried to slide it on to my finger: it was too small.

'Oh, it doesn't fit,' I said, disappointed.

He looked at it more closely and chuckled, 'It's expandable, yer duck!'

I was with him a lot today. We went to the basement together with the lights out. Afterwards he congratulated me but still complained that 'we can't do booger all in a lift'.

On a later journey we had a laugh at a rather snobbish bloke with a beard who got in but wouldn't answer Frank when spoken to. He asked where the hostel is in Victoria and did the number 36 bus go there.

I hope he isn't going to appear suddenly.

Louise and I dealt with the correspondence and told each other ghost stories.

I have accepted a command, phrased as an invitation, to visit Auntie Phyl in Dorset to make up for my not being at Chipstead when she visited.

The City Lit lecture tonight turned out to be a showing of Tony Palmer's film, *All My Loving*, which I had seen on television before. Palmer doesn't have any theories though, only observations. He was very suspicious of [singer-songwriter] Donovan, saying, 'That man is a Fascist.'

23rd – Wednesday

Passed one of those nights, imagining the new Mr and Mrs Browne's honeymoon, but I did get some sleep in the end.

Walked to work, went up with Frank. He was reading poetry again (*Cromwell's Return From Ireland*). He told me he thought George Bernard Shaw was a great man and the Potato Famine was terrible ('For it did reduce the population'). At lunchtime I bought him some Polos and we split the packet. He was delighted as he had been eating onions.

Went down to the basement, but this time not to the foot of the lift shaft. Frank has worked out that if he stops the lift so that the top of it is just below the ground floor, the bottom of the lift is just above the top of the door to the basement, and there, in front of the lift doors, is ... solid wall.

Nobody can see in.

So he very carefully positioned the lift this time, and ... Oh Christ, I suppose it had to happen, but I didn't want to do it!

He was so close, it was so intimate; it was almost all the way. I didn't feel anything special and there was no real pleasure in it. He asked me afterwards, of course, and I didn't know what to say to him. Anyway, it made him far more affectionate and sort of grateful though, which was nice.

Well, once in a while I would go that far, but no further.

He wanted us to go out for the day.

No go.

'T'ink of me as now you see and do not me forget. And in a while you know that I'll be sleepin' widja yet.'

No go again.

Did I know any riddles?

No, not after the last lot you told me.

Silence.

An affectionate goodbye.

Canteen supper, felt slightly sick and stunned.

I should feel happy, shouldn't I? Not worried.

Came back still feeling weird about Frank. I don't want any more; I don't want to be involved with him.

24th – Thursday

This morning Frank gave me a short speech entitled, 'Where Do the Dead Go?' He has calculated that heaven, hell and purgatory couldn't possibly hold all the millions of people who have lived and died, so reincarnation is the only logical answer. Death, he thinks, fits in with everything else in life. Like plants and seeds, man is born over again, man in his children.

I stood in the lift at the sixth floor listening to all of this, and couldn't help thinking what a good face he has. I didn't say anything about yesterday, and neither did he.

I made a complete bish of some copying, and he was very consoling. Later, I couldn't get the top off a new bottle of

Snopake [correction fluid], so I went out to the lifts and pressed the buzzer. He appeared, and I asked him to open it for me, which he promptly did.

I would call him a gentle man, but not a gentleman (that always sounds like a public convenience).

Louise and I are getting on well. Apparently, Gill overheard her having a long chat with Frank.

In the evening I bought a copy of the new Beatles album, *Let It Be*.

25th – Friday

Blood test at the Institute. Dr Poirier struggled to locate a vein, alas.

Got back to Langham at 10.45 to Frank's delight. We managed very well: one passionate kiss and the rest was affection. Today's lift lecture, at lunchtime, was on the topic of Love Thy Neighbour. Frank proposed, Gill spoke up for An Eye for An Eye. I moderated between the two of them.

Frank asked if I considered him a kind man. I said, 'Yes, I do' (to my possible peril).

There will be somebody else one day; it won't be Frank forever but for the last couple of days he has been different, very tender and much more sensible.

Maybe he understands he got it wrong on Wednesday.

We couldn't say goodbye tonight, there were too many 'spies' around.

Janice finished today.

Came home to play the new Beatles LP.

26th – Saturday

Usual shopping expeditions. Listened to new Beatles record.

27th – Sunday

Keep forgetting how much eye stuff I have put in.

28th – Monday

Train journey has taken a new turn. Sue Moriarty was very terse, but it seems that she is now going out with Richard, formerly known as 'Little Weed'.

Frank said he'd spent the weekend 'workin'' and that, well, somebody had to do it. His wife can dress herself but has to have him lace her into the boots she wears to walk.

Madly busy. A new temp replacing Janice came in, took one look at the office, said she had a terrible cold and went out again.

Frank, who normally stays in his lift all day, put his head round the office door a little later on and asked if I was OK. I said yes, wondering why he was asking.

He came over and half-sat on my desk. I glanced at him and went on typing.

Frank: So, who was dat woman?
Me: 'That woman' is supposed to be typing here in
        my office.
Frank: I'm in your office now.
Me: Yes, but you're not typing.
Frank: No. (Chuckles) Pencilling.

I threatened him with my notebook. He kissed me and went out again.

'That woman' never came back. Frank was concerned because he thought there was something odd about her.

We had a pretty wonderful session after lunch, stronger but more gentle. On the way back up, I complained about his stopping the lift suddenly with a jolt.

'Why?' he said, prodding me in the belly, 'you've got nothing in there.'

'Oh, Frank,' I sighed, 'you get more and more like an Irishman every day.'

I got him his tea when I went down for Louise, and neatly avoided Carol.

At ten to six, I summoned Frank, who came all the way up from the basement to take me down, with all the necessary ways of saying goodnight.

He asked if I had a regular boyfriend.

'No, you know I haven't,' I said.

'Well,' he said, 'I can satisfy you at times.'

'You do,' I said, skipping away quickly.

Then on the Tube I started crying because I care about him so much and it's all wrong.

29th – Tuesday

I didn't see Frank until lunchtime and then quite a bit in the afternoon. He bought me tea – he thinks the tea from the vending machine is better than the tea from the Club. In fact, he says the BBC Club smells of stale kippers, old socks and rotten fruit.

Going down for lunch, I got into his lift. He picked up various people on the way down. Somewhere on a lower floor he sent the lift in the wrong direction, to howls of 'FRANK!' from the other passengers. When I thought about it, it is pretty remarkable that he doesn't do that more often.

The usual kisses and hugs, but he was worried when Miss Sheridan and then Mr Roberts nearly caught us and he was right to be.

A new relief turned up during the afternoon to be shown how to operate the lift. That didn't deter Frank, though.

He held my hand behind our backs while carrying on a conversation with the man as if nothing was happening.

Superb, huh!

Chatted to Louise. She said she was afraid of moths. I threatened to bring in a jam jar of moths for her, and she said that if I did, she would finish me by writing me a lousy reference!

Missed Frank in both senses at 5.45.

HELL!

Walked to City Lit. Fantastic talk from Tony Palmer about Zappa and then we saw the film he directed of Cream's last concert at the Albert Hall.

30th – Wednesday

Went up early. Frank and I had a tremendous session. It was all very friendly, too, which was nice, and he led me out of it gently, saying he wouldn't try to go any further.

I don't think he has any false teeth.

I told Frank he was very efficient; he misheard me and thought I said he was officious. I called him gorgeous, he called me 'me dahlin'.' He was looking very satisfied (so he should). We split another packet of mints. 'So,' he asked, 'if you won't go to bed with me, would you go with a younger man?' I said, 'Nope, I only go for OAPs.'

Frank said he liked my new 'gardening' dress. Gardening dress? Yes, for it has all the flowers on it. I wouldn't mind a day out with him, if only I could trust him. And so it goes on.

He said he will take Friday off to do some shopping because his daughter is coming up from Basingstoke.

Jack was off. The skinny man who was his relief said to us, 'What's between you two, you're always in his lift?'

I had lunch with Gill in the Salad Bar, giving Leah a firm brush-off.

Frank had a bad headache again. He said his head felt heavy and I noticed he nearly fell over himself opening a lift door.

Worried.

Curry. Chat with Zelda about teaching.

July

1st – Thursday

I was only just awake when Zelda knocked to collect the sheets for the laundry. Felt groggy, and crawled to the office.

Arrived to find Frank in Jack's lift, eating a bun. He bought me a roll and two butters. We had a pretty fantastic time together. When we finally arrived at the sixth floor we discovered the relief man in Frank's lift was reluctant to give it back. I saw Frank briefly again at lunchtime and made a few excuses to see him in the afternoon. To the basement for one kiss, the rest as usual. I told him I was too fond of him and that he didn't deserve it. He laughed.

I told him about Auntie Phyl, whom I am going to visit tomorrow, and when I said she had never had any children, Frank asked if Gill was 'frail' and if that was why she didn't have any children herself. I said I didn't think Gill was frail – in fact, she is quite tough. Also, she knows a lot about him and me, but is broad-minded. He said that was good, but I should look after her because I am bigger than she is. I said I thought it was more a case of her looking after me.

He wished me a nice, quiet weekend with my aunt.

I told him to look after himself and to behave.

He wanted to take me down to the basement at six when he left, and asked would I stay until then? I said I couldn't because I was having a drink with the 'frail' Gill.

Back to Chipstead. Vera was terribly miserable because Father was being bolshy again.

Madly in love with Frank.

2nd – Friday

Up early; a rushed packing session. Went to Croydon with Vera. Father in bloody mood still and terribly upsetting for her. She and I compared and contrasted the relative merits of Frank and Father. Frank won hands down (!!).

After lunch with Penny, I went to the Institute to change the dates for my appointments next week so that I would have to come back to London on Monday, thereby pre-empting any efforts by Auntie Phyl to delay my return.

Set off for Dorset from Waterloo; there were a lot of Americans on the train. Finished reading Christopher Booker's *The Neophiliacs*. We rattled past Basingstoke. I can't say my heart leapt – it's not a very inspiring place.

Auntie Phyl swooped on me at Gillingham Station and drove me to her country cottage. It's miles from everywhere apart from the smelly cowsheds opposite, a barn of a place with a thatched roof, odd-shaped rooms and lots of awkward steps and stairs. I suppose you would say it had character, a bit like Auntie herself. We had a glass of sherry and then she took me to Bryanston School, where we had a delicious meal and a lovely concert by the Paul Tortellier Trio.

3rd – Saturday

Auntie treated me to breakfast in bed, after which she drove us to a smallholding in Hansford for peas and home-baked bread. Then we picked strawberries together. Back at the cottage she cooked a superb chicken lunch and then went upstairs for a rest.

As it was an afternoon of quiet sunshine I went on a walk to Hambledon Hill. On the way back, I met a strange man with no teeth accompanied by a small boy; they were hunting for fossils. He directed me to Child Okeford, but I became lost and couldn't find the right path. In the end I found a phone box and rang Auntie. I felt like I had walked ten miles in three hours.

I hope I lost some weight.

After tea Auntie drove me back to Bryanston School for a performance of The Water Music at the Bathing Place. A beautiful summer evening, and of course lovely music, but it was all a bit too 'tirribly' civilised for my taste. Also, I rumbled Auntie's cunning plan, as before the concert she surveyed a group of sixth-formers, cooing, 'The Bryanston boys are always such *nice boys*, don't you think? *Such nice boys.*'

To please her, I agreed.

Afterwards we had soup and strawberries for supper and saw the news on TV. She tried again on the subject of the Nice Young Men at Bryanston but they are schoolboys, for goodness sake, and I've got an Irishman who is an expert on what can be done in fifteen minutes standing up in a six-foot square lift. Of course, I'm keeping very quiet on this and most subjects. Auntie Phyl is notoriously inquisitive, a shocking gossip who specialises in exaggeration.

4th – Sunday

Didn't get up until twenty-five to twelve, which was an excellent way to kill off the morning. Ate a very good meal of roast beef and a gooseberry pie. The weather was hotter and more close today.

Auntie went for a rest, well deserved after all that cooking, so I went for a walk around the roads on what I was sure was a foolproof route. I picked some wild flowers and saw a funny little animal.

The trouble with Auntie Phyl is that she was brought up in the Edwardian era, when a woman's only ambition was to make a good marriage with no sex outside the door. Divorce was also outside the door – in fact, much further down the garden. She assumes the only possible thing a young gel could be interested in would be to get married, as if everything else in life is secondary to that goal. Annoyingly, I have to sneakingly admit that I am, of course, looking for a Nice Young Man but I'm damned if I'm going to let her know.

And where is this Nice Young Man anyway? Not at the SBC, or the City Lit, or wandering the streets of London. Perhaps Auntie Phyl more than anyone thinks that young men fall down chimneys.

The other problem with her is that although she somehow got on with my mother, she is very critical of Vera. She even said something about Vera being a gold-digger. I don't really understand this. As far as I can see, Vera puts up with such a lot from my father and is very kind to me.

Auntie Phyl even told me Uncle Ron teased her when she was a little girl until she cried, and then she got a squint. Well, she hasn't got one now, although her eyes are different colours.

There is something very odd about our family.

5th – Monday

Breakfast in bed again. Once I was up and had heard Exactly What Auntie Thinks about Edward Heath, which is Not Much, I thanked her and made it clear that I couldn't possibly stay in her lovely cottage any longer because I needed to be back in London. Thus Auntie drove me to Gillingham Station and I was released from my niecely duty. I shouldn't be too cruel – she was generous and cooked me huge quantities of food, but her company is very wearing.

I travelled back, reading T. S. Eliot. There was a group of schoolgirls from Salisbury in the carriage who were bound for Majorca.

At the Institute, after the usual check up, I was introduced to a medical artist who had been brought in to paint my left eye. After a bit, we got talking. He told me he trained first as an artist and then went into science afterwards so he understands all the medical terms and what it is he has to make sure he gets into the picture. I asked him why the doctors needed paintings, and he said that not everything shows up as well in photos. He showed me the completed painting afterwards.

A very nice guy, who was interesting to talk to.

Back to Chipstead. Father was in a good humour and so was Vera.

Auntie must have phoned in a report of good behaviour.

Wondering, is it a woman's business to appeal to men, and for men to compete for the best? Outdated, or just too basic?

6th – Tuesday

Up at 6.20 to have a bath, etc. Attempted to catch and missed the 7.50 train, so I had to wait ages at East Croydon for the next one. When I got to Victoria, I trotted along to the hostel meaning to dump my stuff, only to discover that I didn't have my keys. Panic! I rang the bell and in the end the housekeeper allowed me in and gave me a spare, but she was very ungracious about it.

There are too many miserable old women in my life at the moment.

Rushed up to the Langham, pausing on the way only to buy a packet of Polos for Frank. He was delighted to see me, and I him. We'd been apart for four days, and after a quick chat about the weekend and my ophthalmic well-being, during which he announced with heavy innuendo that he too was a specialist, I was whisked off to the new inter-ground-floor-and-basement secret place and the lights went off. He put one arm around me and with the other hand he brought my face to his for a loooong kiss, which I thought would go on forever, and rather wished it had. It was warm enough for him to have his jacket open. Very close, it was. I'm not kidding. There was a lot of giving, respect, sympathy. I can tell he's not just out for what he can get from me.

Had my first pay rise, annual increase of £65.

The final lecture tonight at the City Lit. Tony Palmer, who turned up in a purple Mini, played some records and talked about how he saw the future of pop music. Basically, he hedged his bets and said it could go in any direction: electronic, big band, orchestral, film music, but he emphasised its energy and satire. I asked him if he had read *The Neophiliacs* and he said he had, but disagreed with some of the arguments.

7th – Wednesday

Fabulous day. Summer at last, the weather hot and sunny.

All the bosses went off to an education officers' meeting, which left me plenty of time for further discussions with Frank.

We began by talking about the price of food, which is going up again. He said he spent £13 on food at the weekend, £3 of which was on meat. But then he had bought sweets for his grandchildren.

I asked him to describe his council flat. It's in Alfred Road, near the Royal Oak Underground station. It's on the ground floor of a small block, and has a bedroom, bathroom, sitting room and kitchen. The sitting room is 16' by 9'. He said he prefers squarer rooms because they are easier to furnish. He said perhaps I'd visit it sometime.

He is taking annual leave to go to Basingstoke with his wife and we are taking holidays at different times. Curses.

He suggested he might come to see me in the hostel one evening, but I explained that men weren't allowed in.

'That's OK,' he said brightly, 'I'll dress up as a woman.'

And then, guess what, he asked me to go to bed with him. I refused, but this time explained that if we did do it, I would probably have to leave my job because I wouldn't be happy working in the same building with him, and apart from how he and I might manage afterwards, it would become obvious to everyone else.

He looked concerned and said, 'You know I know the ropes. I like you, you know I want you and I won't do you any harm,' and then he said much more that I didn't understand, like 'You only do wrong when you let it go.'

(What?)

I asked him what line I should take in the event of us being caught.

'Don't worry,' he said, 'I won't let you get into any trouble.'

He said he wouldn't ever get married again because it ties you down, and murder is the worst possible sin. I was a bit worried about this train of thought, but he brightened up again and recited a rhyme about impertinence and countenance or possibly incontinence, which I didn't quite get, and a rude one about King Harold of Munster, who did something with a youngster.

Adrienne came to lunch and told us about her women's encounter group.

Later on, Frank was laughing about the men from religious broadcasting. He said they get into the lift and are so tied up in their thinking, they can only say 'yes – um – no,' to him when he speaks to them. I can't help thinking how handsome he is and what a fabulous elastic face he has, with all sorts of expressions. He is a really lovely fellah.

Hooray for the education officers' meeting.

Met Penny in the evening. Had a super Chinese meal, walked to St James's Park and then on to her room. We had a real good laugh (about pelicans and people's legs), then I took the bus back.

It was a lovely day.

8th – Thursday

Louise was out this morning, and when she came back in the afternoon she was flaked out with the heat.

I went in early, went up to the Institute to be photographed again, and came back.

Frank super. Two early-morning feeling sessions. Before I had said anything to him, he already knew about my 'condition', which was odd. He had taken his jacket off, which facilitated things, and afterwards we had a conversation about bras.

It was odd to be discussing them with a man.

He gave Gill and me a Crunchie bar each, which he got from the machine – he said it was by accident and refused to take any money for them. I bought him a tea and changed his money for him in the afternoon.

I bought a pound of strawberries for 10p and ate them all at lunch.

Celia told me she decoded stuff during the war; Frank told me he liked listening to ITMA [*It's That Man Again*, popular BBC radio comedy at the time].

We had a silly 'Yes, yes, yes, yes, no' conversation and started laughing again.

But it's all terrible, terrible, terrible, terrible, terrible.

Curry. Zelda still in a mess over her German, who hasn't contacted her for ages and seems unlikely to do so ever again.

Frank told me today there are fifty-two ways of getting a woman.

9th – Friday

Frank came into the office first thing for a couple of kisses. He was very pleasant mostly but got rather fruity in the afternoon, making the usual suggestions again. I said, 'It's sad, you're the right fellow, but at the wrong time.'

A man may have seen us together in the evening, enjoying an extended goodbye and a bit of cuddling.

Louise and I had a long discussion about *The Neophiliacs* book, Illusion and Reality, *The Iceman Cometh*, the First World War and Gallipoli. Germ warfare got in there somewhere too.

Gill in a panic about a science thing, so I offered to help her by working overtime.

Jack is off next week. Frank spent some time with a broom clearing plastic cups, which people had chucked down the shaft, off the roof of his lift. He said he hoped I would enjoy going to 'Wording' tomorrow.

Home.

10th – Saturday

Picked up Penny from Purley Station and drove to Chanctonbury Ring, which is on the South Downs near 'Wording'. It has to be my favourite place in the world, with views to the sea on one side and London on the other. I try to visit it every year, and thought Penny might appreciate the ancient, mysterious atmosphere among the trees. The views were obscured a little by haze but otherwise it was well worth the climb. Then we drove to Angmering, parked down a side road and shook hands with the sea.

Travelling back along a dual carriageway outside Crawley the exhaust pipe broke. I pulled over to the side and we were wondering what to do next when a young man stopped and fixed it for us. We thanked him effusively and he drove off. I suppose he was spoken for ... Anyway, he shot off once the job was done and didn't ask for either of our phone numbers.

Had supper at home and then took Penny to the station.

11th – Sunday

Terribly hot weather.

Oh, Frank! Having said to him that we have no future, am I making too big a deal about the whole thing? I can't imagine ever wanting to do anything with anyone else, so why not just go ahead with him? What's the difference when we have already done what we have done?

But I don't think I love him and I won't do it.

Should I go at six with him one evening or not?

Can I stop him if I did?

Yes, I should think so, dear.

Should I not go at all?

Yes ... No ... I want him.

Do you want him?

I don't know.

In that case, you don't.

But I don't know what he would do to me, or rather, what it would feel like, so I don't know whether I would want it or not.

I can guess.

You are fantasising.

Is that wrong?

No, it's a different point altogether. I mean, I think I love ... something, and that something is part of him.

You are losing your self-control.

12th – Monday

Went up with an incommunicative Sue Moriarty.

Perhaps The Weed has sprouted.

On arrival, Frank announced that he had not spent a pleasant weekend. The hot weather had made his wife very sick with sweating and mild fits, and he had to 'keep her quiet' for fear she'd go into a coma. He hadn't any energy himself to conserve.

I was busy with typing and didn't see him again until after lunch, when we had a terribly affectionate session.

Louise went home in the afternoon. She had toothache and said she had overdosed herself with paracetamol. So when I went down to the Club for a cup of tea, I bought one for Frank as well, only when he picked me up at the ground floor, I saw he was already finishing a cup.

Me (getting into the lift with him):
        Oh, do you want this tea? I see someone else
        has got you one already.

Frank: Oh, dat's Waites' girl on the fourth floor.
        She buys me tea sometimes.
      (I give him a straight look)
      (He looks back at me)

Frank: But I don't buy tea for hor.

He closed the gates and started up the lift. As we got to the sixth floor, he turned round to me and said quietly, 'Sarah, you know you're the best t'ing I've got – you're great!'

13th – Tuesday

Since January, Frank and I have had eleven weeks together – which equals the eleven weeks he was away with the hip operation. Was he really away for so long? It seems I have known him for ages, and the time he was away never happened.

We had a very all-stops-out session in the morning.

He asked why I hadn't reported him. I said I wouldn't because I liked him.

Louise was off with toothache so I typed most of Harris's *Science Box* guide, including all his infuriating spelling and punctuation mistakes.

Carol told me she thought she had got Frank into trouble about something, but she didn't say what it was. I wasn't sure if she was bluffing to get me to admit something.

Walked around Regent's Park for a while as it was a pleasant evening. Frank was very affectionate all day, although I didn't see him so often. He's got it badly at the moment.

If I put my hands to my face even now I can smell him, so clean and sweet.

14th – Wednesday

Arrived at nine to find Frank talking to a man, whom he bundled away with indecent haste. He took me up and we had a very intense session in the office. He wanted it desperately but we did what we had done before and as we finished, he muttered with a smile, 'Well, at least I didn't come.'

Worked all morning on *Science Box* and had a busy day, really.

Had lunch alone.

Frank working solo because Jack was away somewhere. He was in a very chirpy mood; he said it was because of us in the morning, but I doubt it. He was pulling faces a lot – he said he had an itchy nose, which meant 'some bleedin' booger's talking about me'.

I told Frank that Jack had been very good to me when he was in hospital. Frank said he buys Jack a lot of things – tea, fags, newspapers and so on – and they got on pretty well.

When I left at ten to six he had already changed out of his uniform as if he was going home, but he said he wasn't leaving yet – he had been asked to work on late.

I hope he wasn't planning to take someone else down to the basement.

I walked back to the hostel and tried to find the Westminster Bridge Fortes, which Frank said he once decorated, but I couldn't see it so I suppose it has gone. He told me that once, when he was painting the cafe, he got lost in Westminster.

15th – Thursday

Another hot day. Had a session on the *Springboard* material with Mr Jones – he refers to sunbathing as the 'Burning of the Virgins'.

Didn't see so much of Little Frank. A trip to our basement hiding place was curtailed by a loud buzz from below. Frank let me go, we did our emergency clothes fix and he dropped down to open the door. There stood an elderly man in painting overalls, holding a couple of paint pots and some brushes.

'Go round to der bleedin' Goods Lift, wouldja?' said Frank fiercely.

The man started to argue, but Frank pointed out the way to go and shut the lift door. I felt a bit sorry for the guy, but Frank said he should have known not to use the passenger lift – I don't think he liked being interrupted.

I told him I would like to go to Killarney sometime. He said it's a good place to go to: if it rains, the people take you in. Although some of his family are still in Ireland, the country is too poor to support everyone, so you have to leave to find your fortune elsewhere and from then on you must 'paddle your own canoe'.

We discussed headaches. He gets his pills on his wife's payment-exempt prescription because he takes about six a day, and it would cost him several quid a week otherwise. This is because of the brain injury he had from The Fall.

At the end of the day, I asked him to take me down to the basement again. He was only too pleased to oblige, and gave me a beautiful goodnight kiss.

Frank:	So, didja come down here for dat?
Me:	No, no, I was just going home through Cavendish Square.
Frank:	Are you still in love wid me?
	(Silence. Frank thinks I am mulling this over but actually I haven't heard him properly)
Me:	Pardon?
	(Frank looks at me and we both start laughing)

And off I went, walking back to the hostel down Park Lane. Curry. Zelda.

16th – Friday

Busy in the office. Miss Sharp not amused by illiteracy of the *Science Box* guide either.

Frank has been given some important files to read: A *House Services II* list and a *Productivity Manual (Phase Three)*. He said carrying them gave him cramp.

Madly wanted him in the afternoon, and in the evening got it up to the borderlines of what we've ever done before.

The details too personal even for this diary, but he was amused at my going a bit red.

Frank: I am going to give you everything.

He waved goodbye to me from the steps of the Langham, and even though I felt a little sick on the train afterwards, he was fabulous.

Home.

17th – Saturday

Met Zelda at Purley and had a day out together in Kent. We went to Tunbridge Wells first and then on to Penshurst Place – I wouldn't mind living there myself. It was a long day and I dropped her back at the station around 6 p.m.

18th – Sunday

Think we should abolish towels and have hot air blowers in the bathroom instead.

Read a very good book on the Murder of Charles Bravo. He did it himself, accidentally.

Right, I am giving up making rules about what I should do with Frank because it's impossible to do anything but play it by ear. As for him, I reckon he is 55 per cent out for one thing, 10 per cent fatherly concern and affection and 30 per cent (does this make 100 per cent?) a good friend. And 5 per cent don't know.

Where do we go from here then? It's all a bloody shame, really.

I am sorry this diary has consisted of 'He said' so much.

19th – Monday

Went back to London but had barely anything to discuss with Moriarty.

Frank was even better looking than usual.

Is the light in the lift flattering?

He didn't mention Friday, apart from asking obliquely was I all right? I said yes. We split a packet of mints and exchanged a few kisses during the day. Nearly missed him at five to six – he was going as I left, so we didn't do anything special.

I don't blame him for any of this. He's a silly old man, you know.

Gill and I had lunch together but with the ubiquitous Leah so conversation was limited.

20th – Tuesday

Walked up to the office. Frank said he is getting a new uniform, which he doesn't particularly want or need. He said the BBC is good to him in the things that don't matter; instead they should stop the sack barrows going up in his lift.

Celia summoned me to her office to make an appointment for an annual interview with Mr Roberts. She asked how long did I want with him. I said however long most people had, so was put down for twenty minutes. While we were talking, Mr Roberts came out from his office and offered me a glass of sherry. When I told Louise about that she said it means I've arrived.

I was debating about saying yes and going out with Frank in the evening, but in the end I went down to the basement and he was ever so gentle and warm, although his hands went everywhere. He asked me about taking off my pants, but I said I didn't want to make it easier for him and after all, he wasn't doing too badly. I told him he was incredible. (He is.)

He could have done with a shave, though.

Went to Little Portland Street Library and borrowed *Ulysses* (Irish) and Thomas Hardy.

21st – Wednesday

Annual Interview today; it lasted about ten minutes. The report, written by Louise, was a bit embarrassing. It opened with, 'Sarah is the best secretary I have ever had,' and extolled the virtues of my shorthand, phoning, time-keeping and enthusiasm for work. I had to keep a straight face when I read, 'Sarah continued to come into work to assist in the Department even when she was suffering from an eye disease' (if only she knew!). She did say my typing was sometimes inaccurate and Roberts asked me about that. I said I wasn't very mechanically minded. He asked me about playing the guitar and my writing, and said obviously I would be moving on soon and that he and Louise would be sorry when I did.

He is very intelligent-looking; a big man, with a bald head and very blue eyes.

Frank told me he has always had good reports. I asked how anyone could know how he worked, so he explained that supervisors come over at odd times to watch him and Jack. Somehow we got on to the railways, and he told me how when he was working on the roof of Paddington Station during the Second World War, he saw doodlebugs flying over, and about incendiary bombs falling around his house.

Felt really fond of him.

Devil.

'Praying and sex,' he said, 'they both get you in the knees.'

Frank: How many children do you t'ink you'll have?
Me: Thousands.

We had a good time together today.

Louise and I in hysterics about a club that cares for white mice, and about old mice in the radio studios.

Supper at BH. Walked back.

22nd – Thursday

Frank busy today, me not so. Louise must have overdosed because she became distinctly lethargic in the afternoon.

Valerie, Gill and I retreated to the pub for lunch to discuss Sharpy and other highly confidential rubbish about staff at the SBC.

Louise said to Frank how nice I was (Frank and I thought this was a bit fishy) but I was glad to hear he was gentlemanly enough to agree with her. He has decided that, since we are all animals, we should all go about naked. I said this would be a bit chilly, but he said it would be beautiful.

Supper with Penny and Gill, discussing humanism and falling down. Walked back with Penny to Charing Cross, and then through St James's Park.

Wondering how long I can defy the might of the little over-sexed Irishman, but feeling rather self-indulgently happy and satisfied.

I'm very fortunate, really.

23rd – Friday

This morning, Frank announced to me that I was a good girl and was doing 'the right thing' in not agreeing to go too far with him. In fact, he was really sweet all day, although he was tired because he was working on his own. He had to dash out at teatime to buy a birthday card.

Louise was sleepy all day – I don't think she is very well.

Gill and I had lunch together. She was surprised to learn

what Frank and I talk about. After lunch, I had a chat with Frank about jobs, etc., while he munched a buttered bun. He tried to talk me out of leaving the SBC, which was flattering but a bit pointless. He was so kind and gentle all day. He 'let me go' in the evening, with a funny little kiss and a request that I 'take it easy'.

I do so love him.

And he seemed genuinely fond of me, although he did suggest I took a look at Room 26, which has a bed in it.

I didn't fall for that one.

24th – Saturday

Tony Palmer has written an article about Yoko Ono ['Grapefruit', *The Spectator*, 24 July]. I don't think he could have done much more with the subject, to be honest.

Listened to *Let It Be* all afternoon, and rewrote some of my poems.

Madly – no, not madly – deeply in love again with Frank.

25th – Sunday

Dull. Uncle Ron came over. Cleared up all the poems in case Father finds the ones about Frank.

Longing for tomorrow, and I've been thinking a lot about his wife.

26th – Monday

Sue Moriarty and I travelled up together in profound silence. Hurried in to see Frank, who kissed me for good behaviour. He said he had walked into a post over the weekend while he was reading, and had come to work without any of his painkillers.

'Is it snowing?' he asked.

I wasn't sure if he was joking or whether he had done some real damage to his eyesight. I wanted to cuddle him and maybe he felt the same but anyway, we didn't get the opportunity. I didn't see half enough of him.

He proposes taking Wednesday off to do some business, which he will explain to me tomorrow. Got properly upset over that. Then I realised with a horrid shock that in two weeks' time he is going on leave.

Oh, Christ!

I had supper in the BH canteen overlooking Regent Street. Looking out of the window, I saw Frank hobbling away down the road to Oxford Circus. Deeply, genuinely, painfully, stupidly, sadly love him today. I can't bear not being with him.

Walked back, took a look at Jules Bar and then went into Westminster Cathedral, which is beautiful and rather moving, although I don't go for all those bleeding (literally) statues.

I said a prayer for Frank.

27th – Tuesday

I had a series of dreams, some of them I had had before, about Frank.

The morning was sunny, but it rained hell's drizzle in the evening.

Went up at nine. Frank and I went into the office and had one of those intimate sessions. I told him I loved him, because I honestly did/do. He didn't refer to it again during the day. He refused to say what he is doing tomorrow, only that he was 'getting meself sorted out, s'all'.

We discussed the Irish. I said I agreed with Catholicism in general, but that it wasn't kind to people on specific things like contraception.

Some people, Frank said, just like to believe what they are told.

I asked him what he believed in. He said, 'In every man for himself, and to live according to your own conscience.' I said I would miss him tomorrow and wasn't happy at the prospect of our only having four days together in the next five weeks.

We talked about my future and leaving the SBC. I said I didn't want to work for a commercial firm, and it was a shame I couldn't take him with me when I went.

'Well,' he sighed, 'it's a shame I can't be with you always' (or words to that effect).

'You're still a lovely fellah,' I said.

He was tired and sleepy towards the end of the day, either because of his head or the pills.

We got on very well today, on a friendly basis, and the conversation really flowed. But because I love to spend time with him, I think I am in his lift too long.

I would go out with him, but (1) he hasn't asked me for a while and I don't want to mention it first, and (2) I don't honestly feel I can trust him, or myself. I let him have this morning (it feels like five years ago now) because I wanted it as much as he did, but honest to God we surely can't go much further? I felt so much sympathy, pity and love for him.

It's the situation that is impossible, not us.

28th – Wednesday

Although it was a day without Little Frank, and even Jack said he missed him, it passed quickly.

Louise and I talked about swearing in school programmes and why is it necessary. She explained the background to the sex education programmes and how they had been recommended because so many children don't get any sex education at home. She said the level of ignorance about sex among even teenagers was worrying. I agreed.

We also talked about plays, mythology in modern life and radio panel games. We both like *My Word* and *My Music* but she thinks Clement Freud is conceited. I stuck up for Kenneth Williams. After that, we spent about an hour discussing Harold Wilson, referenda, Michael Foot, the House of Commons, the British and Australian forms of government, the Common Market, Chinese restaurants and telephones. All that lasted from ten minutes past two to twenty minutes past four – there wasn't so much work to do today.

I have discovered that Active Holidays is also running a week for 'Young People' in Coniston. Carol says it's a great place for a walking holiday and A.H. is a good way of meeting people.

Gill and I had a drink after work, and at first we talked about her job being up-graded, then we got on to Frank. I said to Gill, 'I have grown three years in one year. I'm not even the person I was in January.' She said it was all the result of my sheltered upbringing and not knowing any blokes. I must have brightened up Frank's life, but he is a romantic old Irishman and I should be careful because I could hurt him a lot. Also, we really mustn't get caught together. The natural way for it to end would be for me to leave the SBC and the Langham. I agreed with her.

I'm afraid the version I gave her of what we have been up to was a bit bowdlerised, though.

I have tried to work out how old Frank is. At first I thought he was about forty-five, but maybe that's wrong. He was on the railways for 21 years and with Fortes for 8 years, so has worked 29 years. I don't know how long he has been at the BBC. If he was sixteen when he left Ireland, he must have been born 1914–16. Thus he is in his late fifties, which makes sense.

I see nothing wrong in loving a man of that age at all – it's the personality that counts.

He told me he wasted his life on the railways and not to do the same thing, i.e. I should leave the SBC.

Anyway, although I might have fallen into this thing with Frank because I don't know any other blokes, it doesn't mean that I love him any the less, does it?

Little Portland Street Library. Chicken curry.

29th – Thursday

I got into the lift with Frank first thing, but with a crowd of other people. He greeted us with his usual 'Come into the parlour' as we piled in. One of them, another secretary, asked him where he had been yesterday. He said he had been 'sick, sad and sorrowful'. When he was on his own with me I asked him again, but he wouldn't say more than that he had been travelling and waiting. I suspected a hospital visit, but who knows?

He bought me a roll in the morning, and Gill and I did our Houdini disappearing act at lunchtime to go to the pub, thus avoiding the others.

I had a long talk with Frank in the afternoon. We started off on money: he asked how much I was saving and how much was my rent at the hostel. He said he got married on 80/- a week, that it was rotten to be tied to a marriage because you fancied a girl and couldn't have her unless you wedded her, because a man could always hold back, even in the heat of the moment.

I wondered if Tuesday morning could be described as being 'in the heat of the moment'.

A woman he called Sheila got into the lift, and they had a conversation in Irish. I asked him about speaking in Irish. He told me how to count to ten: ain, doo, tre, car, quig, shae, shocht, hoct, no, ver. I think that's right. Then, when I had collected Louise's tea from the Club and we were on the ground floor, an obviously pregnant woman got into Jack's lift, which was being driven by a trainee. Frank said he felt sorry for her, travelling with him because he wouldn't be able to stop the lift smoothly.

'Well,' I said, 'You bump the lift sometimes.'

'So, are you telling me you have a baby in there as well?'

I laughed, and he started to sing a song about loving me.

Up at the sixth floor he asked me, 'What is this shorthand that you secretaries do, how does it work?' I began to describe it, not very well, and then said, 'Wait here.' I collected my notebook from my office, went back to the lift and showed it to him. I explained how the symbols are phonetic and what some of them meant; I even wrote out his name in shorthand. He took the book, studied it for a few moments, and then said, 'Oh yes, I understand, this says, "I love you, I love you very much ..."' – at which point Carol bustled up to the lift and we hastily changed the subject.

He is a wonderfully good-hearted man. I must not take him too seriously, though.

30th – Friday

Arrived to find Frank and Jack walking down the stairs from the first floor. Frank was quiet today and I started to wonder all sorts of miserable things like, is he through with us? Is there another girl? Why did I take him so seriously? We had a kiss in the basement and a couple elsewhere.

'How about fitting a red light in the lift?' he said.

He asked where my home was, where do I travel from and how long does it take. However, he doesn't like classical music, for ''tis for der highbrows', it is boring and it goes on and on, like cricket. He's not keen on pop either, although he admitted the Beatles 'have the music'.

I asked him what kind of music he liked, and he said brass bands.

He had a dream about writing a cheque. 'Well,' he said, 'funny things go on at night.'

Back home to plague Vera. Reading Aldous Huxley.

31st – Saturday

Things not too bad at home, but I'm having second thoughts about going on the Isle of Wight holiday – I am not all that keen on a week away with people I don't know.

Everything I am with Frank, both the reality and the dream of being with him, is what is important to me now. It is right for both of us, at the moment. It has its incompleteness, but it isn't a lie or sordid.

It's a funny love – sad, and good.

August

1st – Sunday

Listened to some dreadful pop music – I could almost do with Frank's brass bands.

2nd – Monday

[At the top of the page: Bloody Monday, bloody week]

Went up with a slightly more chatty Sue Moriarty. Force of circumstance, I think, as Richard wasn't around.

For the first time I was fed up with my job. It all seemed old hat and there wasn't a lot to do.

I missed seeing Frank after lunch, but we had some interesting conversations. Funny how his lift is the right size for a confessional booth.

Frank:	Well, I suppose in a few years' time some young fellah will come along and you'll settle down.
Me:	I suppose so.
Frank:	Would you rather be an old man's darling, or a young man's slave?

(Pause for thought)

Me: Neither. Perhaps an old man's darling would be
         better – I don't want to be anyone's slave.

Frank: Neither, nayther, nevertheless ... You wouldn't,
         you know.

Me: No?

Frank: All this, it means nothing. It's only a bit of
         flirting. It doesn't matter. I know I get a bit ...
         angry ... but ...

Me: That's only natural.

Frank: Yes, that's the way it is. But I wouldn't want to
         hurt you or [some phrase that meant getting
         me pregnant] or upset you. You get a bit angry
         too – well, that's what it's there for. But it
         doesn't matter. I wouldn't do nothing bad to
         you. Oh, crikeys, no!

He said he felt bitter that the BBC had questioned his 'productivity' – 'But I don't worry about it. I spend me time and money on the drink. I fill me head with nuttin'.'

I told him I like him better with his hair a bit longer – short hair makes his ears stick out. 'Humph,' he said, 'as long as that's the only thing.'

Walked back to the hostel through Green Park, and began to wonder whether I have been a colossal fool to think I mattered to Frank, his saying that what we had done 'didn't matter'. Perhaps he and his wife are more happily married than I can imagine. Ended up in tears down Buckingham Palace Road.

Paid an enormous amount of money for rent in the hostel. Can't stand living here anymore. I can't summon up the courage to go anywhere else because I am alone but I don't want to admit that.

Oh God, what am I to do?

3rd – Tuesday

It bucketed with rain and I was soaked on the way in. Frank bought me some breakfast, which has gone up to 3p for a roll, and he also gave me half his biscuit.

A strange woman came in and hung around by the lifts for a couple of hours midday. She was removed by one of the commissionaires.

On return from lunch, I mentioned to Frank how miserable I had been yesterday evening. At first he said it was probably down to natural causes, then he said he thought a lot of it was because of my parents. He said not to be too depressed about things.

'Is your father Irish?' he asked. I said no, but I almost wished he was because the Irish seem so much more friendly. 'No,' he said, 'some Irish are rotten.' Most of his best friends are English.

'I'll think up a formula to get you happy,' he said.

But if he did, he didn't tell me what it was because the next time I saw him The Fat Trainee was in the lift with him. I bought Frank a cup of tea though, and he managed to tickle my palm behind his back.

Felt a bit down, but better than yesterday.

Curry.

4th – Wednesday

Miserable again. I can't think why this happens so suddenly.

I rang Father about the car insurance, but he didn't recognise me or my name and put down the phone. I left it a bit, then rang again and spoke to Vera.

Over lunch, Carol told us she will be leaving soon as she is moving to a new job at 35 Marylebone High Street. Gill has been made up to a Grade SC6, which is good news.

Louise a bit cheesed off still. I think something has gone wrong, her friend the psychiatrist rang her today.

Frank had The Fat Trainee with him again today, but managed to lose him after lunch when I went for the *Radio Times*, allowing us a very passionate kiss in the basement. Otherwise we were reduced to looking and tickling. He said he wanted to get me with child. I said that wasn't a helpful suggestion, in fact I nearly spat at him in fury. He knows damn well what I don't want.

I'm not being coy, I just Don't Bloody Want It from him.

Gill, Penny, Carol and I had supper together, discussing SBC trivia. Afterwards I walked back to Charing Cross Road with Penny and we abandoned our plan of going on holiday together to Dorset.

Should I have taken Frank so seriously? He's away next week on holiday, which makes it worse.

5th – Thursday

In a bloody lousy state, so I don't think I will be coherent.

1. Georgina Fox rang to say she's moving into a flat, and I'm furious because I've been waiting and hoping that she and I could get a flat together.
2. The *Science Box* guide has been buggered up and the whole thing will have to be retyped.
3. I had a headache all day.
4. AND FRANK'S GONE.

When I got to work, I was worried because I thought he might be after a bit more than the usual, but instead nothing at all happened because he had The Fat Trainee in his lift. And it had taken him an hour to get from Euston Road to Great Portland Street, having had to change trains and wait in the rain. In fact, he only arrived at the same time as I did.

The Fat Trainee is really dense.

I didn't see Frank again until later in the morning, when I went to the shops for Louise. Bought mints. Came back. Gave mints to Frank. He followed me into the lift with The Fat Trainee and tried to return half the packet as usual as we were travelling up. I said no, because I wanted him to keep them all.

Then he followed me out of the lift and said, 'Look, I'm going home because I feel lousy. I won't see you for a month.' 'Three weeks,' I said. 'OK,' he says, 'three weeks.' Blows me a kiss, gets back into the lift and is gone. And I actually waved at him as he descended – how ridiculous.

I felt awful at lunch. I came back to the office and cried intermittently through a very long afternoon.

Louise must have realised how I felt because towards the end of the day, after she had given me some dictation, she and I had a chat. I told her I thought I would look for another job soon, and that I was thinking of moving over to administration in BH. She thought production might suit me better. Then I said that I wanted to move out of the hostel but wasn't sure where to go. She gave me some advice about flats, e.g. be brazen and make sure that even if you are sharing a flat, you have your own room – it was worth the extra cost. Then she said why not think about moving into a bedsitter, which is one room in a house, usually with a shared bath and maybe kitchen. She said she was in a similar situation when she separated from her husband, looking for jobs and accommodation.

'Just join everything going,' she said.

I walked back to the hostel and went into Westminster Cathedral. A choir was singing, so I sat down and listened for a little while, and then I went into the chapel of the Irish saints and lit a candle for Frank.

6th – Friday

Cold. Office dead quiet. And it has been confirmed that, Bloody Hell, some old Flossie will be coming to share my office next week. DAMN! Things are going from bad to worse.

Lunch with Valerie and Gill discussing modern art, egalitarianism, etc. Gill to the right, Sarah left of right, Valerie moderate. Asked Valerie and Gill for advice about flats – how to find out what's available and so on. Apparently the BBC has an Accommodation Officer who finds places for staff, so she might be able to help me. I asked Louise if she knew anything about this person.

Chatted to Jack, who was very kind towards me. Perhaps he guesses how I am feeling.

Back home to announce flat and job plans to Vera. She agreed.

How quickly can three weeks go?

7th – Saturday

Chipstead.

I have been mulling over the Isle of Wight holiday and decided against it. I feel it's better by far to cancel than to go on a holiday that I don't want and can't afford. Of course I realise it would mean letting down Zelda and it would be the most rotten, awful thing I have ever done to cancel it now. In fact, if I were Zelda I'd be bitterly upset and angry. I shall have to face the consequences with her, but that's only fair. To be honest, after last week I can't face being away from work when Frank comes back from leave.

Usual shopping. Father bloody.

8th – Sunday

Talked with Vera and destroyed the letters I wrote out last night, cancelling the Isle of Wight holiday. I'll only be away for a week and it means my integrity remains intact.

Saw a programme on TV that brought the Icelandic saga stories to life, and felt I could do with a bit of Odin-worship.

9th – Monday

Weather dull and overcast, which could have made the atmosphere cosy but instead it was grey and flat. Office quiet, and in the absence of Frank it seemed terribly empty. I'm not saying that having him there always makes happy situations, just more interesting ones, and it is always nice to know what he is doing. Made a determined effort and almost managed to ignore his absence, in a sort of necessary-for-survival way.

Flossie Frogspawn (or as Carol has it, Frogsperm) arrived to take up residence on the other side of my desk. She is an overlarge, middle-aged woman, with hair escaping in all directions. My typing deteriorated – I can't concentrate with someone else in the office.

Gill and I escaped at lunchtime and Valerie joined us later. We had a good laugh about Miss Sharp and Miss Malcolm.

After work I walked down to the Haymarket and bought a ticket for the theatre for tomorrow and then came back through St James's Park. I sat and listened for a while to … a brass band (cough) … the Band of the Irish (cough) Guards.

Is life like a lift? We are on the ground floor when we are born, and reach the top floor when we die, and in between we go up and down at different speeds, stopping at different floors.

10th – Tuesday

Terrible news about Belfast: three young, off-duty soldiers from the Royal Highland Fusiliers have been killed. Father was in that regiment during the war.

Lunch with Valerie, Gill, Carol and Leah in BH canteen. Turns out everyone detests one of the officers and consequently he received no congratulations when he was awarded an OBE.

Carol told me Frank had been very 'unforthcoming' about her job move.

Louise said that if I was thinking of applying for other jobs I should write my will, which sounded a bit drastic until she explained she meant I should write down for the next incumbent how I do my job.

I went over for supper at BH and shared a table with a girl who works in the Engineering Department. She said, don't apply for a job in Engineering, it's boring, and then said sensitive people shouldn't work in a production department.

Does this rule me out?

Walked to the Haymarket Theatre and saw *A Voyage Round My Father* by John Mortimer, with Alec Guinness playing the father. English summer garden atmosphere, and very much Guinness's play. Some very funny lines. Refreshing night out.

Twenty more days to go. Ugh!

11th – Wednesday

Mrs Frogspawn's 'work' was of such high standard that I only had to retype three out of four pages. She and I are enjoying a mildly pleasant antagonism. As I did her corrections, she told me that she is going to be moved to a clerical job working for Miss Sharp rather than this 'ordinary secretarial post'. I don't think she is a trained secretary. Oh well, I suppose I can tolerate her. Just. I am more worried about her being given the menial chores, like taking down the photocopying and getting drinks from the Club. I can't allow her to take those over because they require journeys in the lift.

Louise exasperated about the *TV7 Guide*, which came back wrong again.

After work I went to Westminster Cathedral again. There was a concert on, so I bought a programme and joined the small audience. There were a lot of pieces of music and it went on a long time. The choir was good, the soloists were a bit ropey and the organ was so deafening there was no option but to be spiritually uplifted.

12th – Thursday

At last, a day that went by quickly.

Louise a good deal more cheerful now and we had a good laugh in the evening about the filing.

Mrs Frogspawn told me that her new clerical post is going to be announced shortly. I wasn't aware that Miss Sharp wanted a clerk, but maybe she does. I'm really worried about the dogsbody duties being taken away from me.

Lunch with Gill, and we went on a half-successful hunt for art materials for Kaz but couldn't find a litho pencil anywhere, even though we went to the dramatically named Bleeding Heart Yard.

Carol is to leave on 27 August while I am away on holiday, which is a shame. I'll miss her leaving do.

Gill and I had supper together. She was upset because a flat she was after had been taken, and cross because Kaz leaves it all up to her. Meanwhile, she is hunting for ways of publicising Kaz's art work. Papers? Letters?

13th – Friday

Pouring with rain.

Reorganised the Outside Borrowers file to the accompaniment of Mrs Frogspawn tapping and splattering on the typewriter.

A mix-up over trains meant I got home late. Nearly finished reading *The Canterbury Tales*, which I am enjoying.

14th – Saturday

Bought black boots for walking in on holiday. I can hardly believe it is in a week's time. Read Chaucer while sitting in the car, waiting for Father in Coulsdon. Vera seems terribly tired and strained.

15th – Sunday

Conversation at lunch:

Vera: That meat you are eating cost thirty shillings.

Father: It would cost more at a restaurant.

Vera: Yes, but it would save me the preparation and clearing up afterwards.

Father: I'll do that.

Me: But if you did, she would still have to clear up after you.

Father: Well, I will pay for you and Vera to go for a meal at The Midday Sun.

Me: But we want you to come too so we could go as a family.

Father: Rubbish.

Father: I thought things had hit rock bottom when that little nit Suzanne [my aunt] started on at me on Wednesday.

Vera:	Saying what?
Me:	She's not a little nit.
Father:	You only say that to curry favour with Vera.
Me:	I am sorry you think I am such a shallow person that what I say is only to curry favour with someone. It shows how little you know me.

Is it right for a family to be this way?

Read *The Boston Strangler*.

It's fifteen days before Frank and I meet again.

16th – Monday

When I got in to work, I learned Mrs Frogspawn had made a huge fuss about the typewriter she had been using, saying it caused her to make far too many mistakes. She had swapped it over with mine because apparently mine 'works better'.

Louise noticed and is taking action so I can have mine back again.

Valerie and I decided we would join the BBC amateur dramatic society together – it's called the Ariel Theatre Group.

Walked back. Curry.

In the future I won't be able to imagine or understand all of this with Frank but nothing will be the same again. He has changed the part of me of which I am most aware.

17th – Tuesday

Jack's latest holiday idea is that he takes Louise and me to Torquay.

The battle of the typewriters was resolved in my favour.

Valerie and I decided Miss Sharp would be an unsuitable person to invite to an orgy, and anyway, she would never go due to pressure of work.

Gill was upset. A couple of the other girls had a go at her, saying she was odd because she hadn't booked up a week's holiday. But with an unpredictable artist husband she can't do that kind of planning in advance.

After work, Gill and I went to Westbourne Park to look at a possible flat for her and Kaz. It was a grotty area. We were off to a good start when the Cypriot landlady said she didn't like the English, but was a bit happier when Gill said her husband was Hungarian. Gill was undecided but I wouldn't have touched the place with a barge pole. I would hope to do better for the money (£12).

I came back via Paddington Station, stopping to look up and admire the roof. I wondered whether any of Frank's handiwork was still up there. Then I called in at Westminster Cathedral again. There was some sort of service going on. I bought St Patrick a candle and said a little prayer for Frank.

It's utter hell without him.

18th – Wednesday

Worked solidly all day on the *Springboard* Study Unit, which was exhausting, although I enjoyed typing out the Mummer's Play.

Lunched with Valerie and Gill. We discussed men and marriage, emotion and reason.

Miss Handley has asked me to supper. I do not want to accept.

Discussed modern poetry with Louise.

After work, Penny and I had a substantial and well-cooked Chinese meal for 93p. Not bad, eh? She told me about conversing with a drunk in Lambeth Church, and different ways of understanding people and how one matures by understanding others.

Back to the bloody old hostel.

19th – Thursday

Hot. Walked up. Gill overworked, but the rest of us weren't too busy.

Went to the Marble Arch M&S with Valerie, and bought another long black cardigan.

Had a word with Frank's temporary replacement, who was keen to give me all the details of Frank's injuries. I mentally gave him a score of 10/10. However, either he didn't know about, or didn't mention, the bullet wound which Jack claims to suffer from. And Jack told me his next-door neighbour in Paddington keeps wanting to hit him.

Bernard Levin has written an article in *The Times* today about Edward Heath being a sailor, which is along the same lines as Louise and I discussed the other day.

Lit another candle in the Cathedral. Frank would probably regurgitate if he knew I was doing it, but I honestly mean it.

I feel the same about him as I did two weeks ago.

20th – Friday

About to go on holiday so the office was madly busy. Typed another Loan Scheme thing for the *Merry-Go-Round* programme [TV series for primary schools, which included three controversial programmes: *Beginning*, *Birth* and *Full Circle*]. Attempted to get Carol sloshed as it was the last day that I would be working with her. We ended up discussing smoking and drugs, and of course Sharp and her secretaries.

Had a talk from Gill about Frank, especially about how things are on his side, his wife and so on. But I am very mindful about his wife. Crawled home in the pouring rain, and took a taxi from Chipstead Station, which I shared with someone who said he was an ex-MP.

Vera quite cheerful.

21st – Saturday

Off on holiday to the Isle of Wight. The travel plans worked successfully and we even passed through Basingstoke again. I gave it a little wave and thought of Frank being out there somewhere. Zelda and I arrived at Yarmouth, not knowing whether it was Cowes or Lymington, and found we were wrong on both counts.

We camped down in the A.H. house in Freshwater in a room shared with another girl called Ruth from Manchester. It's very large, with a big window and a view of the sea. The house is on a cliff above Freshwater Bay, with a swimming pool and gardens all round. Zelda said, 'It's Manderley.'

We had supper with Ruby, a telegraphist from Tooting. Most of the other people on the holiday are middle-aged or elderly. After the meal, we adjourned for barn dancing. The atmosphere is very friendly and we got to meet everyone as we swung them around. There was one partner I could have done with, but of course he isn't here.

22nd – Sunday

The disaster of the day was that I lost my beloved John Lennon leather cap somewhere; otherwise the day was good. After breakfast and a morning service we went for a walk along the clifftop to Compton Bay and came back along the beach. A large lunch was served in the house. I went to the shops and bought postcards for the parents and Louise, and visited the little thatched church of St Agnes.

I watched some people play tennis and had a go on the mini-golf course under the instruction of Ruth's dad; her parents and boyfriend are on the holiday with her.

I then had a chat with one of the walks' leaders, whose name is Norman. He was formerly a football referee until some man ran his studs down his leg after a controversial decision went against him. After supper about five of us went to the pub down the road.

23rd – Monday

The walking begins! We went up Tennyson Down and I was bitten to pieces by midges. The view wasn't up to much because it was close and misty. We walked on to The Needles and then down to Alum Bay. After that, I went out and played a game of tennis with Ruth against a couple of the older ladies. Supper was followed by more country dancing, and then I went to the pub again with Zelda, Ruth, her boyfriend and a couple of other people, including an older bloke called Len.

24th – Tuesday

We went by coach to Steephill Cove and walked to Ventnor, then by coach again up to a cafe and walked over the fields to Briddle Inn. After supper, another walks' leader, a former teacher called Gary, invited Ruth and her boyfriend, Zelda and myself to see his photos of the 1970 Isle of Wight pop festival. We went into the smallest lounge, he put out the lights and showed the slides through a projector on to a screen. During this film show, he poured each of us several glasses of Merrydown cider.

I was hoping to see pictures of the groups, but they were mostly of the audience. As the festival went on, a lot of them took off their clothes so there were lots of slides of naked young people on the grass, on the beach and running about in the sea.

When we got to the end of the slide show, Zelda began talking about her long-lost German boyfriend. Gary was very consoling. For some reason the whole thing made me feel a bit odd, but that might have been the amount of cider I had drunk.

Bed at 2.30 a.m.

25th – Wednesday

We took the coach to Cowes and visited Queen Victoria's old home, Osborne. It was full of Victorian junk, but the Swiss Cottage was rather sweet. Len came round with Zelda and me, and pointed out that the Queen is still making money out of the place.

Back at Freshwater, I played tennis, a silly game of cricket and then we gathered on the beach for a barbecue and fireworks. After that, I went to the Albion pub with Gary and a couple of the other older chaps. Gary asked me if I had a boyfriend and I told him yes. Which is, sort of, true.

I didn't go into details.

26th – Thursday

Today, the walk was to Brook. I spent a lot of it with Len, who is Jewish and comes from the East End (his grandfather was a leather-worker in Russia). I'd put him in his mid-forties so almost eligibly young for me. We had an interesting conversation about immigration. He told me that his family had lived 'like rats, in the sewers' during the Blitz. Over lunch I talked to one of the other blokes about Tennyson, while Len chucked peanuts at me. One of the women told me tales about all the suicides that jump off the Clifton Suspension Bridge.

Back at the house we had an after-dinner concert, with people doing comedy sketches about *Coronation Street* and graveyards, after which Len and I went down to the Albion, had a couple of Merrydowns and talked about *Oh! Calcutta!*, which he has seen but I haven't.

He said it was rubbish.

27th – Friday

Walk from Shide to Arreton Manor, where we had lunch and
I snoozed for a bit, keeping an eye on Gary, whom I don't
entirely trust. Then walked from Brading to Ryde and took
the coach back.

Tonight was Fancy Dress Night. Zelda and I dressed up as
hippies – Zelda looked very pretty, with a headband, beads
and a short dress. Len lent me an old T-shirt and I wore that
with my jeans. A couple of blokes dressed up in funny wigs.
More dancing and then a large crowd of us went to the pub.
Len suggested we took a bottle back to his room, where he
began to kiss and cuddle me, but I asked him to stop.

Len:	Ah, you have a boyfriend?
Me:	Yes.
Len:	What's his name?
Me:	Frank.
Len:	Lucky Frank!

Having come to a full stop there, we joined a party in the
Boot Room, where several of the old boys were singing
wartime RAF songs. Len did 'Any Old Iron' to great applause.
One chap did a Max Miller number and another one did a
song called 'Cocaine Bill'.

When that broke up, Len and I went into the ballroom, and
sat in the dark, finishing up the bottle of Merrydown
and talking about his former marriage. He is separated but
not divorced (too expensive, he said). He asked me about
Frank but I didn't say much, only that he was an Irish bloke I
knew at work. Len asked if we might meet again and I said
I'd think about it.

Len is forty-seven, so younger than Frank but hardly the
Nice Young Man.

I got back to the bedroom at about 2.30. Ruth was fast asleep but Zelda was awake, steaming with rage. As I came in the door, she smacked me in the face, and said how dare I carry on with Len like that. I said it was nothing to do with her and got into bed. Then she started crying, and said Gary had taken her into a cupboard or room some-where, tried to get her clothes off and assaulted her. I thought that was a bit unlikely and I wasn't quite sure what she meant by 'assaulted'. Anyway, I was very tired by then and said couldn't we just go to sleep and leave it until the morning.

28th – Saturday

I got up to go to breakfast but Zelda stayed in bed, under the covers, not talking. I went to breakfast, it was sad to say goodbye to everyone. Len came over and said, 'Don't give my love to that lucky Frank, will you!'

When I got back to the bedroom Zelda was up, packing her things but still not speaking. Ruth had already gone.

The journey back was unpleasant. I had a bad hangover and was very tired. Zelda said not a word to me the whole way back and I didn't care. I had enjoyed the holiday, was glad I went in the end, and felt everyone had made a real effort to make us younger people feel part of the group. I didn't want Zelda spoiling that.

I noticed that mentioning Frank had been useful in warding off uncomfortable advances.

29th – Sunday

Slept until 1 p.m. Told Vera all about the holiday. She said, 'Why not write to Len, he might be fun to go out with?' I hadn't thought of that.

I'm not sure about getting in touch with him now – it would look as if I was chasing after him.

30th – Monday (Bank Holiday)

Went on a walk on Farthing Downs with Georgina Fox to pick blackberries.

There weren't any.

We listened to records back at her home and watched TV and then had chicken for supper.

I am staying at home this week and commuting to London. Miss Fenn said that they could re-let my room if I gave it up for three weeks, so that has saved me a bit of money.

31st – Tuesday

Drove into Purley and took the train up from there with Georgina Fox.

Frank was overjoyed to see me and said he had been missing me. I told him I had thought of him when the Isle of Wight train went through Basingstoke, and said I had had some lousy weeks without him. He said it had been the same for him too – his holiday wasn't up to much, his wife had been sick and the children were around all the time.

We were all over each other again in excitement until Miss Sharp nearly caught us. He was very conscientious about a strange man who came up in his lift asking for her, checking that she was expecting him.

London Weighting has bumped up my pay.

I didn't see a lot of Frank today, and am not sure I want all the Frank-type problems back again.

September

1st – Wednesday

Collected my photos of the Isle of Wight from the chemist, but they were rather disappointing.

Louise and I had a laugh about a character called Mandrake, who appeared in a series of novels she read when she was young. He had a girl sidekick called Nana and a Nubian slave called Lotho, and in a moment of crisis would 'gesture hypnotically'. We wondered if this tactic might be useful at the SBC.

Frank was all over me again in great delight, repeatedly kissing me. I'm fond of him, but … oh, I am such an idiot. Anyway, he left early to take his wife to the doctor.

It's all so confusing. I even started wondering if Len might phone me, he knows where I work.

Train home was crowded and Vera has gone away, leaving me in the house with Father. Wrote a letter to her.

2nd – Thursday

Wondering whether I should have made more of Len on holiday. I feel rotten towards Frank – he's making real attempts to be friendly, and I am awfully fond of him until he grabs me. I just don't want him like that anymore.

I can't see any jobs at the moment that I would want to apply for.

3rd – Friday

Bought a shirt at C&As. I only saw Frank three times. He wanted me to wait in the basement for him at the end of the day but I didn't want to, so I left. I feel so awful about that man, I could cry.

Came back on the train and in my confusion accidentally got off at Purley Oaks, a station too soon. Rather than wait for another train, I walked into Purley and picked up the car.

It was weird being home this week without Vera.

4th – Saturday

My second holiday – off to the Lake District. Read *Puckoon* on the train. Perhaps it was something to do with Spike Milligan, but I was surprised that we didn't go uphill all the way to the north.

I had to wait for two and a half hours at Ambleside for a bus to Coniston so I sat in a little cafe. While I was there, sipping tea and eating a buttered bun, Rachmaninov's Paganini Variation, the very romantic one, came on the radio and I couldn't help thinking about Frank. Oh dear! Anyway, finally the bus came, but I missed the drop-off point at Monk Coniston and had to walk about a mile and a half back to the house.

So, where do all the Young Conservatives go for a holiday? Let me tell you: A. H. Young People's week. Lots of shiny fresh faces and knitted pullovers. Alas, there was no community spirit like that on the first night at Freshwater, it was all a bit subdued with nobody talking and everyone looking nervously round the room. The trouble with a group of young people on holiday is that we are all Going To Be, not Have Done, so we don't have much to talk about. A bloke called Pete from Newcastle finally chatted me up a bit but I didn't fancy him.

5th – Sunday

I went for a walk around the house first thing, beginning to wonder what I was letting myself in for. Going into the churchyard nearby, I had a nasty moment when I spotted a gravestone with my own name on it.

The morning service was followed by a walk to Tarn Hows, which, we were told, is the most reproduced view in the Lake District. You can see it on boxes of chocolates, tea trays and calendars. In which case, I wondered, why had we gone all that way to see it? You can't really say that on a walking holiday, though, can you? In the afternoon a group of us took a boat on the lake, one hour saw us round it. Had a look at the shops, played croquet and assembled for a talk on mountain safety, which didn't happen because the bloke giving it was out rescuing someone. At 10 o'clock everyone upped and went to the pub, where things brightened up a little.

Not enjoying this holiday much.

6th – Monday

Walked to Langdale and Elterwater, I think. Visited a slate quarry, which was interesting although I couldn't hear what the man showing us round it said because of all the quarrying. Still, he was a brilliant hand with the axey thing. Walked about eight miles, beautiful scenery but tiring. Had a rest until supper and after that went to the pub (four of us in a Triumph Spitfire), which was fun.

People being a bit more chatty now.

7th – Tuesday

Coach ride to Dungeon Ghyll, where we had a tough, hot walk uphill past several lakes to a wasp-infested pub for refreshment, past the quarry again and back along a ferny, boggy but very pretty valley. The views were superb. I walked most of the way with a couple called Joyce and Dave. Fell asleep on the coach coming back.

Supper was followed by a half-hearted game of dominoes, and as soon as it seemed decent we made a dash to the pub. I still don't know most people's names or anything about them – it's taking ages for people to mix.

A letter from Vera has arrived, hoorah!

8th – Wednesday

Spent the day out with Dave, Joyce and a chap called Michael. We went in Dave's car to Windermere and Kendal. The funniest bit was when we took a boat out on Lake Windermere and nearly ran it aground. Mike kept talking about intelligence and Eysenck [German psychologist].

There was a barbecue in the evening, which didn't really get off the ground. Even though some of us had already been to the pub, had a few drinks and brought back bottles of cider, everyone sat around nervously. I perched on a dead tree branch next to a chap called Alastair, who was dark-haired, bespectacled and very quiet.

He seemed a Nice Young Man.

9th – Thursday

Went to Easedale Tarn with the C party (the easiest walking group). It was a steep climb, with good views of a waterfall. We visited the Wordsworths' Dove Cottage and Grasmere.

Dorothy W. was a bit weird, wasn't she?

In the evening I went back to the Mucky Duck (or whatever the pub is called) with a few of the others, including Nice Alastair and drank lager. Mike started on about intelligence again, and on the way back, Alastair and I held hands in the back of Dave's Anglia.

Wow! Could this be It?

He even managed a tiny kiss before I went to bed about midnight.

10th – Friday

Alastair joined me for breakfast, which was promising after last night's romantic episode, but as he went off on the A walk to do twelve miles up a mountain I didn't see him for the rest of the day. Instead I joined the C group on a walk around the Grizedale Forest. We visited a Forestry Commission site, but it was quite cold among the trees and I couldn't follow the technical stuff in the talk. Then on to Hawkshead, where Joyce bought a sheepskin rug and we both bought some perfume. We saw some deer on the way.

I had supper with Alastair and a couple of the others, watched a table tennis competition and went down to the pub. But no further action from Alastair, who is probably concerned that last night he might have gone a bit too far.

11th – Saturday

Fabulously sunny day; the summer not yet over. Had breakfast with Dave, Joyce and Alastair, with whom I exchanged addresses. I travelled back to Euston with a couple of the others.

I wouldn't be surprised if I never saw Alastair again – he was a nice chap, but very reserved.

12th – Sunday

Another fabulously sunny day. Bored Vera with an account of the holiday and did my washing and ironing. Vera said that Aunt Suzanne invited Father to supper last week but he declined, saying he had a previous commitment, which of course he hadn't.

I don't know how I will have the courage to face Frank tomorrow.

13th – Monday

Hannah (Mrs Frogspawn) is still in my office. She is in the throes of obtaining a Jewish divorce and was faffing on about some papers. It seems to be very complicated.

Louise was in a good mood and Gill was back, hooray! We escaped for lunch together to the Yorkshire Grey and exchanged our news. I rabbited on about my holidays, about meeting Len and Alastair – she thought they both sounded like good prospects.

Poor old Frank! He left early to take his wife to hospital – she has suspected gangrene. He said Louise had told him she had had a postcard from me.

It was a busy day, but when I got back to the hostel I realised what a bloody awful place it is. The long, dreary corridors, the smells, the old women shuffling about in their grubby dressing gowns in the evening …

I decided to take the initiative with Len, and looked him up in the London phone directory. He has an unusual surname so he was easy to find. I called the number from the phone downstairs in the hostel and a woman answered so I left a message. At about 9.45 someone banged on my door and shouted, 'There's a bloke called Len on the phone for you downstairs!'

We had a nice chat – it cheered me up no end. He took my work phone number and said he would ring me next week, asking if he would be able to recognise me after my holiday in the Lake District as I must have lost a stone with all the walking. 'Oh, by the way,' he said, 'that was my sister who answered the phone when you rang.'

When I got back to my room Zelda, to whom I have barely spoken since we came back from the Isle of Wight, shouted across the corridor, 'Have you been speaking to Len?' but it was in a slightly nasty voice so I said no. I felt a silly afterwards for lying but had no desire to talk to her.

Afterwards, I wondered whether it really was Len's sister who answered the phone.

14th – Tuesday

According to Frank, Jack has 'gone up the Matterhorn. Or, it might be the Harrow Road,' thus leaving him as the only lift man today.

Frank's wife has gone into hospital so he is on his own in the flat. He suggested it might be a good idea if someone called in and cooked his supper. I declined the invitation. Poor Mrs Browne!

Louise gave me the extension number of a Miss Twitchett. At first I thought she must be something out of a Beatrix Potter story, possibly a large tabby cat in a gingham apron. No, it turned out she is the BBC's Accommodation Officer and she might be able to help me find a bedsit.

15th – Wednesday

Finished the reel in the camera and took it to be developed. I would have liked to have taken a photograph of Frank, but I couldn't get him on his own in enough light without making it obvious what I was doing. He invited me to go out with him on Saturday, but I said no. I feel sorry for his poor, helpless, gangrenous wife.

Arranged to see Miss Twitchett on Monday.

Walked back to the ****ing hostel.

It's Frank's birthday on Wednesday next week.

16th – Thursday

Weather turned a little warmer, although it has been lousy all week. Autumn is here.

Lunch at BH with Valerie, Gill and a couple of others. Busy in the office doing distributions, i.e. mailing out advertising matter and publications to all the schools.

Frank asked if I had lost my virginity, as well as my hat on the Isle of Wight. When I said no, he invited me to go to bed with him, got the usual answer and then lowered his sights a little and suggested a drink instead. He also told me proudly he had done all the ironing at home and would be willing to demonstrate any number of other domestic skills.

Gill got him a cup of tea and he paid her for it. Didn't see much of him. Actually, I have cooled off him quite a bit since I went on the holidays. He must be aware things have changed.

Louise most kindly invited Gill and me for a drink with her after work. We discussed ageing and facelifts.

Went shopping and found a decent dress in D. H. Evans – blue corduroy, but at nearly £10!

Caught the bus back. Ignored Zelda and listened to The Rite of Spring.

Tired. Must write to Alastair.

17th – Friday

Left the hostel this morning thinking anywhere has got to be better than that place.

Frank was involved in a hilarious performance over a non-functioning lift, which was very entertaining. Still asking me to go and see him at the weekend but to no avail.

Masses of distribution to do, so busy all afternoon.

Picked up the photos of the Lake District and showed them to everyone at lunch. Alastair met with everyone's approval – what a Nice Young Man, etc., etc.

Travelled home. Neither the oven nor Father was working.

18th – Saturday

Walked round Reigate Heath golf course with Aunt Suzanne, more or less keeping pace with Cliff Michelmore [broadcaster], who was playing a round. Went back to tea with her and chatted about my mother. She showed me some old photos, which were hysterically funny, including one of Mum's 'Nazi boyfriend', Otto. The war intervened, of course, and my mother married Father in 1939.

If Hitler hadn't invaded Czechoslovakia I might have been born half-German. In which case, of course, I wouldn't be me.

Aunt Suzanne married when she was twenty.

19th – Sunday

Wrote and re-wrote a letter to Alastair.

Went to see Georgina Fox and got the plot of two films: *The Raven* and *Bananas*, which is a Woody Allen pic. Had tea on the lawn and then went to her room to read *Mad* magazines and listen to *Pick Of The Pops* in great disgust at the low standard of music.

Talked to Vera about a flat. She suggested I had my own room, preferably in a small flat in somewhere like Belsize Park, Camden Town or St John's Wood.

Thinking it over, I realise Len is not the answer. He is younger than Frank and good company but realistically is too old to qualify as a Nice Young Man. (Father would have a fit if he thought I was going out with a Jew.) Alastair lives in Huddersfield, which might as well be Timbuktu.

20th – Monday

Interview with Miss Twitchett, who was perfectly OK and not furry at all. She offered me a room in Norland Square, which was odd because that's exactly where Louise lives. I said no. Then she mentioned a place in Cricklewood, which might still be available. Otherwise she said she would be in touch if anything came up in North London.

Posted the now-notorious letter to Alastair. One of the secretaries told me there's a cholera outbreak in Huddersfield, so if I don't hear from him again I will know why.

Got everything wrong at work and had to resort to two cups of hot chocolate.

Apart from the usual suggestions, met with the usual refusals, and further one that I give him some new pants or a big kiss for his birthday, Frank was good company today, although I think he is concerned about his wife being so ill, and it seems she is getting worse. Poor chap. He was leaning against me in the lift and suddenly yelped because his hip went funny.

I hope I cheered him up.

Frank (glumly):   You're not lacking anything, Sarah. It's me that's lacking it.

According to him, all the Jews were off work today.

Curry. Hostel a little more bearable now that I am thinking of going. I may have to give one month's notice, which presents difficulties. I may have to pay two lots of rent for a week or two while I move from one place to another.

Listened to *The Turn Of The Screw*. Don't laugh.

21st – Tuesday

Len hasn't phoned.

Louise wasn't in until the afternoon. Wore a jacket and was greeted by commendations.

Hooray!

Carol phoned up to see how I was getting on. Her new job is notoriously a tough post, but she is sticking at it.

After much evasion I finally found out how old Frank is. At first I had thought he was about forty-five, then revised it a while ago to fifty-ish.

As it is his birthday tomorrow, I asked him how old he would be. He made me laugh, saying, 'Twenty-four,' and then 'Thirty-six,' but I persisted. Finally, while we were berthed at the Entresol, he pointed at one of the doors and said, 'See der number on dat door? Dat is how old I will be tomorrow.' I looked at the door and the number was sixty-two. I swallowed a 'Christ Almighty!' because I didn't want him to see how surprised I was. Then we had a nice discussion about how one can live happily in one's old age.

But, Christ Almighty, he's sixty-two!

Supper at BH. Went to see Timothy Dalton in a play called *The Samaritan* at the Shaw Theatre. It was awful, bordering on the banal. All the characters were made of cardboard.

Still, it made a change to have an evening out.

22nd – Wednesday

Frank's birthday. He wasn't in in the morning as he went to the hospital about his wife.

I was kept busy clearing out old Loan Scheme files, stopping to chat with Louise every five minutes, and then had lunch with Valerie, Veronica (temp replacement for Carol) and Gill. We had a good laugh about Sharpy and sleeping with men.

Frank arrived at about 2 p.m. I gave him a birthday card and a packet of mints. He was a little overwhelmed but showed his gratitude.

Me:	I've been to see the Accommodation Officer and she is going to let me know when a room comes up in North London, so I can get out of that hostel.
Frank:	Nort' London, eh? I tell you, don't go to Kilburn, 'tis not a good area.
Me:	Really? I thought it was full of Irish people.
Frank:	Aye, 'tis, and dat's why you should avoid it.

His wife is better, but he still seems rather miserable.

I said, 'Do you realise we have been at it since January?'

'Oh,' he said, 'that's time to have had two miscarriages.'

He asked why I fancied him.

I said, 'I don't know, Frankie, I just do.'

23rd – Thursday

I didn't wake up until ten to nine, which was worrying as I had promised myself I would get in early to see Frank. Instead I took the Tube up and had to put up with the crowds.

Hannah is very cheesed off with Miss Sharp, so I expect she will be going soon. That clerical post never materialised.

Louise was in late and was rather short with me about my reading a magazine in the office. However, we got on well subsequently when reorganising the files, discussing the film *Taking Off*, which she had seen recently.

Gill was rather despondent. She said she was getting to the stage when she wanted to make Kaz jealous, but on reflection I don't suppose she will do anything about it.

Conversation with Gill at lunch:

I said my affair with Frank might be seen as a mistake by some people, but I thought it had done me a lot of good.

Gill is frustrated by Kaz's lethargy. She feels he has had a second chance in life and isn't using it – perhaps he needs a tougher wife? He always wants things instantly. After having been a refugee (he escaped from Hungary in 1956), he is accustomed to insecurity, so he doesn't see any need to think ahead.

We discussed whether insecure children were more likely to take the blame for things later on when they are adults, and how surprised we both are when other parents are more affectionate with their children than ours were with us.

I wasn't able to be with Frank much. He seemed very depressed at lunchtime and when we went to the basement together at the end of the day, I felt sorry for him.

I am so fond of Frank.

Had a quick supper with Penny and Georgina Fox at the Chinese restaurant.

I have only exchanged a few words with Zelda since we got back from the holiday. I know she is cross with me for not supporting her over Gary, but there wasn't much I could have done about it. I did suggest she write a letter to the A.H., giving all the details, but I'm not sure she wants to.

Wondering whether Alastair will have written back to me yet, or whether he is in the grip of cholera.

24th – Friday

Scrambled into work.

Frank was affectionate, supplying me with mints and a Coke at lunchtime. Feelings were running high by the afternoon, and I felt more generous towards him than I have been since I came back from holidays.

Hannah surprised me by saying she would like me as a daughter.

No, thanks, I already have enough parent trouble!

Then Veronica said Mr Jones had praised me. I have an eclectic bunch of followers, that's for sure. Then a rude woman from Publications phoned and harangued me, which was upsetting and brought me down to earth again.

But Frank stole the day for me, hanging around on the sixth floor on the off-chance of a chat. The only disappointment was that we couldn't manage a proper goodbye at the end of the day as John the Post got in the way.

Came back to Chipstead to find Vera on her own – Il Papa had gone out to some Masonic ritual. A letter from Alastair had arrived, but it was very formal: 'I note you are now back at work and that things are going well', and so on.

There is no prospect of my seeing him again soon.

25th – Saturday

Up early and went with Vera to … London! Collected a frying pan from John Lewis and then went on a semi-successful shopping expedition. I bought a blue wool coat in a military style at Selfridges and a dress at Marks. We were home by 3 p.m.

I sorted out some old letters and photos and watched TV. Three variety shows in succession: Harry Secombe, Des O'Connor and Glen Campbell.

At least they got better as the evening went on.

Followed by a great football match: 2–2 Liverpool v Manchester United.

Retired to bed, feeling fond towards Frank again.

26th – Sunday

It isn't real country here, it isn't real town – it's a suburban nowhere, a nothing, a nightmare. All I can hear now is a barking dog, rustling leaves and the distant growling of aeroplanes, plus [English countertenor] Alfred Deller, but he is hardly part of the usual scene. And now I am going out for a walk because I've eaten far too much and am getting fat and heavy again.

Saw a TV programme about a yachtsman called Moitessier, who started to sail around the world and couldn't stop. Mr and Mrs Andrews by Gainsborough – what a couple, they look like they could have lived in Surrey all their lives!

27th – Monday

Frank overjoyed to see me; he was frisking about merrily. It's not only about me, though – I think he is lonely on his own at home. At least, he keeps inviting me to go back there for tea, or to go for a drink with him at the Royal Oak. I am hell's fond of him, but I have to refuse as I can't trust him.

Frank: You can trust God.
Me: But you're not God.

(I don't trust myself either.)

I told him it was my birthday soon.

Miss Sharp upset Hannah by telling her off for not coming in early. Poor Mrs Frogspawn was already unhappy about the large amount of typing she'd been given. Valerie and I helped her finish it.

Back at the hostel, I overheard Zelda talking to one of the other girls so I hope she has given up at last and will leave me alone.

I was thinking about changing jobs and began looking at some of the ads on the vacancies noticeboard, but realised I couldn't bear the thought of leaving Frank.

28th – Tuesday

Hannah arrived early, anxious to redeem herself to Sharpy, and was rewarded by being pounded with more work.

Frank was bolshy. He was displeased when I asked after his wife and was generally cheesed off. Well, if he's annoyed with me for not accepting one of the many recent invitations to enjoy sex in his flat, he should consider all that 'It's only flirtin'' stuff. Tough.

At lunchtime Gill, Valerie, Leah (surprise!) and I went to 35 Marylebone High Street to see how Carol was getting on in her new job. Carol embarrassed me by talking about Little Frank, so I shrugged and changed the subject. Gill did say afterwards she thought Carol had become a bit more adult and more aware of things.

Over supper, Gill and I laid plots to get Kaz to do more about finding a flat and getting paid work. She was very sympathetic about Vera and Father, especially about Vera rotting away in Chipstead when she is such a bright, warm little person. As Vera said, Father seems to have lost the art/will/need for communication.

OK, so Len is not going to phone me, which may be just as well. This leaves ... Frank.

29th – Wednesday

Walked in early. Not feeling very affectionate at the moment, maybe I don't feel affection first thing in the morning? More annoyance, perhaps.

Frank had his annual interview this morning, and it passed off without a hitch. He is, so he was told, 'alert, courteous, efficient, good-humoured, conscientious ...' ('Oh,' I said, 'so they missed off "funny ... sexy ..."?') At least no one has reported him for mischief with a secretary.

Office fairly busy.

Supper with Penny, who is planning to move to a job at The Psychic Institute. I told her at length about my holidays, which reminded me of Alastair and I began to wish more had happened with him. This is all probably due to some disenchantment with Frank.

Sad.

30th – Thursday

Frank was a bit better today but he is getting awfully randy. Again, he asked me to go out with him. I am tempted, and would do if I could trust him not to try to get me into bed with him. The trouble is that outside work there would be more scope for him to realise his fantasies. He would have the time, the place and the opportunity, things could easily get out of hand and I bet I wouldn't have the heart to refuse him. Afterwards he would probably want us to stop doing what we are doing at work, which might seem like a good idea until you realise that work imposes limitations which make it easier for me to handle him.

No, it's not on.

He gave me a 50p piece [£7 today] and said, 'Here, take this and go and buy some chocolates or tights for your birthday.'

It was really thoughtful of him – he can be wonderful at times.

Excitingly, Hannah is at daggers with Sharp and Valerie over a stencil. Valerie and I went to lunch in the Salad Bar, growling together about her.

Bought *Old Possum's Book of Practical Cats* on the cheap at a closing-down sale at a bookshop in Regent Street.

Joyce from the Coniston holiday and I had a meal at the Old Kentucky and talked about our holiday memories, especially of 'her' Dave and 'my' Alastair. She has been seeing 'her' Dave a lot, and I am glad they are getting on well. They are going to the November reunion, but I doubt that Alastair will go.

October

1st – Friday

Frank produced a photo of himself taken about thirty years ago. I think it might have been his wedding photo, as his wife was by his side and sitting around them were what looked like friends or relations. I didn't think they looked up to much. Frank was dark-haired and very smart, standing up straight like a 5'2"guardsman; but, oddly enough, I didn't think he was as attractive then as he is now. His wife is, or rather was, a biggish woman. Not surprisingly, she is taller than him, with a round, pleasant face. It was a rather touching photo, though.

I sat on his tip-up seat in the lift as I looked at the photo with him, leaning against his knees while he tickled my ears.

He asked me again if I would go out with him next week; I said no.

I would go out with Frank the person, but not Frank the situation.

He can't understand why I am not having a birthday party (neither can I).

Hannah has lost her wedding ring. That hardly matters, she is divorced. She said she would buy another one.

Gill bought herself a pair of shoes at Freeman Hardy & Willis.

Home again. Father bloody, of course, and Vera a little better. It makes me miserable when she is sad.

Rang to thank Aunt Suzanne, who has said she will buy me tickets to see *Going On* at the theatre for my birthday.

2nd – Saturday

YEURGH!!

A plan to go out to lunch tomorrow to celebrate my birthday has foundered. Papa made it quite obvious that he wasn't keen to go, regarding the prospect as a bore. I didn't want him to have it all his own way again but he managed it. Vera and I then rowed, which made me miserable. I think I frightened her, talking about driving in bad weather.

Lunch was a silent affair.

I went for a two-hour walk round Markedge Lane and bloody boring it was too, apart from passing a courting couple in a steamed-up car.

Came back and read *Borstal Boy*. Brendan Behan. Irish (cough).

Father bloody awful and I have only said about six words to him all day. Vera says he's like that all the time now, except for when they are arguing. I really feel like sticking a knife between his shoulder blades. He's a selfish old git and he makes life so miserable for everyone else, especially poor, long-suffering Vera.

3rd – Sunday (My birthday)

Opened cards and presents. Then Vera and I set off together to find somewhere for lunch. We got as far as the outskirts of Horsham but it was so misty by then we had to give up and come home. Pottered around. Weather got colder. Played the guitar and watched TV.

I am now twenty. I wonder where I will be at thirty?

4th – Monday

Frank said he had a quiet weekend but a 'strong' one, whatever that means. I said I had missed him and it had been dull. I gave him a piece of my birthday cake. He asked me to visit him – he said he wouldn't hurt me, it would just be a lark.

I 'considered it' but stuck to my guns and refused.

> Frank (with a sigh):
> Never say die.
> Me: Nor will this die.

Office busy and dull so I didn't see him often.
Later, it got sour. We were parked at the Entresol.

> Frank: So why won't you come and visit me one
> evening?
> Me: I can't because your wife is in hospital, and it
> would be mean to be taking advantage of that.
> Frank (picking at a thumbnail):
> Well, 'tis mean anyway, what we're doing.

(Which is true.) I said he made me more miserable than anyone else. There was a long pause. Finally, I ran out [of the lift] on a lie, but when I came back, I told him I still loved him. In a serious voice, he said he wouldn't bed me but would have me some other way. I refused, and he took the lift away without saying more.

I walked down to the ground floor, feeling lousy and near to tears. I felt so muddled and depressed.

I WILL NOT sleep with Frank, or fiddle about. He may be upset but I know my mind. It feels as if we're pulling apart like this, but at least we have had something to pull apart from. Of course, and it's right, he's more fond of her than me and I mean less to him. OK, but that makes me sad. He deserves a kick in the balls but I can't bear the idea of being unkind to him. He knows I'm fond of him, but he knows not how much I owe him. I couldn't have gone this far and felt nothing for him. It may be a result of my boring, lonely life and he is just someone I have attached my feelings to.

Maybe I should change my way of life; I'm trying. But I love him, I do.

Gill said, 'You need Alastair to come down from Huddersfield and distract you.' But he shows no sign of making the journey unprompted, and I'd be more miserable again if that fell through (which I feel it would). I wish he had been less reserved and more like Frank.

Some good news: Hannah is leaving.

Veronica's gone already, and a new person has arrived to work for Mr Jones. She is called Pam, middle-aged, a bit dumb and aloof. Not youngish like us.

Curry.

5th – Tuesday

A fabulous day of Frankity. His wife's better now, but has had too much insulin. I showed him some old photos of my family, and he pronounced me a nice little kid. We discussed long hair, which he dislikes on grounds of dirt – he said short hair looks neat. He told me about his son-in-law, who works for an American company in computer engineering and earns £80 a week. His daughter married at twenty-one. He said he couldn't stop her, though if I tried the same thing he said he would chastise me!

I told him he should have heard my speech to him last night while I was walking back to Victoria.

He asked if I would come with him tonight and I said no. He said, 'OK, I am not going to force you.'

'Isn't it strange,' he went on, 'that men can carry on siring children into old age but not women?' I said, 'You mean, like Charlie Chaplin?' He said, 'Yes, but I wouldn't want to be having children who were half-monkeys.' I asked him about Brendan Behan, and he said, 'Oh yes, that's the fellah who died of the drink.'

Hannah told Louise that she was leaving; and then told Miss Sharp, who asked her to give two weeks' notice. One of Hannah's causes for complaint was Valerie, which was a bit unfair. I told Louise about My Plans to Right the SBC.

Busy day in the office.

At lunchtime I needed to go to John Lewis, so I opted for the Chandos Street route down to the basement with Frank. He asked me again to go out with him. I said no, and instead he and I got together, all over the shop. He sighed we hadn't gone far enough, and then consoled himself by muttering, 'Still, some fellahs only get it standing up once a month.'

On my return I hugged him and said I loved him, and he laughed. We decided (surprisingly) to cool it down. He claimed his hip was much improved and he could now run upstairs. I said, 'Go on, show me then,' and he did. He ran up the steps from the basement to the ground floor and then strolled back down, beaming. I gave him a round of applause.

He is a wonderful, cuddly, warm, maddening, lovable Frank.

Supped with Gill. Looking at the old family photos with Frank reminded me of my brother, who died when I was young. I can't believe I had a brother and I never really knew him.

I wish he had lived.

The Mall looks great with all the flags out for Emperor Hirohito.

6th – Wednesday

Went in to work all smart because I was going out for a meal this evening. Frank said first thing that I looked nice and he would not be exerting me (shame). Hannah grumpy; Valerie and I getting on well.

Went to C&As with Gill and bought a fur hat for the winter.

'Shot the cat?' asked Frank when he saw it, 'you look like a Rooshun spy!' He was singing the 'Eriskay Love Lilt' today, which made a change from the usual Irish stuff like 'The Mountains Of Mourne'.

Down to the basement and another session as 27 July, but he didn't get as far and he complained about my wearing too many clothes.

Poor Frank!

We got on well afterwards, though.

I must be odd.

To Charing Cross, and had a fabulous meal at a restaurant with Vera, Penny and Georgina Fox to celebrate my birthday. It was expensive but the food was good. I think Penny felt a bit unwell and out of it, but Vera was very friendly towards her.

Afterwards I went back to Georgina's new flat in South Kensington (a bit awkward as I had to choose between the two friends). It made me want to leave the hostel even more.

7th – Thursday

Frank asked if I could get something photocopied for him, and I said yes. He handed me a sheet of paper with a prayer written on it. I went to Copying Services and got it done.

He was very pleased and grateful – in fact, he was very loving and didn't push me into anything at all.

I think the copying was for his wife.

Then he asked me again to go back to his flat. I said no, but with greater reluctance, gazing into his lovely blue eyes …

He asked if it was because I was frightened about what might happen to me and explained what he had in mind, saying he wouldn't hurt me – 'Not even when I was a youngster did I leave the girl to carry the can.' Then he gave me some instructions so I could avoid any 'danger'.

'Look Sarah,' he went on, 'there is always the danger of us being caught if we are doing something in here. It'll only be just this once, I won't harm you and that's the Gotstroot.'

I stood there in the lift for what felt like ages, with him looking at me hopefully. I was tempted, honestly I was, but what about afterwards?

Saying we would do it 'just this once' is a two-edged sword. What if I wanted more? What about the whole situation?

Me: Frankie, I would do anything for you …
Frank: I know dat.
Me: But not That. I'm in a hell of a mess with you already without making it any worse. I can't.

He looked at me sadly and nodded, and I damn nearly changed my mind.

At lunchtime, before the others came on to the landing to go for lunch, I instinctively hugged him. No one noticed, I hope. When they all piled into the lift, he called out, 'Backs to the wall!' which made everyone laugh.

Awful lunch, with hordes of people; very stiff and without conversation. Leah sullen silence, Pam lofty silence; Hannah being Hannah. I came back early to the office. No, they are not that bad really, but not my chosen company.

Shopped. Tried on a dress at C&As. Thought about Frank. Was I wise to refuse? Does wisdom come into it? How would it affect me afterwards if I did do it with him? What sort of an experience would it be?

8th – Friday

Incredible day.
  Neither Louise nor Hannah were in and I wasn't busy.

Frank: While the cats are away, the mouse is dancing.

I was so glad to see Frank this morning, and grateful to him for being so easy with me yesterday. At midday, he took me down to the basement, hungering, and tried something that would have got him further but it didn't really work, and I felt terribly sorry and upset for him.
  It's so hopeless.

Me: Frank, we've gone too far.
Frank: What a funny girl you are! 'Tis because we
          haven't gone far enough.
      (Pauses, sighs)
          Well, maybe 'tis better to stop larking around
          because I don't want to hurt you and 'tis all wrong.

For him, this was quite an admission, but done so tenderly, with his hand on my arm. I agreed and we kissed in a friendly way.

Frank: 'Tis not der people dat's wrong, 'tis the place
          and the time, and so on.

At half past four I was done for – I was so tired, I felt like falling asleep – so I went out to have a chat with him. He gave me a brief lesson on how to kiss a young man so he didn't think, 'Aye, here's a lassie that's been somewhere before'. It felt as if he was preparing me for the future without him.

Mrs Browne may be out of hospital on Monday.

Will our relationship last? I'd honestly like it to now.

Back home to Chipstead.

Dull.

9th – Saturday

Went into Croydon with Vera, bought a photo album and new shoes. Lunch.

Read *The Female Eunuch*. At first I was really shocked by it – I mean, all these years I have been trying to be what I thought I should be, i.e. good and nice to other people, and now [Germaine] Greer is suggesting that kindness and willingness to help others should come second to doing things for yourself. I can't see how this is right. And are all men as horrible as she seems to be making out? I mean, men like my uncles or the blokes at the SBC? She seems to suggest we should all go and live in a commune in Italy or something, but I can't speak Italian and it would be too hot.

Wondering if it really is all over with Frank and, if so, what happens now? Surely we will still be friends? Maybe I've got it all wrong. Suppose he moves on to some other girl and she says yes to him, and I have to stand there in the lift, trying not to notice while he holds her hand behind his back?

Read a book about Queen Victoria.

Louise is away next week, which will give me more freedom of action during the day, but I don't know what I'm going to do with it.

10th – Sunday

The weekends are such a waste of time when I consider how I might be spending them. By no stretch of the imagination could they be called 'fun'.

I wrote a funny little song to Frank:

*You were there at the beginning, and you'll be there
    at the end,
You are my saintly devilmaster and my ever-loving
    friend,
Though there isn't all that much of you, what there
    is I know,
Because you are so warm and kind I couldn't let you go,
And if you're my guy, I don't know why.*

*Though there's someone who depends on you, and
    who needs you more than I
I still tell myself I'm yours, and I still make the long
    goodbye,
We never shaped this movement, it was a joke from
    the beginning,
But we found a circle round us, and the whole thing
    started spinning,
And if you're my guy, I don't know why.*

*So we sing against the morning feet a humble liturgy,
Sharing twisting, heaving shufflings and some cups
    of lousy tea,
The more we pull each other we perform social
    disguise,
I can swear I have discovered more than blue in your
    eyes.
And if you're my guy, I don't know why.*

I am not miserable, like yesterday. I daren't think about it because I'm so afraid he will want to end everything, Kaput. I'm sure he can take leaving me more easily than I could take leaving him.

Last week must have been something of a crisis. It feels as if what happened on Friday was important.

How do I play tomorrow? And how do I not hurt him – or me, either? A mutual separation is no answer. Separation wouldn't be mutual anyway, not on this side.

11th – Monday

Went up with Moriarty, who seemed upset because she said Richard had been rude.

Things are not well in the Garden of Weed.

Frankie was not in, so I assumed his wife was coming out of hospital – just when I really wanted to see him too.

The day went much faster than I had expected. I was very busy in the morning, and at lunch Gill and Pam got into a discussion about business, efficiency and the difference between generations.

Went shopping and pottered around in the afternoon, chatting with Gill and Valerie. There was no work, really – I just had to keep that knowledge from Miss Sharp. However, there was a great hooroosh about the vending machines on the fourth floor. Gill has written to *Ariel*, the BBC staff newspaper, about them.

Jack was being almost paternal. Without seeming to make a meaningful point, he told me that a BBC lift man is not permitted to touch passengers, and if he did so, he would be dismissed instantly. That made me worried about Frank. And yes, I can see why he would be so anxious to get me round to his flat instead of us struggling in the lift.

Well, that won't happen now, not with Mrs Browne there.

I can see how Frank and I are at cross purposes. It's strange: sometimes it feels like I am being very intimate with someone from another planet. Maybe Germaine Greer is on to something.

Gill and I had a drink and talked about Kaz and Frank.

Phoned Georgina, who is in a difficult situation after losing her granny, whom she was very fond of.

Curry supper.

12th – Tuesday

Involved day.

Frank was back. He said he had a headache at the weekend and there was a lot of confusion yesterday about Mrs B, but anyhow she's home again. He described a randy dream he suffered from on Sunday, in which whatever randiness was taking place, and it involved me with very few clothes on, was interrupted by Louise suddenly entering the bedroom. I suspect this was also his way of telling me he still wants me … or rather, It.

I asked him if he had told his wife anything about me and he said (shocked) no. He asked me whom I had told, and I said only Vera and Gill. That surprised him, so I hastily and half-truthfully explained that I hadn't told Vera what we'd done together, only about him as a person, and that I wouldn't tell anyone I didn't trust.

'It's a female failing, needing to tell your friends about things,' I said.

'Aye,' said Frank, 'and men boast to each other about havin' sex.'

He was very affectionate, especially after I gave him some mints, and said he would have come into the office to see me if Hannah wasn't in there. He is very cuddly.

Lunch in the pub with Gill and Valerie, discussing Germaine Greer. Having thought about her book a bit more yesterday,

I said she had some good points. Gill was against it and Valerie was in between. Some men sitting nearby overheard us and were nudging and smirking unpleasantly.

Mrs Chambers [Photocopying Service] thought I looked nice in black.

Rain. I went to see *The Go-Between* after work with an old school friend. Dialogue Pinteresque, music good, atmosphere good, unhealthy social situation well suggested. Boy's view of adult world and their reactions interesting.

It made me melancholy about Frank, his emphasis on bedding me as if it were the only thing we could do together. This morning I felt happy because I wanted him for the best reasons. Now I wonder whether I feel more for him than he does for me, and it makes me sad.

13th – Wednesday

It drizzled all day and the wind was chilly.

Hannah was bitching about Miss Sharp, but at least she had been given an open reference. Hannah read it out loud to me. When she reached, 'Hannah works at a speed never before encountered', I had to clap my hand over my mouth. Full marks to Miss Sharp for that one! Anyway, Hannah finished today, thank goodness, as she is taking leave tomorrow and Friday.

Louise will be late back from being away because she hasn't gone yet.

Frank seemed to have been a little lost without me this morning and glad when I turned up. I told him all about the story of *The Go-Between*, about the lovers meeting in secrecy and how they were found out.

Sort of a cautionary tale, I suppose.

He said, 'Make sure you come in early tomorrow morning.' We went down to the basement twice and on one of the trips had two very beautiful kisses. I told him he looks like a gnome; he told me he wears glasses at home.

Valerie and I went to the BBC Ariel Theatre Group General Meeting. There was a variety of people there from various departments, including a Yorkshireman called Alan. Much of the talk was about administrative matters and the group seems to have been having a few problems.

Another drink with Valerie; back in the rain.

Reasonably cheerful, happy with Frank.

14th – Thursday

I got in early, but Frank was late because the trains were bad again and he had to walk all the way from Baker Street station. He and I went down to the basement together for the usual. Looking at him, his age struck me for the first time: the small lines on his cheeks, and his lower eyelashes. He was very affectionate; he held me close and told me I have a lovely figure. Alas, I am 'unwell' – which he had to know about, of course – and as it came on suddenly I had to nip out quick at lunchtime for some shopping.

At 4.20 he dared to stroll into my office (Hannah gone, Louise away). He sat on the desk and asked what I was doing. Which was something pretty dull so I showed him the book of Irish (cough) verse that I was reading. He said he used to read a lot of poetry in his youth. Apparently he was a kind of pupil monitor/teacher at his village school as he was good with the younger ones.

'Some of dis is good,' he said, flipping through the book and reading out the odd verse.

He likes W. B. Yeats, but it turned out neither of us knows much about J. M. Synge.

Then he asked again if he could come and see me in Victoria but I said no.

IT MUSTN'T HAPPEN.

How odd, both him and Father trying to get into the place.

After work, I went to see *The Music Lovers* with Georgina Fox. God, it was far worse than I had expected! The product of an unbalanced mind, I think. A vehicle for effects and sensation that left me battered. It was even absurdly funny in parts because it was so extravagant. Afterwards I couldn't go to sleep because I was so frightened the old women in the hostel might drag me down the corridor and shove me into a bath of boiling-hot water.

At least Frank is wholesome.

15th – Friday

Arrived at work to find Frank 'havin' a roll' (a bread roll). He wasn't happy that I brought him a tea without sugar from the vending machine, and destroyed the plastic cup afterwards to make a spiderish sort of animal with which to attack me. He calls the BBC the 'Big Black Cat'.

He said his wife will never get better but he doesn't complain about it – it's not 'in my nature'.

It finally dawned on him that I have a guitar.

'Do you play Bach?' he asked, out of nowhere.

We went down to the basement again. He was very gentle and affectionate. We got on really well and I was sorry to leave him in the evening.

Hannah called in and said goodbye to Gill and me, but not Valerie. Not sure why she bothered. I had hoped to have the office back to myself again but no, we have a new temp coming on Monday to replace Hannah – oh, YEURCH! – just when I am enjoying my privacy again.

BLAST.

Gill was abused by the Head of Catering about her letter about the vending machines.

Went home. Father seemed a bit better after a trip away with the Press Association.

The house is cold.

16th – Saturday

Vera accused me of not helping her enough and only talking about Frank; and she is quite right, of course. After lunch she went off to visit a friend of hers who lives down in the valley, whom my father has banned from visiting the house.

I sat upstairs and read the book of *The Go-Between*. I was upset for Leo's mother – she sounded so nice.

Spent most of the afternoon and evening upset because I want to be with Frank, although I don't want all this being furtive stuff.

Am I still the best thing he's got?

17th – Sunday

I imagine Frank would call today a 'quiet day'. So would I.

Did the ironing for Vera and helped with the lunch. Managed to spill a glass of beer at lunchtime in a panicky fit and it was awful, a sort of impatience coupled with clumsiness, and frustration at not being able to co-ordinate properly.

At least we have *Morecambe & Wise* on TV this evening to look forward to.

18th – Monday

A Sue has arrived to take Hannah's place. Oddly enough, Hannah herself rang in, fully expecting us to beg her to come back, so I had to explain that a replacement was already in situ. Anyway, she is working for an estate agent from next Monday.

Good luck to them!

Most of the day Frank was around. He asked after Vera, saying how she is a mother to me, although I think of her more as an aunt. He said he had a quiet, 'routine' weekend, but had wanted me.

'You were an innocent little t'ing when I started widja,' he sighed. 'Still, someone had to show you the difficulties of life.'

He said he had always been one for the ladies, making it sound like a mild affliction.

He was very strong in the morning and we managed two beautiful kisses, but really suffered because there were so many 'snoopers' about.

We discussed budgerigars ('You're my budgie') and people in the office.

Gill has foot trouble, which seems similar to my finger trouble.

Will Louise be back tomorrow? I am enjoying my freedom from her supervision.

Back to the hostel at about 9.30 and paid the rent – £32 since August.

19th – Tuesday

Frank asked me what I thought love meant. 'Like a circle,' I answered, 'a giving and receiving.' He said, 'Yes, love should be equal on both sides.' I said, 'You'd need to be a saint to manage that, though.' He dislikes the word 'love' because he thinks blokes use it to get in quick with a girl – he prefers 'fond of'.

'Love,' he said, 'means a back door and a full belly.'

I've been telling him that I love him, so I felt a little hurt.

We went downstairs twice, once leading to his purposely jamming the lift so that it didn't seem suspicious that it was out of action for so long. He was enthusiastic but it was bloody painful, so I said so and he stopped at once.

He said, 'It's no good in here, we have to meet outside the office sometime.'

He'd heard that a girl at Yalding House, who was 'out for everything', was sacked because the other women were jealous of her.

I suspect there is another side to that story.

Gill's foot pretty bad and the poor lass can hardly walk.

Valerie and I were insulting each other.

Gill got the vending machine man sorted out.

Louise probably in tomorrow.

I'd like an evening of Frank's company, if only he'd behave.

Curry. Also ate a lot of raisins.

20th – Wednesday

Took my guitar to work with me today as I was going on to the ATG audition in the evening. I showed Frank the words to 'Gilgarra Mountain' and was very surprised that he didn't know them – I thought it was an Irish song.

Louise was back, arriving at the same time as the postcard she had sent me. I told her I had been to see *The Music Lovers* and had found it disturbing; she said, 'Ken Russell is a charlatan.'

Gill not in, presumably because of her feet. I missed her company, and Valerie and I had to take turns sitting in her office, guarding her phone in case it rang.

Boring.

We grumbled about it together over lunch.

Radio Times day, so off Frank and I went to the basement, but much more successfully this time. Frank got what he wanted but I remained 'safe and sound'. It hurt a bit, but he was much kinder. Anyway, he was very affectionate, and later in the afternoon he followed me into the Club and bought me a cup of tea, being very friendly, smiling and patting my arm and so on.

Wonderfully gentle, kind man – I know he is 'fond of' me now.

Went to an audition for the Ariel Theatre Group with Valerie. They are putting on a children's musical show just before Christmas called *The Owl and the Pussycat Went to See* ... [sic] based on the Lear poem.

I sang a couple of songs not well, but played the guitar reasonably and joked my way through the rest. It felt funny, singing in front of strangers.

21st – Thursday

Frank is worried about his tax. His wife should be certified as blind, although she is actually only very badly sighted. I typed an envelope for him. He seemed rather upset, and in the afternoon he took me aside and said he was sorry we'd been too far yesterday. I said I only wanted what would make him happy.

'So near,' he sighed, 'and yet so far!'

We spent quite a long time examining the woodwork in the lift. The inlaid wood panelling is a work of art, but nobody looks after it, and oil from the cogs and chains above the roof is seeping in and spoiling it. Frank said it was a real shame. We chatted on about jobs, staying, moving, flats and the audition. In the evening we finished up in the basement and I know he is still very fond of me, and warm.

Gill is still away. Kaz rang in in the morning, he sounded very grumpy – perhaps it was too early in the day for him.

Meanwhile, Miss Twitchett has come up with a bedsitting room in a house in NW6. It might be too expensive but I said I would go and take a look at it.

Wondering if I could try the P.A. Training course, or do I have to be twenty-one to apply for it?

Carol says I have missed a job vacancy in Publicity. If I went to 35 MHS, I wouldn't see Frank every day.

No, it's OK, I will have to move on sometime. Better things are ahead. And I can always come back and see him.

Hey, look, optimism!

Oh – his full name is FRANCIS JOHN and his signature is a big, old-fashioned copper-platey thing – I saw it on the tax form.

I went round the shops, bought a book and a ring at Selfridges.

Oh, Frank, how fabulous that I will see you again tomorrow!

22nd – Friday

When I arrived, Louise was already by the lifts on the ground floor, eagerly scanning the board of job vacancies.

Interesting.

Frank and I exchanged meaningful glances and he took us both to the sixth floor.

Our opportunity came later on – Hallelujah in the basement and he bloody nearly choked me with my bra, which made us laugh.

Gill was back, but I was horrid to Leah so that we could have lunch alone (I feel lousy about it). Anyway, Gill's feet are a little better, I think.

Sue foxed over repeatedly typing the same letter.

Frank upset because he didn't get a sleep in his lunch hour. He said he couldn't find a dark hole. I asked him what he would be doing at the weekend, and he said, 'Working.'

Not at the Langham, of course – at home.

I'd like to approach him about an evening out but that might look a little odd now.

I am spending too much money.

Sometimes I see life semi-objectively, critically, as if I'm reading a book about myself and am powerless to control my fortunes. Most weird – I ought to try to write about my life sometime.

Chipstead; Vera relatively cheerful.

This is a funny place.

23rd – Saturday

Croydon with Vera; bought another black skirt at Marks.

Lunch, then back to London: to the National Film Theatre with Valerie to see *Triumph of the Will*. It was lengthy and dull, with an awful lot of marching. Hitler looked like a born loser – insignificant, and more German than I had expected. All the Nazi leaders looked like crooks. I was surprised that they let through some of the taken-unawares shots of Hitler. Perhaps it was an attempt to make him appear more like the man in the street. In fact, he only seemed to come alive, or be worthy of any attention, when he was speaking in public.

Bed late, but slept well. Reading Norse myths. Why death? In the sense of, Why not pause in one place for a while if one wanted? Why do we grow old? Why do seasons change? Is there a death wish?

24th – Sunday

Warm, sunny day. Worried about my fingers: five are infected, three on the right and two on the left.

Torn about Frank. Everything I take from him feels as if it has been stolen from his wife. Sometimes he seems very fond of me, at others he is quite detached. Some of his comments get to me because they are so true, others are just his Walter Mitty fantasies. He has never said anything that hurt me though, and I think that if I have suffered at all it has been because of my own preconceived ideas.

25th – Monday

Up on the early train.

Frank greeted me most affectionately and we discussed my possible move into a bedsitter. He warned me it might be expensive and to be careful about how much I was charged. Didn't see him often, but we did talk about his wife's toe. He's gone off *Morecambe & Wise*.

Sharpy called me into her office first thing for dictation because Valerie was off with 'normal monthly causes' and she needed to dictate some 'aide memoires' about ORJENT matters. However, Valerie was back by lunchtime, happy to embarrass me by pointing out Alan [from the Ariel Theatre Group] in the BBC Club.

After work I went up to Finchley Road and saw a bedsitter in Canfield Gardens. The area isn't bad at all, rather like Coulsdon. All the residents in the house work for the BBC. The room is on the ground floor, with a bay window overlooking the street, or at least the dustbins. It has a bed, a huge wardrobe, a little cooker, fridge and a sink. There's a table and a chair and an electric fire with a meter you feed with shillings. The room is huge compared to the one at the hostel. I think I will take it – I can always move out again if I don't like it, or even go back home for a little while. Mike, who is in the room at the moment, works for the Cashiers – he is going off to one of the regional offices.

Came back to check my money with Miss Fenn at the hostel.

There is a reunion for everyone who went on an A. H. holiday this year in London on 6 November. Joyce and Dave are going and have written to ask if I will too. I wrote back to say yes.

I don't expect Alastair will be there, nor will I suggest it to him.

Fingers are bloody awful – I need to be referred to a skin clinic. I also want to be with Francis J.B. all day.

All Day.

26th – Tuesday

I discussed the bedsitter with Frank, and a rather distant, sad-sounding Vera on the phone. In fact, when Vera first rang up, Sue answered and thought she was Hannah. She nearly rang off.

Louise also asked about the bedsit, so I described it to her and she thought it sounded OK. I phoned Mrs Rawbone, the landlady, and said I would meet her tomorrow.

Gill's feet are better now.

Frank was cheerful enough, still convinced I'm 'hot', but concerned to see my fingers were bandaged up again. He's the only one who notices.

At lunch we had a long discussion about Women's Lib. Valerie has read Greer's book now and agrees with me; Gill said it had all gone too far. Graham, the Technical Officer (unusually he had joined us), said, 'Isn't it the same for men too?' Leah even uttered a few words – she perks up when Graham is around.

I'm looking forward to moving into Canfield Gardens, and the possibility of going to a pub with Frank, but I don't know if that is wise. He's being very kind and affectionate now and, although he thinks I'm a bit of a kid, he means well.

27th – Wednesday

This week is going quickly. Frank and I discussed pills and potions for Vera, who sounded awfully miserable and in pain over the phone. I got the name of the painkillers he gets on prescription in case they help her. Even better, it is looking hopeful that we might find something to do together outside work that doesn't involve a bed.

Down to the basement in the afternoon (*Radio Times*), the usual. He laughed and said I was warming up. He was very solicitous about the bedsit.

Bought Frank some mints.

If I could keep the people and lose the job, that would be fantastic.

Typed a Method and Ops memo, which had a very flattering passage in it about myself. I wondered if that was why they gave it to me to type.

Drink with Gill and then off to the Finchley Road again. As I arrived a Mouse Removing Man was just leaving, so if there were any mice in the house there won't be any now. Paid a week's rent in advance to Mrs Rawbone, came back to the hostel and handed in my notice. I am moving out on 6 November.

I am worried about Vera.

28th – Thursday

Frank busy, so there wasn't much sex education for me today! He was disgusted that the part-time cleaners earn £3.50 an hour when he gets £5 a day. If that is true, he earns more than I do. He says he gets tired working more than a few hours non-stop, which I can understand. According to Frank, Jack has a girlfriend, but he wouldn't say who she is. I am not sure I believe him.

I had lunch with Valerie and a couple of her neurotic friends in the Salad Bar.

In the afternoon I wandered into Frank's lift only to find him whispering to one of the secretaries from another floor. I was very composed and didn't say anything – after all, I felt I could hardly complain. (I'm glad I am not his wife.) He obviously noticed how I'd felt though, because after that he was very warm and smiling towards me, which cheered me up.

I am afraid the Common Market fails to interest me, and I don't see it will make much difference either way. I suppose emotionally I am against it, but rationally I am for it. Perhaps it's a last resort for dealing with the trade unions.

Met Penny in the evening. We were both tired; she was depressed about changing job next Monday but, having seen me talking to Frank, was interested to hear about him.

29th – Friday

Weather a bit colder: winter is on the way.

Had a long chat with Frank on the sixth floor. He saw a play last night on TV with a naked woman (I mean, she was in the play!) of which he strongly disapproved.

He was intrigued as to why I didn't report him all those months ago, and we had a bit of a laugh about that; and then he asked about my fingers, offering various remedies ('Is that eczema, do you need to wear gloves?'). We agreed he wasn't responsible. He gave me a couple of his headache pills to give Vera tonight.

I went over to the Surgery but the nurses there couldn't refer me to a hospital for my fingers. They said, 'Get a London doctor,' which is logical but a nuisance as I am about to move.

Had lunch in the BH canteen with Gill and Valerie. Pam joined us.

I left at four because I had a dental appointment with Uncle Rupert. He said my teeth were sound and I have a good mouth (although he would not have been aware that I was wearing a beautiful goodnight kiss from the pill-donor).

Vera not looking at all well. I can't get through to her, I wonder if she is unhappy because I rely more on the advice of people like Louise, Gill and Frank nowadays. I do still trust her opinion nonetheless.

30th – Saturday

Did all the shopping. I also went to see the doctor about my fingers. She was bloody rude and unsympathetic. Anyway, she gave me a prescription to tide me over until I find a doctor in London. She wouldn't refer me herself.

Attempted some writing and could only produce trash so abandoned it.

Watched television.

31st – Sunday

Weather pleasant – pale blue sky, dark green grass, the leaves turning yellow.

Nothing else much. Vera not at all well, I think.

November

1st – Monday

Went up with Sue Moriarty, she is so tiresomely conventional. No sign of The Weed anymore.

Frankie depressed, picking at his nails and speaking in short sentences. His daughter is moving house on Saturday week.

Louise made me a present of a copy of Katharine Whitehorn's *Cooking in a Bedsitter*, which was awfully kind of her. She is attending a course this week with the education officers. One of the things they all have to do is a radio interview, and Mr Chaplin asked Louise if he could interview me. It would be about education and he'll do it on Thursday. Terror! But Louise said I should do it and seemed to have faith in my ability, so I said I would.

There was a bomb scare at about 11.30. Masses of police appeared at BH and the Club was shut in the afternoon. Various people were joking around the lifts, saying, 'Are you up to something, Frank?' and to begin with he played up his Irish accent with a lot of 'sures' and 'begorrahs' although, as he pointed out, it could have been anyone, not necessarily the

IRA. But after a while the joke seemed to wear a bit thin. He said quite seriously to one bloke, 'No, I would nivver plant a bomb on anyone.'

Went to the basement with him in the afternoon, and we had a long, tough, close session (that's an awful way of describing it), interrupted by a trip to the third floor. He was very warm and grateful afterwards.

I went over to the BH Surgery, showed them my fingers, explained my position and asked if they could refer me to a doctor. I was given an address and went off to this illegible street. The doctor there seemed quite decent and wrote me out a prescription. He had a nervous twitch.

Too many patients.

Back to talk to Miss Fenn at the hostel about my leaving.

2nd – Tuesday

Frank and I had a disagreement. He said he thought the monarchy was redundant and unnecessary, I said I thought it performed a necessary function. This led on to newspapers. He used to read the *Daily Herald*, but says now the *Morning Star* is the only paper to print the facts. I disagreed even more strongly, but neither of us wanted to fall out with the other so in the end we compromised by saying all papers told lies. He then asked, solicitously, if I was all right, because I seemed a bit cross and hurt.

He thinks he is starting a cold. We went on talking about bells, batteries and the BBC, pay rises, bearded commission-aires, working hours, Fortes, Jules Bar and drinks (he drinks ten to twenty bottles of Light Ale a week – I think he said a week, anyway).

Late in the day Louise gave me a tape of an interview to type out for her, so I carried on with that and missed saying goodnight to Frank. Ghastly. Had a drink and supper with

Valerie, feeling upset. She and I are depressed about the SBC. Now Sue is getting cheesed off with Sharpy.

Suppose Frank isn't in for the rest of the week with that cold? And I have to work in the Recordings Library tomorrow. Bloody hell! No lift opportunities from there.

3rd – Wednesday

There wasn't a lot of work to do for the Recordings Library in the end, so with Louise away on the course, the mouse was dancing.

Frank wasn't touching me today. He says it was because he had a cold. I wondered whether he was upset because we had disagreed about the monarchy yesterday. Today's topic was one of his favourites: reincarnation and how he believes you are reborn into your family. After that we went on to what on earth Adam and Eve had found to talk about.

Later, we had a heart-to-heart about families. His daughter is called Elizabeth (he calls her Betty) and she was a secretary at London University before she married. He never remembers his father, but remembers his mother well, and with affection. His brothers and sisters, he says, are only concerned with what he's got, and he says he has better friends than that.

He told me, 'In all troot', I am soft as a willow, and I weep easily. The only one t'ing I feel guilty about is playin' about wid you ... although 'tis only wrong in the Scriptures.' I tried making the sign of the Cross, like priests do, and he laughed because I got it the wrong way round. He showed me how to do it the right way, and the pair of us stood in the lift, signing crosses at each other. If anyone had seen us they would have thought we were mad.

I knew he was soft a long time ago, but to hear it from him was an admission.

He was so tender and friendly. Today (and I have only just

realised it) must have been the first day for ages that he hasn't kissed me.

Long talk with Gill about her brother's girlfriend. Apparently she enjoyed *The Music Lovers* and wanted to go to it three times.

Results of the ATG auditions – nothing for me, but Valerie has the part of a Jumbly Girl.

Oh well.

Went to the NFT to see the film *Orphée*, interesting. The main man was awfully hairy. Nice touches and some good jokes, but the end was unconvincing.

4th – Thursday

Frank warmer and very affectionate. Discussed language (church sayings in Irish).

He said his wife was a very kind and gentle person who gave him good advice and how 'she wouldn't be hurtin' a fly'.

They sound like a lovely couple – I wish my parents were like that. I mentioned Vera has back trouble; Frank promptly offered to rub her back for her. I said, 'Well, you are both quite short.' 'In bed,' he said, 'there are no height problems.'

I don't think he meant being in bed with Vera.

Gill and Valerie have both volunteered to help me move into the bedsit on Saturday.

Nothing much to do at work. Mr Chaplin, who is one of the more friendly and approachable of the officers, interviewed me in Louise's office about my schooldays and history. It didn't take too long and I quite enjoyed it.

In the evening Gill and I went to the BH canteen, and over supper I showed her my latest poems. Her main criticism was that she found inconsistency in the subject. She said I was writing stews, not cakes. And rather sloppy stews too.

Went to the theatre via HMV and met Penny. We saw *Getting*

On by Alan Bennett, extremely funny, but I got muddled, trying to work out any deeper meanings. Was Bennett saying that unconventionality is, in itself, now a convention and you can't escape it? Maybe someone else thinks that one can be unconventional by being 'conventional'?

I want to be with Frank but I don't want anything to come between him and his wife. I hinted that we might go for a drink together one evening, but he said he doesn't like leaving her at the moment. Anyway, goodness knows where we would go – Boots the Chemist?

5th – Friday

Woke up from a strange dream about Frank and a dead baby.

Tomorrow I will move out of the hostel. I cleared out the stuff in my room and packed it – it only took about an hour, if that. I am dead keen to leave this place.

So I had time for a farewell walk to work. Up Buckingham Palace Road, past the expensive cafe, which is always full of people having delicious breakfasts, past the Palace (Hello Ma'am, I supported you), through Green Park to Piccadilly, Bond Street, Regent Street, Oxford Circus and on to Portland Place. I can't believe it is the last time.

Mr Chaplin gave me a tape with a copy of the interview on it. He said he had been told it was the best interview that anyone on the course had done, and suggested it would have been even better if he had cut himself out of it.

Louise, who had done an interview with someone else, said it had been a useful course and she had learned a lot about herself. The person running it said she thought she 'really knew' me after listening to Chaplin's tape, but Louise felt it was only one side of me. I agreed with her.

It's a superb tape recording of a defence mechanism in action.

Frank was wonderful. He was acting a bit nutty ('I don't care if it's the bleedin' Papal Nuncio,' he said for some reason when I was talking about who owned the hostel). He hoped the weather would be fine tomorrow for my move. He wanted to help with my rent and my moving out, but I thanked him and said I was OK.

He gave me his roll at breakfast and we went on chatting about all sorts of things. He got a bit cheeky, and at the end of the day we descended to the basement, where we had a little kiss between us, and I know he is fond of me.

I hate being away from him.

6th – Saturday

Had a terrible night. It was freezing cold, and around midnight there was a lot of shouting at the back of the hostel, from the pub on the other side of the wall. I looked out of the window and saw a man holding a knife, and someone else doubled up. There were a few other men standing around. Gradually they all split up and moved off, taking the victim with them.

In the morning I wandered around the shops in Victoria for a bit, and then waited in my room. Kaz phoned up to say that Gill was drunk last night and had a hangover, so they weren't able to come. However, Valerie and her boyfriend did turn up. They helped me bring down my stuff, load it into a taxi and go to Canfield Gardens. We were unpacking it all when someone called Ken, who has one of the rooms on the floor above, came down and had a coffee with us.

Valerie's boyfriend had been promised a curry as a reward for helping with the removal, so we walked up to the Finchley Road and studied several menus. We ended up in the Golden Curry, where we had a not very exciting meal. Then they left and I came back to my room.

During the afternoon Penny called in. We had a cup of tea and she helped me rearrange the furniture.

Finally I went to the A. H. reunion. It wasn't all that fantastic. I saw few people I recognised and spent most of the evening with Dave and Joyce. The only person from Freshwater was Gary, the man Zelda said had assaulted her. I had a brief chat with him. He seemed OK and I couldn't really mention the incident. Even if I had, he would have denied doing anything wrong, wouldn't he?

He didn't ask after her.

7th – Sunday

Caught the 9.28 down from London Bridge and saw veteran cars on the Brighton Road as the driver obligingly halted for us on the bridge at Coulsdon.

Vera seemed much better. She found a spare saucepan and frying pan for me, and a few other useful bits. I hope she will come and see the bedsit soon. Father has improved too – he was playing my LP of Verdi's Requiem. We even had an interesting discussion about pornography and obscenity, which he thinks should be licensed for use at home in the same way as alcohol is.

Vera said Louise 'has done you a lot of good in drawing you out'. So she has, but maybe she's not the only person to be involved in that.

Saw *Morecambe & Wise*. Glenda Jackson has a bitchy mouth.

It was the first day I have enjoyed being at home since God knows when.

8th – Monday

Went back to London, armed with some food and other nice things from home.

Frank was very affectionate all day. He asked about the bedsit, how was Vera's back, and gave me some advice (of course) on how to look after myself.

He reckons it would be better for me to come to work on the Tube via Great Portland Street. You have to change at Baker Street, but it means you avoid the crowds at Oxford Circus. I'll give it a try tomorrow.

I said Vera ought to rename our budgie Frank, instead of Fred.

'Oh,' he replied, 'so we're both cocky then?'

I asked about his weekend, and he said he got through over £3 on Saturday night because he was buying drinks for his friends.

Gill was most apologetic about not coming to help on Saturday, but it was OK and she said she would come over to see the bedsit soon.

Louise rather sombre (Valerie's word). I had supper with Valerie, and we sat for ages discussing sex, homosexuality, British nationality, Oz, etc.

Got back to the bedsit at about 8.30 and pinned posters on the walls.

I feel as if I have been here in the bedsit for quite a while already. I am getting used to the musty smell as you come in through the front door. Although I don't like having to go up a floor to use the bathroom, I am learning what is the best time to nip in there for a bath, and there are no old lady hairs left in the tub.

I'm so glad I am no longer in that awful hostel.

9th – Tuesday

I left plenty of time to get to work because I wasn't sure how long it would take me to get there. I took the Bakerloo Line to Baker Street, and changed on to the Circle Line for Great

Portland Street, as instructed. It was nice walking down the street thinking Frank had walked down it a few minutes earlier, but it was still only 8.45 when I got to the Langham so I wandered around Cavendish Square in the cold until nine. I was frozen by the time I finally got in.

The office was extremely cold too. At midday Frankie appeared with a cup of soup (fabulous stuff) to warm me up and wouldn't take any money for it. He was very gentle, warm, funny, friendly, stupid, cuddly, all day.

Louise was also more cheerful. We had a letter from someone today enclosing a prayer which the writer thought should be included in *A Religious Service for Primary Schools*. Louise read it out to me. It was about how we should all be kinder to animals, and could do this mostly by not poking them with sticks.

I saw little of Gill. She had been upset at lunch by a couple of the others who had joined forces to tell her 'Kaz can't live off you forever'.

Frank suggested we might go out together on Saturday.

After work I went to see a film, *The Lost Continent*. There was a hilarious moment where Eric Porter lay on the ground gushing blood, and a woman rushed over to him and shouted, 'Are you all right?'

Back to the bedsit to cook supper. This was scrambled eggs on Ryvita, and yoghurt. I think maybe you are not supposed to put scrambled eggs on Ryvita, and there wasn't a lot of the yoghurt as most of it had leaked into my handbag.

10th – Wednesday

Arrived too early again.

I went up to the sixth floor with Frank and it all started well, but then he started to explain to me how to tap an electricity meter so you didn't have to keep putting shillings in. That's fraud, isn't it? Or stealing? Anyway, I walked out of the lift.

The next time I saw him he looked a bit sheepish and said, 'You didn't like to hear me talkin' like dat, didja, bein' a rogue?' I shook my head. There was a pause; he looked at me with a tilt of his head.

'So, have you fallen out widjerself?'

Something metallic fell out of the buzzer casing. He picked it up, held it out to me and said, 'D'you fancy a screw then?'

Down to the basement for the *Radio Times* and more desperate closeness, with hands everywhere. Both of us. Looking at me appraisingly, he said, 'You have better legs than Miss World, you know. You could be like Marilyn Monroe.' Frank's fantasies may be a bit wide of the mark, but God he makes me feel good! He was so affectionate all day. It feels as if we are becoming increasingly together in things.

'Me and you,' he said, pointing at us in turn, 'you have a bit of brain and I have the bit of brawn.'

'Let's go out together on Friday night,' he suggested. I said I'd think about it.

He doesn't know what to do at Christmas as his wife is still not too good, but he will probably take a week off then.

Lunch in the pub, drank with Gill and Valerie in the evening and then I had a subdued supper with Valerie at BH.

11th – Thursday

It's getting awfully close now.

Frank and I pottered about together for part of the day. He was very loving, giving me things, asking me about work and home, chatting, showing off, wanting to help me. He's decided against us going out on Friday (I hadn't said yes, mind you) because it meant lying to his wife. I was relieved when he said that, and made a pompous little speech about us not being unfair to her, etc., which in the circumstances was so unnecessary. Instead, he said maybe we could take a half-day off work later on, to which I agreed (may God forgive me).

Frank (holding both my hands):
        Are you in love?
Me: Yes, I suppose I am.
Frank: I suppose I am too.

This bloody situation. He regretted being so much older than I am. The poor bugger wants me, I know, and I want him. And we both respect each other's feelings and love, etc., but it's so bloody. He loves me – he did today, anyway.

I give up.

Went to the canteen with Gill for lunch, and with Valerie for supper. Valerie is worried about her flatmates, and the play rehearsals, which are not going well.

Sue and I were laughing about Geoffrey Curtis's secretary, who always yells 'What?' at me on the phone.

Frank calls Jack 'The Invisible Man' because he's not at work as much as he should be.

Had a nosebleed at 5 p.m.

That dream last Friday still bothers me.

12th – Friday

Arrived at the right time at last, having left the bedsit at 8.30 and went up with Little Frank. He was very passionate in his greetings, asking if I'd go down to the basement sometime. I said maybe.

Lunch with Gill and Sue. Louise is thinking of applying for the Prospect job. If she got it, would I apply to go with her? Is that wise?

Valerie stapled my pullover while I was in her office talking to her.

Finally went to the basement with Frank and had a passionate session. He asked afterwards if I was OK. Oh yes, I was! We were nearly caught by a man who kept peering through the door – I think Frank had stopped the lift high enough above it so he couldn't have seen anything.

Went for a drink with Gill and Kaz (Frank said he would come too, but I couldn't say yes) and argued madly. Kaz is rather too cynical (like Father) and sees bad in everything but himself.

13th – Saturday

Woke up with a lousy sore throat and felt crummy. Crawled back home. Fixed the car with anti-freeze and took El Supremo to the shops in Purley and Coulsdon.

Crept into bed and slept on and off, listening to the radio. Bad night.

14th – Sunday

Didn't wake up until about 1 o'clock. Came down to lunch feeling a little better, so stayed down. Read the papers and watched TV (*Morecambe & Wise*, Richard Burton in *My Cousin Rachel* and a little bit of Duke Ellington).

15th – Monday

Up at nine with a bit of a cold. Thanks, Frankie! Had breakfast with Vera, then rang the office and explained to Louise I wouldn't be in. I rang Gill, who said Frank was in so I asked her to let him know I was off sick.

Pottered around. Listened to Verdi's Requiem and read

The Reality of Monarchy. It was rather dull and I gave up with it. Chatted to Vera.

16th – Tuesday

Went back to work wondering whether I should or I shouldn't (typical). For a change Weedy Richard was at the station today, but not Moriarty. I avoided him.

Frank was pleased to see me and was very solicitous about my health. However, his wife had become worse at the week-end, and she had been crying. I asked if there was anything I could do to help, but of course there wasn't.

Frank maintains the Irish are stupid because they are too quick-tempered and never listen to reason. He was very cuddly today, in one of those moods. I couldn't stop hugging him.

He said he doesn't keep letters or diaries.

In the afternoon he bought me a bread roll and a packet of juice, and when I offered to pay him, he said no, because he owed me a lot.

(Huh?)

I noticed there is a secretarial job going at *The Listener* magazine. It's on the next grade up, and if I got it, I would still have an office in the Langham but on the 't'ird' floor. I asked Frank what he thought about it. He chuckled and said, 'Well, you wouldn't be escapin' any danger.' He gave me some advice about the people at *The Listener* (some of them are 'pansies') and said he would find out what he could about the job.

Jack wants to hold a Christmas party in his lift. He is only going to invite people he likes, and apparently this means Louise and himself. If he wins the football pools, the party will move from his lift to a hotel. Gill asked, 'Do you mean the Langham?' And he said no.

In the afternoon Louise suggested I ask Frank about the people at *The Listener*. I said, 'Oh, do you think so?' I wasn't falling for that one. And anyway, little did she know we'd already had the discussion.

Leah gatecrashed lunch again. It's awful; if she comes with us, she is an encumbrance, and if she doesn't, we feel bad about leaving her behind. Supper with Valerie, discussing Christianity (she is an atheist).

What I need is a good screw. Hah!

17th – Wednesday

Quite a day!

Went up with Frankie, who had suggested I should come in before anyone else was around and while Jack was on the fourth floor, supposedly phoning his woman.

Frank asked how I was, and we went down to the basement but it was difficult because we wanted to avoid kissing each other and him catching the cold again. He was seriously disheartened by this cramping of his style. He asked me to go out with him on Friday. I said I would go, but it seems obvious what he is after. Kind of him, of course. Still …

His watch is at the menders, so I lent him mine. It's an old one my Uncle Rupert picked up in the RAF in the war, so it's OK for a man to wear. He thanked me but said afterwards he found it difficult to read.

Gill told me she had had a dream last night about finding a rabbi in her office. Later, we checked over a draft together and had a good laugh reading the bits that were emphasised WITH EMPHASIS.

Met Penny and went over to the BH canteen. Ended up playing with sugar lumps, matchboxes and cigarette packets, but discussed her job, the Kabbalah, etc.

Back to the bedsit. Bought some groceries including lemons:

a lemon drink for my cold. Made a poster out of old Beatles'
photographs.

This is one of those Victorian-type rooms with high ceilings,
so it is difficult to get it warm with only two bars of an electric
fire.

18th – Thursday

Went to the basement with Frankie for the usual. My cold is
a lot better, and he was very hot (phew!). Afterwards, he
presented me with a bread roll, which was sweet of him.
However, I wasn't so pleased at losing a button off my new
coat.

BLAST.

Jack was considering removing the School Broadcasting
Council nameplate on the wall on the sixth floor. Frank said
no, turn it upside down, and promptly read it out backwards
to me.

He still hasn't resolved the problem about what to do at
Christmas. I offered to buy him a Christmas present and he
said the only thing he needed was shoelaces. He said he is no
good at buying presents, he gives his daughter £10. We talked
again for a while about Ireland and his past.

I am still worried about the problem of Leah attaching
herself to us at lunchtime. Today she tagged along with us
even though we were discussing theology, although I had
hoped that might put her off.

Frank didn't wait for me this evening. He was gone by the
time I finished and I was a bit upset. Anyway, I pulled myself
together and went off to Marks, where I bought a dressing
gown, a nightgown and some tights – bit of a spending spree.

Decided that Frankie has made me more vulnerable. For
301 days I have been thinking of him.

19th – Friday

Crawled into work. Frankie had had a look around his lift for my coat button but not found it. Instead, he offered me one he had found at his home – unfortunately it turned out to be too small.

Valerie was a bit off. Gill said Pam told her she thought I was 'intelligent' and 'would go far'.

Which is encouraging.

Bought *Who Moved the Stone?* from Mowbrays. ('Who moved the stone?' said Frank, reading the cover, 'I did!') He was very cuddly and we discussed how he would manage this weekend and what was the best way to fry chips – he's cooking fish and chips tonight. No rolls in the machine today and he considered going out to Fortes for one, but didn't.

He and Jack decided to start a brass band together, Jack on the trombone or sax, Frank on the flute or, he suggested, 'the fiddle'.

Had a drink with Gill, talked about Frank and Kaz.

Back to the bedsit to cook a curry – very, very slowly – on the little Belling cooker.

Cold got a bit worse today.

20th – Saturday

Got up at nine and went round the shops at Finchley Road, Woolworths, John Barnes, etc. I bought a copy of the *Ham and High* (local newspaper) and found a report on a lecture given by Louise's psychiatrist friend. I wondered whether she had seen it, and whether it would be cheeky of me to take it in for her. Maybe I am not supposed to draw any conclusions from the phone calls.

Gill came over to inspect the bedsit. We went up the road to the Golden Egg and talked about Kaz and Frank, and she told me about her past escapades. On returning to the house I discovered I had left my keys in the room. A man called Dick Hughes, who has the flat in the basement, came upstairs, and when we explained our predicament he went back, reappeared with a screwdriver and forced the door open. It only has a Yale lock.

After that I came back to Chipstead. Vera reckons Frank is more considerate than other men, especially younger ones. It's a pity he isn't younger and the situation isn't different.

I read *The Girl with Green Eyes* (Irish).

21st – Sunday

Quite a pleasant day, the weather is really wintry now. Got up late.

Fingers looking ominous at the moment, but cold is receding.

I took the car out for a run over to Purley, past where I went to school, and then back home. Purley reminded me of so much, especially of the grey afternoons in the winter of 1964, sitting in Uncle Rupert's waiting room doing maths homework and eating Bassett sherbet fountains. Mother was in hospital in those days, it was just before she died. I must have had to get a lift to school with one of the families in the village, and I imagine Uncle Rupert brought me home in the evenings when he finished work. I can't really remember now, and it all seems a long time ago.

Anyhow, it is quite dark now, and cosy in the house once the fires are lit.

22nd – Monday

Very cold travelling up to London. Frankie not in. Worried.

It was so cold in the office that we papered up the cracks

again and shivered. Louise and I kept warm by filling in job application forms.

Both Gill and I went to the shops and bought a pair of boots.

With Frank away, I didn't bother much with the lifts. A man called Jimmy was working on Frank's lift. I had to keep stopping myself from telling him when to stop it, how to slow it down – I felt absurdly protective, and didn't want him damaging Frank's lift. However, I missed the man himself less than I thought I would because I knew he would be coming back and that he cares about me; and anyway, there was so much to do today. It felt like it did when he was away in hospital. I hope he and his wife aren't ill(er). I suppose it could be to do with his daughter's visit, or he may have picked up my cold.

Hope he's back tomorrow.

I mistook Mr Roberts for the cleaning man. He hugged me, the old devil.

23rd – Tuesday

I didn't wake up until 8.15, far too late! I had to sprint down as fast as I could from Great Portland Street station so that I could get in before everyone else arrived.

Frankie was in. But Louise had a dreadful-sounding cold so she didn't appear. In her absence, I dealt with a phone call from a very voluble lady complaining about the sex education programmes. Her main objection was based on the premise that 'all men come from the gutter' and she spent forty minutes explaining why children had to be protected from sexual knowledge. I sort of knew what to say to her, because I had heard Louise deal with so many calls like that. I took her details and promised I would pass on her comments. Then I typed up a record of the conversation and gave it to Miss Sharp. She found it of 'great interest and value'.

Yippee.

Then I typed my application for the vacancy at *The Listener*, went out to the lifts and asked Frank if he knew where I could find the office to hand it in. He promptly took me down to the 't'ird' floor and we went on a hunt together; he knew more or less where to go.

He said his wife was very ill on Sunday night and he didn't get much sleep, so he wasn't fit for much yesterday. He lost his hat in the wind on Saturday.

I told him about Roberts hugging me. 'Poor old man,' he said, so I shook him.

He asked about Vera, and when I told him how she was, he sympathised but I don't think he quite understood.

When we got back to the lift, he said he had a poem for me. I know quite a bit about Frank's poems by now, and they are usually filthy. Anyway, this one wasn't and, although I can't remember it all, it ended with, 'I love you best of all'. Then he asked if we could have a little time together soon. I said yes, possibly.

It became more saucy in the afternoon. We were down to the basement as usual, and after several passionate kisses and so on, Frank said half-jokingly that we should have a stripping dare. Whoever took off the most clothes would win.

I hesitated for a moment and then thought, damn it, I'll call his bluff. Anyway, it was easy for me, my shirt and bra were already hanging about, so I simply took them off and stood there in front of him, half-bare, my back resting against the wood panelling.

His jacket was undone and his tie loose. He undid a couple of buttons on his shirt, and then stopped. 'No, 'tis no good,' he said. ''Tis my uniform. You win.'

For what felt like a couple of minutes he looked over what was in front of him, and then said quietly, 'Cover yourself up.'

He went over to his seat.

'You're very sexy, you know. Very hot.'

He stared out of the lift door.

I put myself back together again, saying, 'But only with you.'

His face lit up with surprise, even delight.

I felt strangely proud of myself and better for having done that.

It was really freezing this evening in the bedsit.

24th – Wednesday

We decided not to go down to the basement first thing because it was so cold. Frankie bought me breakfast instead and we sat at the sixth floor, drank tea, chatted and ate our bread rolls. He said, 'You know, 'tis a strange thing but the English can't make Irish stew as it's made at home (sic) because it needs a lot of spuds and turnips cooked in with the meat. And another t'ing, the Guinness is too sour in England.'

Louise was back. She was impressed by my report of the telephone complaint. However, Gill's boss pointed out to Sharpy that 'a secretary' should not have had to deal with the call. I can see his point, but I did it, and did it well.

Louise has sent in her application for the job at *Prospect*. She thinks Sharpy will have a fit if we both leave at the same time.

Went shopping in Marks (again) for tights. Frankie offered to buy them for me as they were to replace the ones damaged in a moment of passion yesterday. I refused to let him.

Jack wants to come and visit me one Sunday. Frank said he (Jack) would if I let him.

God help us!

Supper at BH and back via Great Portland Street.

Frankie tender all day. We went down to the basement for the *Radio Times* but the Eunuch prevented anything happening.

Actually he isn't a eunuch, Frank says, he's just a bit tubby and talks in a high-pitched voice. He pushed barrows around down there – no one seems to know what his job actually is.

Frankie said he'd been thinking about my changing jobs, and how we could still go on seeing each other, even if I end up working outside the Langham.

Valerie told me Pam had said she could imagine having a good night on the tiles with Frank.

Looking back at the beginning of this diary, I wouldn't wish for that time again at all.

25th – Thursday

On arrival, went to the basement with Frank and had quite a long session. He asked afterwards whether I was angry, and I said no, I couldn't be angry with him. I wanted to tell him how much I cared about him, but the opportunity didn't come about.

Went shopping in the evening, feeling a bit melancholy about Frank.

When I got back to the house I met Dick Hughes on the doorstep. He is a large, burly man with a beard, probably in his mid-thirties. He told me he used to be a lecturer at UEA and now works as a producer in the BBC's Further Education Department. His office is in the Langham on the third floor, although I don't remember seeing him there. He was stroking the large ginger cat that belongs to the people next door.

Dick asked if I would like to join him for dinner, along with two former students of his who were to arrive shortly. So I changed into a dress and went down to his flat. His friends, Barbara and Mark, arrived and we had Paella à la Hughes. I hadn't had paella before, but it was very good. The meal went OK, although I felt a bit out of my depth in the conversation and probably revealed my lack of university education because at times the others exchanged looks across the table. Anyway, they were very friendly and a lot of wine was consumed so perhaps they didn't notice my intellectual faux pas.

Barbara and Mark left around midnight. I stayed on to help Dick finish the last bottle. The conversation took a maudlin turn. Dick confessed that he used to go out with Barbara and still fancies her. He said that if Mark didn't exist, he would make a move but can't because they are a couple.

I made sympathetic noises. Dick put his arm round me, conducted me to the sofa and began kissing me. My curiosity about beards was quickly satisfied, in that it wasn't too bad, just a bit scratchy. And I tolerated the mustiness of his wine-soaked breath for the sake of giving him a little comfort in his despair. However, a few minutes later one hand slipped around my waist while the other began an ascent up my thigh and I thought, I don't want this from you. So I stopped him – I said it was getting very late, thank you for the meal and escaped.

Upstairs, I crawled into bed and lay there, thinking, Oh, Christ, I knew it! It's not about wanting to Do It with someone, it's about the someone you Do It with. Why is it that with a man like Dick, whom I don't want, I could have done anything and no one would object? In fact, I would probably get a round of applause from my friends. But if anyone saw the man I do love even giving me a little kiss he would lose his job and my name would be mud, all because of who he is and what he is. And he can't be here with me now because he's married and he's too bloody old.

And I wished, wished it had been Frank there, downstairs, kissing me. I wouldn't have held back. As no doubt Dick, on the floor beneath me, was thinking about Barbara.

26th – Friday

I hardly slept at all, but I wasn't tired. Galloped in to work to meet Frank and told him what had happened with Dick Hughes.

'Oh, Sarah,' he exclaimed, 'you're not to go for everyone!'

He said I should try to be a bit clever and I was too sentimental.

I went up to Gill's office and told her about it all, and later had lunch in the pub with her, Sue and Pam.

Had to type some committee documents for Miss Sheridan, which irritated me intensely because it had to conform to a particular layout with a lot of indentation and numbering to get right.

It was Frank all day. He bought me breakfast and tea, and after lunch we split a packet of mints. After last night I was so relieved and happy to be with him again. I stopped him after a couple of kisses and, holding him very closely, told him I loved him so much, that I knew now it was him I wanted, and all sorts of other silly things; but I meant them. Then *I* even kissed him, to his great amusement. We were inseparable for as much of the day as we could be.

All afternoon he said, 'Come down to the basement with me.' I said I would when I finished work. So at the end of the day we did. I was ready to kiss him as usual, but he said no, and we simply cuddled each other for a while. Oh God, it was so wonderful to be with him! It's hard to explain how much there is between us.

He said he is going sick visiting this weekend at Whitechapel.

I felt a bit sad about poor Dick Hughes, who has no one to console him about his lost love.

Back to Chipstead.

27th – Saturday

I woke up late, and found that Vera had already gone to London, which was odd. Went shopping for her in Waitrose. After lunch I drew some Christmas cards.

It wasn't until yesterday, after the episode with Dick Hughes, that I realised how fond of Frank I am, and I told him how I felt. 'I beg your pardon?' he said, so I repeated it. He smiled and said, 'Yes, I heard you perfectly well the first time, I just wanted to hear you say it all again.'

Cheeky booger!

I'm glad I have done what I did with Frank. I'm not ashamed of any of it at all.

28th – Sunday

Georgina Fox came over in the afternoon and we listened to records.

29th – Monday

Weed-free. No sign of either Richard or of Moriarty.

Weather was warmer at last.

Frank was very pleased to see me and danced about with glee. His weekend was better than the previous one, he said, but had been occupied with thinking about me.

We went to the basement at about four on the pretence of getting cups of tea and had fifty-seven varieties.

'Only priests have to behave themselves,' said Frank.

Back to the bedsit about 6.45.

I had promised to lend my harmonica to Dick Hughes, so I took it down to his flat. He wasn't in, so I left it by the door with a note. Ate scrambled eggs, on toast this time. Faffed about.

Bed at 10.30, later woken up by Dick Hughes outside in the hall, coming in late with some woman.

30th – Tuesday

Frankie still calling me Fuzzyhead and singing songs about Killarney, which is usually a sign that he is happy. He bought me breakfast and tea. Today he was in a literary mood, scribbling things in a small notebook, which he kept hidden. However, he did show me an extraordinary drawing he'd made of us in bed together. I said it looked like we had left our clothes behind somewhere.

Work boring; actually too easy. Louise had a difficult man on the phone. I dropped a hint to her about my not being here the next time we had to do whatever it was, and she just growled rather grimly.

There was a flare-up over the Leah/lunch situation. Miss Handley gave us some hard but probably practical advice about how to put her off coming with us. Valerie was upset about it, but Handley said Leah is not quite so dumb as she seems.

Valerie isn't impressed with the way *The Owl and the Pussycat* is going.

Back at the bedsit, Dick Hughes put his nose around the door, but only for a quick thank you for the harmonica.

December

1st – Wednesday

Saw Frank mostly in the afternoon, when the topics of conversation were Sir Thomas More, reincarnation (again), Belfast (apparently things were worse in 1916 than they are now) and singing. And he wants to come and see me one evening, but not at the weekend because he would like to see me the day after. Then, to confuse me completely, he said I was to take no notice of what he says; and finally suggested we went for a quick drink before Christmas. Undecided.

Louise and I discussed eunuchs, Mickey Mouse, books, diaries and Frank's attitude to religion.

Lunch with Pam, Valerie and Sue. Sue is interested in one of the officers, who is possibly queer and probably not interested, so we tried to put her off.

Had a drink with Valerie, who was meeting Alan (the Yorkshireman) and a girl called Deborah, who are both in the cast of the play with her. Suspect Deborah fancies Alan.

Back at the bedsit I ate a home-cooked Irish stew, with lots of turnip and potato, followed by satsumas and read *The Comedians*, which was very good.

Sarah Shaw

2nd – Thursday

Poor old Frankie. He had a bad night last night because of (a) something on TV that had upset him and (b) his wife. I rang up the Income Tax again for him and they confirmed that she is registered blind. Also, I now know his staff number.

He told me a lot about how Christmas, and what he calls St Stephen's Day or Wren Day, used to be celebrated in Western Ireland. The latter involved dressing up and parading about with a toy wren on a pole singing a peculiar song, which he sang to me. It all sounded like something out of *The Golden Bough*.

He asked me about my evenings, and was I contented? I said no, not really, which made him smile.

Went for a drink in the evening with Pam, Valerie and Gill. Then bought more tights at Marks, fighting through the crowds at Oxford Circus.

3rd – Friday

Still no news from *The Listener* but on reflection I think it might be better for me to get out of the Langham, and then work out how I am going to carry on with Frank.

Louise and I discussed anarchists and Hitler's Germany. Her friend, the psychiatrist, works with Jewish refugees so it was particularly well-informed.

I made her a birthday card for Sunday.

Going for lunch, Gill and I got into Frank's lift. Gill had with her a sheet for her boss's expenses, which she had filled in but not yet added up.

'I'd better put the total in,' she said, and read the figures aloud as she added them.

'Nine pounds, twenty five p.' said Frank, from the other side of the lift.

'Is that right?' Gill asked, and looked at the columns again. 'Oh yes, that's right. You're quick, Frank.'

I caught his look.

Lunch was in the Salad Bar, discussing women's role in society, Victorian love affairs, etc.

Frank was very fond all day, especially in the afternoon. He said maybe we could meet outside work sometime around Christmas. I didn't say no. Went down to the basement with him in the late evening, and he was astonishingly moved and very tender, so I know he cares for me, as I do for him.

Had a chip salad in BH and went back to the bedsit.

4th – Saturday

A disturbed night, with Dick Hughes being on the phone outside my room into the small hours – I think he was phoning a girlfriend in America.

Met Gill at Victoria and went to Twickenham to visit an old friend of hers who has just had a baby. It looks like Mr Chaplin.

Back to Chipstead about 8 p.m. Watched TV, Crystal Palace actually won a match. Also, Sir Kenneth Clark on Seurat – his pronunciation has become even more precious.

5th – Sunday

Well, nothing really. Frightened the cat with the hair dryer.

6th – Monday

Frank and I re-united in the basement after a weekend's absence. It was … beautiful.

'Come to bed with me, Sarah,' he said. I refused. I do want to go out with him, but I don't feel I can trust him when he keeps talking like that – I can't take the risk. When I told him that he sighed, melted a little and said he understood.

Sue, who is lasting a lot longer than Miss Sharp's other temps, asked me today whether there was anything going on between me and the 'little Irish lift man'. I looked very surprised and said, 'Him? Are you joking?' and she backed down.

The improbability of our relationship does have its advantages.

The Tax Office has written to Frank, so he is happy about that. But his wife, poor lass, has been bad all weekend with arthritis in her back, which sounds very painful. He supposes she will always be like that.

We had a protracted farewell on the ground floor in the evening. He asked after my health, and I after his because he said he didn't feel very well.

Borrowed *The Rainbow* from the library. Also read *Dorian Gray* on the train.

7th – Tuesday

I went in to work feeling very warmly towards the man. We sat together for about fifteen to twenty minutes talking about his wife, and his local priest, Father Allwood, who is a regular visitor.

I saw a lucky amount of him today, we were together a lot. He is so very fond of me he makes me feel good.

Having asked the usual with the usual result, Frank and I had a laugh about having children together and what they might be like if we did.

I told him about the girl in the Photocopying Department who became engaged when she was fifteen, and we agreed with high moral tone that this was most unwise.

Frank said, 'Your father is too fond of you, you know. I think, perhaps, I am your little Daddy.'

We're in the basement again, arms around each other.

Frank: T'ink of me.
Me: I do.
Frank: All the time?
Me: Hadn't you noticed?

Although Frank may not try to squeeze it into words like I do, he really does feel something for me. I know because at the end of the day there was a beautiful sunset, the sky turned an extraordinary mauve colour. Gill spotted it first, and came back into the Langham as I was coming down in Frank's lift, so she, Frank, Jack and I went out on to the front steps of the Langham and looked up Portland Place together.

'Isn't it beautiful?' said Gill and we all agreed, while Frank slipped his hand into mine without anyone else noticing.

8th – Wednesday

Masses of work to do, so I had lunch with my typewriter.

Frank and I didn't manage much, and anyway, I had my 'condition', which he was very sympathetic about. He suggested that Gill, Kaz and I go for a drink with him before Christmas, but I couldn't see that working. It's Kaz's birthday on the 17th and I imagine he will want to be with Gill. Anyway, even if Kaz did come, I can't see him hitting it off with Frank. I mentioned it to Gill in case she was interested, and now she is in a quandary about it.

Frank asked if I cared about him. I said yes, and he said he did too, about me. It feels as if we are just beginning again, and that we can't be together enough.

Reading a book about Oscar Wilde (Irish).

9th – Thursday

Louise displeased with Sue's loud conversation – 'You're very nice but you disturb my thinking.' Jack said he was falling in love with me, which I ignored. The Real Liftie was in fine socialist form this morning, talking about railway unions. I was going to argue with him until I remembered he had spent years working on the railways, so probably knows more about it than I do. His wife slept well last night, anyway.

Bloody fizz at lunchtime. Valerie, Pam and Sue all disappeared, dumping Leah on Gill and me. I didn't ask her to join us and was cross. Gill was annoyed with Valerie. Gill then told me that she wouldn't come for a drink with Frank and me, and said firmly I was unwise to go. I wasn't really expecting that she would come, but was sad she disapproved of my doing so.

I told Frank it was no go with Gill and Kaz and we agreed we would go anyway, him and me. That sounds OK. We popped down to the basement together and he was very warm and amusing.

I went for a drink with Valerie and Gill.

Semi-invited myself down to Dick Hughes's flat to watch TV and got stuck down there while he mumbled himself to sleep, having been to the launderette. So I watched a bit more and then crept out so as not to disturb him.

10th – Friday

Although they are a bit corny, I keep thinking of that Paganini Variation and the Carpenters' 'Close To You'.

''Tis Friday all day today,' said Frank. Went to the basement for 'just a kiss, rejoicing'.

Frank's wife seems better and more cheerful now.

We talked about doing things for other people. He's giving

Jack some money so he can go on a Continental coach tour next year. He said Jack only wants to be mothered.

I was annoyed because I was given a pile of stuff from various people in the Department, and I don't take kindly to having random pieces of work dumped on me. Frank tried to laugh me out of it, so I let it go and was OK after a couple of hours.

No further news about Jack's proposed Christmas party, but Frank looked round his lift and said we could hold a tea party in there, with ginger biscuits, 'coppatay' and 'dem dried peas' (he meant peanuts).

The lunch gang was very impressed that an F. E. Producer was living in the same house as me. They said I should make friends with him if not more, what a great opportunity and so on. Why is it I can talk to them about Dick Hughes, who means very little to me, but not about Frank, whom I love and who loves me, and the more it goes on between us, the better it gets? I can't speak to anyone about him except Vera, who is fed up with hearing about him, and Gill, who doesn't really approve.

Supper with Sue at Alpino and went to an Ernest Read concert. Miss Handley was there, which was odd.

The concert was good.

11th – Saturday

Had a long, lazy lie-in. Almost didn't get up at all. Finally, when I did, I bumped into Dick Hughes hunting through the piles of envelopes on the hall table. Perhaps the American girlfriend had promised him a letter.

Went to John Barnes and the launderette and then travelled back to Chipstead. I took Vera to the shops, which cheered her up a bit.

She said one of her friends once imagined an air-crash in the skies above Mill Hill shortly before it actually happened.

Frank told me a story about how a tape recording made in a squash court turned out to be full of aircraft noise when they played it back. Apparently the court had been built on a disused airfield.

12th – Sunday

Weather damp and chilly.

I am still not sure that the BBC is the right place for me to be – it seems to be full of spalpeens, bastards and layabouts. I would like to be in a position of authority (which is ambitious!). Perhaps I will be one day, even though I lack university qualifications.

Morecambe & Wise was good tonight.

13th – Monday

Only just, with Vera's aid, got up in time and crawled to London.

Frankie looked cheerful. His wife is better and he said he slept well over the weekend.

He took me down to the basement twice during the day for the usual reasons.

Frank: Oy t'ink I will put some mistletoe up in me lift.
Me: OK, so what will you do when Jack comes to speak to you?
Frank (curling up in disgust):
        Oy don't kiss men!

He suggested we go to a pub in Great Portland Street on Friday evening, and said he will tell his wife that he is having a drink with a pal, which is true-ish. That all sounded OK to me. Even better, I waited for him after work and we walked together down Great Portland Street, chatting away happily, which is a good omen for Friday. Of course he was out of his uniform, and he looks so much softer and more normal in his ordinary clothes.

He does have beautiful blue eyes.

There is a job going at 35 Marylebone High Street, but I'm afraid it might be too advanced for me.

I'm thinking I will take a week off after Christmas. Frank won't be in then, nor Louise.

I asked Mike upstairs if there was a local doctor, and he gave me the name of a Dr Levy, just up the road. So I went to sign on at his practice and mentioned to him about my fingers. He said he would refer me to the Middlesex Hospital skin clinic.

Cooked sausages for tea and ate some fruit.

Gently in love with Frank.

14th – Tuesday

Woke at about 5.45 after a dream about an idiot wishing to be defenestrated, which reminded me of Ken bloody Russell. Slept again and dreamed of Frankie in the house I grew up in at Purley. He was in the playroom with me, and Mr Roberts was standing in the corridor outside.

I went to the Institute for a check-up, and Dr Darougar ('Are you still not married, Sarah?') played around with my eyes. He told me I had well-behaved veins.

Frank was a little upset at my late arrival, but his passion had not dimmed. We were very close all day. A smell of ammonia in the basement put him off, though.

Gill and I plan to put some mistletoe up outside Mr Roberts' office and see what happens. Celia disapproved, but Mr Roberts seemed unmoved when we mentioned it to him.

Louise out most of the day.

Went for a drink in the evening with Gill and Valerie, we three get on very well together. They both suggested that I should find myself a Nice Young Man. I joked that I only go for older men, like Mr Roberts, and silently dreamed about Little Frank.

It's OK, they don't understand.

It's odd that the current trends at the BBC are all about sexual freedom, women's liberation and promoting the working classes; here I am, a middle-class Conservative, trying to be myself but by rebelling against those trends.

Went to the library and borrowed a book on Bosie to compare with the one on Oscar Wilde.

I told Gill that I had decided to go out with Frank on Friday. She wished me no harm and said she had thought I would go.

I have been refusing invitations to go out with him since February.

15th – Wednesday

Frank very warm and tender today although I couldn't see him often because I was busy, Louise being out. We managed a savage trip to the basement and he threatened to give me money to buy tights. He also wants to go out with me after Christmas but I said no. He is cuddling the thought of Friday and assures me has no evil intentions.

I should think not.

We had a discussion about frisky, risky and whiskey, which, he said, makes you sick when you are well and well when you're sick.

I am thinking he lacks depth, but maybe not.

The Great Trousers Scandal today. Gill had been invited to a tea party with the bosses, but she turned up at work in trousers and was told she wasn't suitably dressed and so she couldn't go.

She put up some mistletoe outside her office instead of Mr Roberts's.

Booked time off over Christmas. There's no point coming in without either Louise or Frank being around. But I have a board [interview] for *The Listener* vacancy on 31 December, and will apply for the 35 Marylebone High Street job as well in case that falls through.

Met Penny for a fattening meal at the Old Kentucky. She told me about her job at the Psychic Institute – her boss says they will work well together as they have the Moon in Virgo in common.

Tired. Crawled home, eating liquorice.

Dick knocked on my door and came in. He'd locked himself out of his room. We had coffee and biscuits. He told me he went to Quarry Bank in Liverpool, the same school as John Lennon, only a few years above him. He once caned 'that Lennon' for a misdemeanour.

So now I know someone who once hit a Beatle.

He looked round my room and said the bedhead was 'obscene'. I hadn't thought it was anything, really.

I said I was going to apply for the 35 MHS job and he gave me some advice about the application form. After a while (and possibly because he drew a blank with me) he went off downstairs to break into his room.

16th – Thursday

Arrived to find Frankie armed with a hammer in his little fist; he was attacking some part of the lift machinery again.

We had a conversation about suicide (he opposes it) and queers (he says Cliff Richard isn't one, but I have my doubts). We got on to marriage.

Frank: If I had been younger, I would have married
        you.
Me: Well, when I do get married I hope it will be to
        someone like you.
Frank: Bit taller perhaps?

He then gave me some advice about choosing the right man to marry – 'A man widda steady position' and 'to have children young so you can be young too'. I was probably looking at him as if this was as much news to me as Noah's flood because he finished with 'Well, dat's only a little fellah's advice'.

Filed pamphlets but otherwise not much to do in the office.

I had lunch with Valerie, discussing a girl in her flat who is suffering a semi-nervous breakdown. We got on better on our own together than in a group – I think she would like to be friends with Gill, but Gill and I got together first.

Jack has put out a tin in his lift in the hope of getting some Christmas contributions.

17th – Friday

Oh, Jeez!

I had the job of lift man's assistant this morning, holding various screws, hammers and other implements as Frank tried to fix the buzzer in his lift so that it was quieter. The result was that it failed completely. Ho, ho, ho! It was nice though, being beside him, helping him.

To celebrate the failure we went down to the basement, but in a restrained fashion because it didn't feel right – I suppose because we wanted to keep something in reserve for the evening.

Louise was very amused to see Jack's tin. She suggested to Frank that he should also put out a tin for contributions (he would get a lot more than Jack). Frank said he thought it was more likely that someone would put a bomb in Jack's tin.

Had lunch with Valerie. She seems a bit bored with the ATG play but suggested that if I was around at the weekend, I could go and watch the rehearsals.

Gill's mistletoe is producing results. Both Mr Roberts and Mr Jones have found excuses to pop into her office and give her a kiss. I was worried Jack might try his luck, but Frank said there is no danger of Jack touching anyone, even though he fancies Miss Sharp and eyes Gill lecherously.

I don't know whether Mr Jones' head was turned by his moment of passion with Gill, but later on he told his secretary, Pam, that she ought to leave and get another job!

Louise left early, which meant I had plenty of time to sit in my office, feeling increasingly nervous and excited about what I was going to do after work. I was fairly confident that Frank wouldn't try to do anything I didn't want to do, but I wasn't at all sure what he had in mind and how it was all going to work out.

So at 6 p.m. I finished up, put on my coat and went out to the lifts. He had already changed into his ordinary clothes. He came up to the sixth floor and collected me, and we went down to the basement together, for once not stopping there. He locked up his lift and we walked over to Broadcasting House and then down Great Portland Street. That's me and Frank, together, outside the Langham. Of course it was dark and he was wearing his hat, so had anyone seen us they might not have recognised us.

There is a pub called The Albany on the corner by the Tube station. Frank took a look inside and said over his shoulder, ''Tis a railway pub,' and sniffed, but it met sufficiently with his approval and we went inside. He bought me a shandy, himself a light ale, and we sat in a corner, huddling up together.

As ever, we talked about Ireland, England, his family. He told me his father was a young railway engineer, but he can't remember him at all. He began smoking when he was four years old, moving on from tea, grass, sugar pulp and anything else he could find to 100 Players a day plus a pipe in the evenings. He gave it up for yearly periods, and finally, on New Year's Eve in 1956, he stopped altogether and hasn't had a smoke since.

When he was sixteen he ran away to London and stayed with a sister who lived in Maida Vale. He met a tart on the street and went back with her, bedded her and on the following morning, when he woke up, he said he looked at her and she 'was an old parsnip'. He was so scared of London that he went back home. He drove a tractor on a farm in Ireland and said he had been an 'old booger', getting drunk, fighting and having women. He used to drink Guinness with whiskey and two raw eggs in it. He doesn't support the IRA or what they are doing in Northern Ireland, of course, but when he was young he thought de Valera was a good bloke and 'during the Troubles' he slept with a photo of him under his pillow.

Then, on to Christmas. He and his wife will go to Basingstoke to stay with their daughter. He has to book a taxi to take them there because she can't travel any other way. It will cost him a lot of money.

He is going for his annual Confession tomorrow. I apologised for being a sin, he said it wasn't much of one anyway, which I found disappointing.

He looked around the pub and pointed out a group of people sitting at another table. He said a couple of them were blind. I wasn't sure how he could tell, but he was probably right.

He was very concerned that he might be boring me, but he was so funny and kind, I was quite happy to let him chatter on.

When he came back from the bar with another round (he absolutely wouldn't let me buy him a drink) and before he put his wallet away, he handed me a £1 note.

'Take this,' he said, 'buy yourself something as a present for Christmas.'

I protested politely, but he pressed it into my hand and insisted.

'I'm not short,' he said.

I looked at him for a moment and then we both started laughing. He hugged me, and chuckled, 'I can always reach up, you know.'

'So how tall is your wife?' I asked.

'Well, I nivver measured hor.'

He said she was blonde, aged sixty, and he was washing her hair when he got home.

I said I thought it had been quite a year for me, and that he had been such an important part of it. He shrugged and said he didn't think I had changed that much.

After about an hour and a half, we finished up. He was anxious that I should stay sober and get home safely, which was very sweet of him.

We went outside into the December night. There were crowds on the pavement, pushing past us. He looked around and said, 'I can't kiss you here, someone from work might see us.' Then he took my hand quite shyly and said, 'Thank you for this.'

I flung my arms around him and nearly knocked the poor man over.

We went down to the Underground trains together.

'Tell Gill,' he said with a wink as we parted at Baker Street, 'she can sleep easily. I have kept you quite safe.'

18th – Saturday

Got up at about 9.30 and did the Finchley Road shops, buying the remaining Christmas presents. Cooked lunch and went down Oxford Street. Bought jeans at Marks and strolled through the crowds back to Selfridges and Claude Gill. Masses of people everywhere of course.

Came back for supper and pottered around. Gave Dick Hughes a Christmas card. And then I sat in my room in a daze. What a fabulous evening it was yesterday, I can't believe it really happened. Frank has spent so much effort over so many months trying to persuade me into his bed, and in the end when we did go out together, we just had a few beers in the corner of a crowded pub; a girl and an old fellow, a tiny part of a London evening in December. Nothing earth shattering occurred; yet being with him, and knowing he liked being with me, made it the most wonderful evening of my life. He was so kind and generous and funny. He is an incredible man, we are an incredible pair, and God, we are so happy together!

Dead on cue, that Paganini Variation was on the radio again tonight.

I am so longing for Monday, it's not true.

I was woken out of this reverie when I went up to the bathroom and met Viv, who lives in a room upstairs. She works on Science programmes for the Open University. She invited me in for tea and cheese on toast, and I had a long chat with her. She warned me about Dick Hughes – she said he has tried it on with all the girls in the house. I wasn't surprised.

Wrote the song 'Bird' for Frank:

You on my hands, you on my brain,
You in the darkness, the sun and the rain;
You in the shuddering, frozen core,
Your song down the shaft, the open laughter,
Bird, I love you more and more.
Because I love you, you love me; because you love me,
    I love you,
Because I love you, you love me; because you love me,
    I love you, Bird.

19th – Sunday

Got up at God knows when o'clock and crawled down the Earl's Court Road in the pouring rain, heading for the rehearsal of the ATG play. It was a lousy journey, with two Tube changes.

It was very dull – well, watching the technicians adjusting the stage lights was OK – but it went on a bit. Had fish and chips for lunch with two other girls in a cafe, with T. Rex's 'Jeepster' thumping in my ear – I may be wrong but it sounded a bit rude.

Came back home at 5.45. Quick chat with Viv and Ken upstairs. Wrapped some Christmas presents, wrote cards and put them out ready to take in tomorrow.

Friday just beginning to wear off. I'm almost afraid of seeing this Gorgeous Beast tomorrow. It's a pity it can't all end on that note.

20th – Monday

Terrors! I didn't wake up until ten to nine!

I hared into work with the cards and Frank's Christmas present(s), which were a packet of mints, a biro, a prayer I had written out for him and an onion, all packed in a small box. He was surprised, but very grateful. There was also a card, which he said was cheeky because inside it said, 'I can't dream of Christmas 'cos I'm dreaming of you'.

Frank has had a haircut – he looks like a convict. He seemed more distant than he was on Friday, but I suppose we were back at work.

Madly in love with him, anyway.

We managed the basement twice.

Phoned the Ariel Theatre Group to buy tickets for Gill, Sue and myself to see Valerie's show tomorrow.

Distributed Christmas cards around the Department, and gave one to Jack, which he appreciated because it was for his wife as well as him.

Frankie liked the prayer – it was a prayer of St Patrick.

21st – Tuesday

At least I arrived in good time this morning, although Gill and Louise were both in late.

I managed some Frank time as well, including a trip to the basement with all stops out. He was a bit awkward today, though.

I wonder if the priest said something to him when he went for Confession? I don't think I can ask him about that, though.

Both Miss Handley and Graham gave him cards and he started to stick them all up on the back of the lift. He said he wouldn't stick mine up because I'd written 'Love from …' inside.

Revised my thought about the Confession later on when he invited me to bed with him and, when I refused yet again, he laughed.

And then I kissed him, because he never gives up.

Jack has had orders to remove his tin.

Gill said Mr Roberts came wandering down the corridor to her office, asking if I was around. She reckoned he wanted to kiss me under the mistletoe. Alas, I was taking dictation from Louise. When I told her, she said she thought Roberts fancies me, because he has been blathering on about my hair to various people.

In the evening, Sue, Gill and I went to Earl's Court Road to see Valerie in the ATG play. I bought the LP of *Imagine* on the cheap before we went in. I did rather regret not having been able to play a part in the production, but oh well … Too bad. Alan played the Quangle Wangle and did a very good impression of Ken Dodd – in fact, they were all good. Valerie was an excellent Jumbly Girl. The children in the audience, of whom there were many, were very excited – lots of screaming and joining in. Despite a few technical hitches, it went off very well.

22nd – Wednesday

Horrible time! I woke at a quarter to nine! I hurled down to the Langham in half an hour, running all the way from Great Portland Street as I was desperate to get there before everyone else. And then, when I did rush up to the lifts, Frankie took one look at me and said I was 'too hot to do anyt'ing wid,' which was very disappointing after all that effort. Anyway, he said he had hit himself on a door this morning, and because the weather was warmer he had a headache for much of the day.

Went to the office Christmas lunch at Pepino's in Great Portland Street with everyone, including Carol, who came back to join us. It was very noisy in there but great fun.

Frank egged Jack on to go and kiss Gill under her mistletoe, but nothing came of it. We knew Jack wouldn't do it anyway.

Me: So will *you* go and kiss Gill under the mistletoe?
Frank: No, not unless she asks me to.
Me: You never waited for me to ask you, before you kissed me.
Frank: Ah, but you were a different proposition.

Jack had a twig of mistletoe in his lift, which I nicked and gave to Frank, with a kiss. In a more intimate moment in the afternoon he told me that he had woken up in the night and found himself 'turning down the sheets' of the bed for me.

'I must have been dreamin',' he said, 'and we were being as gentle as lambs.'

I told him I thought he was good-looking and he sighed, ''Tis all in your imagination.'

Quite fancied going down to the basement but never got it.

Went to the library, and came back to the bedsit feeling madly in love with him.

23rd – Thursday

Arrived to find Frankie cheerful and very tender, the most he has been all week. He bought me a bread roll and did a kind of a double act with Jack, all to do with taking people up in lifts and the sign outside the ladies' loo. Then we had a drink in Frank's lift and wished each other merry Christmas. Once Jack had gone away I gave Frank my phone number, but he said he probably wouldn't be able to call me because of his family being around all the time.

We went to the basement after lunch and were loving each other merrily. He has a marvellous face and strong hands. I said I loved him and was very fond of him, and he smiled back at me. He wished me well, and promised he would try to phone me if he could.

He left at three.

I left at four after a brief chat with Louise, and arrived in Chipstead around the same time as the turkey was delivered. Watched *The Great St. Trinian's Train Robbery*, which kept me from feeling too hollow inside.

Alastair has sent me a Christmas card. Felt awful because I hadn't sent one to him.

24th – Friday

Shopping; completed a song about Frank:

December

'Tis the man from Kerry who has laughed her heart away,
He thought it would soon be done, but as soon as it had
  begun,
Love was growing and he wanted to stay.

When you're feeling lonely or the night keeps you away
You think of you and me, how gentle we could be
And our love is growing and you wanted to stay.

In a bad dream's waking or a cold, unending day,
In crowded streets and trains I think of you again,
And our love is growing, and I wanted to stay.

25th – Saturday (Christmas Day)

Presents. Watched television.

Champagne and salmon made the day a little more luxurious, and there appeared to be a Christmas truce at the dinner table.

26th – Sunday (Boxing Day)

Visited Uncle Rupert and Aunt Suzanne. Ate too much.

27th – Monday

Nothing. Went for a walk with Vera.

28th – Tuesday

Bit lonely. Phoned Georgina Fox. Father reverted to being bloody impossible again. Poor Vera! I don't seem to be able to talk to her about anything except men.

Not expecting Frank to call me, but wish he would.

271

29th – Wednesday

Weather turned colder.

30th – Thursday

Back to London for an appointment at the Middlesex Hospital about eczema on my fingers. I was seen by Dr Bettley, who treated Father for the same thing years ago. I now have a long strip of plaster down my back, with various substances on the inside to see what it is I am allergic to.

I had lunch with Gill and Sue at the Yorkshire Grey. Gill says Christmas went off well, although she had some difficulty with Kaz before they went. Apparently one of the education officers had ensnared Gill under the mistletoe, much to her dislike.

Went back home to Chipstead. It was snowing and I had a slight skid driving up Portnalls Road. Read *The Devils*.

31st – Friday

Went back up to London, reading *Brighton Rock*. At John Lewis I bought a Ronson Rapide hairdryer and a clothes airer, handing over the exact same £1 note that Frank gave me in the pub. I left my shopping with Gill in her office and went for the interview for the job at *The Listener*. Actually, I wasn't that bothered about it. Mr Day, who interviewed me, seemed a bit of a pansy. Mrs Crouch, the Personnel woman, was awfully nice but I don't think I have got the job.

Bought a book of Celtic verse at Book Selections bookshop in Purley on my way back.

Yearning for Little Frankie.

Have actually enjoyed being at home over Christmas.

I wonder how it's going in Basingstoke.

1972–1974

1971 was the only year in which I kept a daily diary. What follows is from memory, and from an intermittent journal I kept between 1973 and 1975.

I didn't get the job at *The Listener*. I had joined the SBC after friendly chats with Miss Malcolm and Louise, so that was my first formal interview. I went in without any preparation and immediately sensed that I was out of my depth, so I wasn't disappointed not to get the job. I remained at the SBC for a few more months.

In late February 1972, I finally agreed to go out on a Saturday evening with Frank.

I took the Tube to Royal Oak. It was a cold, dry winter's evening. He was waiting at the top of the steps, wearing his suit, raincoat and trilby hat. As I arrived, he said he had been wondering whether I would actually turn up, but after a moment he seemed happy that I had. Being there together felt unreal; strange but exciting.

He led me around various streets even though it was so dark I could see little. First, he pointed out Little Venice, twinkling lights reflected in the water, and then we walked along the canal path through a small park. Here, I had a moment of concern because I was on my own with him in a quiet and deserted area and no one else knew where I was. But I took his arm, he smiled and I felt safe. Reaching the Harrow Road, we turned left, passing a tall block of flats. He pointed up at one.

'My wife's in there,' he said.

We followed a footpath over railway tracks, went down another road and reached a pub. I can't remember much about this place because after about twenty minutes or so he told me to drink up quickly; we needed to move on. I didn't ask why. We transferred to another, larger place, which might have been a social club. There was a long bar on one side and seats around tables on the other. Otherwise the room was featureless. We had several beers. I sat on a stool. Frank stood beside me, leaning on the bar, foot up on the rail. Unusually, I found myself looking up at him. 'No Matter How I Try' by Gilbert O'Sullivan and Nilsson's 'Without You' were playing on a jukebox in the background. For about an hour or so we chatted, and when he went off to the Gents he introduced me to a couple of friends, whom he asked to keep me company. One of them immediately launched into a panegyric about Frank: what a good man he was, a friend who always helped anyone in trouble and would never let them down, how he was one of the most popular men in the area, and so on. When Frank came back and his friends moved away, I told him what the man had said. He laughed, and then leant over to me and whispered, 'They all t'ink you're my daughter.'

Around ten o'clock we left the pub. He said, 'I can't take you home wid me, my wife's there.' I didn't know what he had thought we might do next, and he didn't seem too sure either. I followed him a short distance along a straight road before turning on to a piece of wasteground under The Westway flyover. It was hardly a salubrious spot. Old newspapers, cans and other bits of rubbish were dotted around, and up against concrete pillars various couples were coupling.

Frank led me to a remoter pitch and we set about doing what we usually did. The traffic thundered overhead, the other couples cursed and moaned. Someone yelled something at us. Frank turned round, shouted 'Booger off!' then carried on.

It wasn't what I had expected, not that I had expected anything, really. In the cold night air, and uncomfortably uncertain where I could safely put my feet, I leant back and thought of Ireland. After Frank came, he said, 'I'm sorry, I'm sorry,' and was very solicitous about my well-being. Although far from ecstasy myself, pinned as I was against a concrete support of one of London's major arterial roads, I was with him and I had made him happy; and however grim our surroundings that was all I wanted.

Frank packed himself away; we straightened our clothes. After darting off to a nearby road, he hailed a taxi. He spoke to the driver, money changed hands and the next thing I remember is Frank standing on the pavement, waving me goodbye. The driver was silent all the way back. When I got to the bedsit, I asked if I owed him anything, but he simply dismissed me and drove off.

It might surprise you, but I was euphoric. I had done it: I had had an evening with Frank and in itself that was wonderful. I started to feel embarrassed about the way it had ended, I immediately pictured Frank leaning on the bar, smiling at me with those wonderful blue eyes, and was awash with love for him again.

The following day, around midday, the phone rang. One of the girls in the house answered it and banged on my door. It was for me: it was for me! It was Frank! He was on his way home from church and had stopped in a phone box to make the call because he was anxious to know if I was all right. Had I got back home safely? Was I angry with him? I said I was fine, I had enjoyed the evening, I liked his friends, I loved him … I was still swimmingly delirious with happiness.

He said several times he was sorry about what had happened and where he had taken me, but I told him not to worry.

A few weeks later, I finished working for the School Broadcasting Council. At the end of my last day, Gill, Valerie, Pam and I went for a celebratory drink in the BBC Club. I invited Frank to join us, thinking that at last in the company of my friends he and I could be recognised as a couple. Gill and Valerie weren't entirely happy with this arrangement, but went along with it.

Frank was beaming with pride when we entered the Club together. He bought a round of drinks, and to begin with all went well, even if the conversation was a little awkward. It was after the second or third round that things started to falter. Frank would not, of course, allow any of us to buy a round and although we protested, he went back to the bar as soon as our glasses were empty. Looks were exchanged. Valerie was worried that he might not be able to afford it all. We whispered, 'Don't finish your drink,' but Frank continued to pile them up for when we finished the one we had. Full glasses glared intimidatingly from the table. Finally, I could bear it no more. I told him I was sorry but, 'Oh, look at the time, we must go now!' We thanked him and made our way out of the Langham. Later on, in a Ladies' loo somewhere, I cried my eyes out on Pam's shoulder as it finally sank in that between Frank and myself there were, and always would be, too many unresolvable differences.

When I told Vera about this episode, she was angry that Frank had treated us like 'a bunch of hooligans on a pub crawl in Paddington', which seemed a little harsh. The next time I met Frank I thanked him again. He asked why we had hurried off and if he had done something wrong. I suggested he might have overdone it a bit with the drinks. He straightened up defensively for a moment, looked hurt and finally shrugged, sighing that he had only tried to do his best for me.

My next job was still at the BBC, as secretary to a school radio programmes producer called John Parry. Our office was in 1 Portland Place, opposite the Langham so most mornings, before I started work, I would call in to see Frank for a kiss and a cuddle. As time went by my visits became less frequent; sometimes I arrived too late or I had to be in the office early. Once or twice people saw me coming over from the Langham and asked suspiciously what I had been doing there. In the end, I began to feel that starting the working day by canoodling in a lift was … odd. However, he was still a mate, he was fun and we were fond of each other. Some evenings we would meet after work, walk up to Great Portland Street station and travel to Baker Street, where I would change trains and we would bid each other an affectionate goodnight.

In the afternoons, when I went over to the Club for tea with other secretaries from the Department, Frank might sidle in and sit by himself at one of the other tables. Having explained that he was a friend, I would join him for a chat. In time the other girls started asking me how had I become friends with a lift man, why did he always come into the Club when I was in there, and so on. So sometimes I had to dampen their curiosity. I stayed with them, and tried not to notice the man on the other side of the room who, with dignified patience, sat stirring his tea and never took his eyes off me. Then I would have to get up and walk out, passing Frank's table with only a faint nod of recognition, hating myself afterwards for what I had done.

By the end of 1972 I had met more people of my own age, mostly through joining the BBC's Studio Amateur Dramatic Group. I assumed these friends wouldn't understand, let alone approve of my having been so closely involved with a lift man, so I never mentioned it.

21 March 1973

Vera came to the office yesterday. She was very upset and on the verge of tears. She told me Father has cancer and is likely to die within a few months. I wasn't upset, just a bit stunned.

And where's Frank? Still off sick, and has been for the past six weeks or so. I hope he is OK.

28 March 1973

Frank is back after five weeks or so of absence.

He asked if I were married yet.

I said no.

He also asked if I would call in and see him in the mornings before work.

I said no.

'Hmm,' he said, 'so you've gone off that idea.'

And he just smiled.

God, what a man he is!

But I think it is over anyway, at least in the old sense. After all, I am miles away from the person I was in the summer of 1971.

Won't my friends be pleased?

[In April 1973, my father died.]

29 May 1973

I came back on the train with Frank tonight. The little man looked very pale, and said he thinks of me a lot, etc. The poor fellow really love(s)(d) me, I think. At times he still has something, some attraction – I think it's in his eyes. Yet his view of me seems rather limited. In his own way I suppose I'm important to him, which is flattering but I doubt whether his idea of me is similar to anyone else's.

4 June 1973

Little Frank seems to be pining. He told me on Friday about some dream he had had, that he was standing at a railway station and I was at the barrier seeing him off, telling him to stay with his daughter and grandchildren. It then went on into some male chauvinist vulgarity about shelling peas, which I won't put down on paper.

He looked very sad and wistful on Friday. I can't figure out why I still find him so attractive – I think it's his blue eyes.

Miss Sharp drove past us while we were talking together. She grinned fiercely.

22 June 1973

Nothing has been the same as the way I loved Frank, because Frank can still just smile at me and I go weak at the knees, although these days I no longer want to grab him.

13 August 1973

I saw Frank today. He was, by turns, charming, embarrassing, vulgar and whimsical, all in the space of twenty minutes.

Oh Lord, what a fate I was saved from!

11 September 1973

Very sad news. I was meeting Pam in the foyer of the Langham and Cyril, a relief lift man, came over to speak to me. He said that Frank's wife died yesterday. So when I got back to the office I wrote a wee note to him, which probably sounded very formal, but I decided to err on the side of caution. All this just two weeks before he is due to retire. Losing her will leave an awful gap in his life, looking after her occupied so much of his time. I hope he won't hit the bottle or something – it must be such a blow to him. I don't even know if he will come back to work again now.

Poor chap. I feel very sorry for him.

[Frank retired from the BBC on 26 September 1973.]

23 October 1973

Bumped into Dick Hughes twice today. John Parry thought he might be sniffing around me. Felt sick and ghastly, hated it. Dick mumbled on about wanting to visit me, but I'm not interested.

Then, at twenty past five, Frank rang me in the office. Awful, too. Fortunately John Parry had left by then. I couldn't tell Frank it was all over, I just said I was busy. He was rather bitter and terse and then tried to get matey at the end, but I didn't want to hear him, didn't know what to say, and rang off.

Both of them on one day.

Frank then wrote three letters to me, all of which I subsequently destroyed.

The first, which was brief, suggested we meet; I declined politely.

In the second, running to four pages, he explained that he had wanted to meet me because he wanted to ask me to marry him. As the meeting hadn't happened, he made the proposal in writing. He sketched out a romantic future for us, promising he would love and take care of me. Halfway through, he apologised for the letter, adding, 'I think I am a better lover than I am a writer.'

On first reading I was very shocked and hid the letter away, thinking I wouldn't answer it, but a couple of days later, I re-read it and realised it deserved a considerate reply. I settled down and wrote back, thanking him as tactfully as I could for the honour but turning down his proposal on the grounds that I didn't want to marry yet.

Another letter arrived within a day or two. Frank said if I didn't want to marry him, would I consider just living with him for a few years?

I replied, 'Dear Frank, [and in large letters] NO. Sarah'.

In May 1974, I handed in my notice to the BBC and accepted a job at a small publishing company.

29 May 1974

Two days to go before I leave the BBC …

I went to my last studio production this afternoon, a Terry Lynch epic about the seaside, which passed off painlessly. John and Terry went straight for a drink in the BBC Club. I took our stuff back to the office and, when I picked up John's briefcase, I found a note from one of the other secretaries to the effect that Frank was in the Club, and had been asking after me.

There was no escape. I had to deliver the briefcase, so I went over with it. Frank was waiting for me by the door. I said hello, took the briefcase to John and dashed straight into the Ladies' loo, shut the door and tried to collect my thoughts. Then it struck me that Frank might have married again, and anyway I felt guilty about taking the money he gave me last year for a birthday present. So I went back into the Club, only to see that Frank was talking to … Dick Hughes! Horrors! Frank came back to me, and I took him outside the door of the Club. I offered to return the money to him, but he wouldn't have it. He told me he just wanted to see me for a drink, and that what had passed between us before could all be forgotten. He kept insisting that I go for a drink with him, that I should phone him, etc.

I told him I couldn't stay, that I was leaving the BBC (true) and moving away to live up North – yes, even next week! (No, not true.) He said he was moving away as well, down to Basingstoke.

He asked after Vera.

He still wanted me to join him for a drink, and I explained to him that I couldn't, because if I went back into the Club, I would have to go and sit with John and Terry – it was like part of my job and would look strange if I abandoned them and went off with other people. (I also knew that if I joined Frank for a drink, John Parry would hound me with questions about him afterwards.)

He said, 'You look well,' and looked rather sadly at me.

I went back into the Club, left him talking to Dick Hughes and quickly gulped down a drink with John Parry. After that I felt I could not stay there any longer. Frank was buying lots of drinks for people in the F. E Department and if I joined them, I was afraid that he might say something in front of them. In fact, I could foresee him and Dick Hughes getting drunk together, and goodness knows what might be said or hinted at. So that was it.

I left, and walked back through Regent's Park, which was delightfully sunny, and watched some American children playing baseball.

Fancy Frank turning up in my last week at the BBC! Had he come next week I would not have been there, but knowing how things were between us, it's no surprise.

Bet he and Dick Hughes swapped some good stories.

Afterword

I never saw or heard from Frank again. He moved to Basingstoke and died in 1982 from heart disease, nine years after retiring from the BBC. He was seventy-three.

My father's death in April 1973 came as a huge blow as it left me without an immediate family. Five months later Frank's wife also died, allowing him to express his deeper feelings for me and to make his offer of marriage. But I was still at a low point myself, and it felt like an intrusion. Had we attempted to revive our relationship I doubt we would have lasted more than a week together, although that week might have had its moments. One of us had to put an end to it, and I was young and callous. My only regret is that I didn't have that final drink with him but the circumstances were not right.

What happened next? After a difficult couple of years I met the man who became my first husband, and returned to work for the BBC, this time at Television Centre as secretary to Louis Marks in the Plays Department. I took a break from paid work to bring up our two children, later meeting another partner, whom I subsequently married. In the 1990s I gained a degree in Social Sciences through the Open University, and in 2000 qualified as a professional librarian. I retired in 2014 after twelve fulfilling years as librarian of a Cambridge college.

Vera moved to a flat in Reigate, keeping up with her many friends and my uncles and aunts. She eventually went to live in a nursing home, and died in 1997. Gill left the SBC in 1975. After her marriage to Kaz broke down, she studied English Literature to doctorate level and became a tutor in adult education. Penny eventually settled in Derbyshire with her husband and two daughters, and worked at an advice centre for small businesses. Valerie moved on to other roles in the BBC, married, later qualified in social work and practised as a mediator.

The Langham was, like so many of its buildings, sold off by the BBC. It has been refurbished and restored as a five-star Grand Hotel, patronised by the late Princess of Wales and Lady Gaga, among others. The floors have been re-numbered, and the offices converted into luxurious bedrooms; those where Louise and I worked are now part of a large suite. The west side lift shaft and stairwell are still in the same place, but the old birdcage lifts have been replaced.

So, what do I think about the diary now, more than forty years on?

In 1971 anyone over thirty would have remembered the 1939–1945 war, and you can see that it still cast a shadow over people's lives. Like others my age, I was struggling to reconcile traditional values with the new social attitudes of the 1960s, especially feminism, which was a new concept to me.

It might surprise you how naïve girls were in those days. Information about sex wasn't that easy to find, and I never read women's magazines, hence my resorting to poems and novels. I completely failed to spot that Frank was stealthily moving step by step towards 'getting to know' me; and for example when I wrote down, 'He said he was in a state last night and had to get up at five in the morning', I had no idea what he had been trying to say. Nor did I understand that he used 'getting angry' to mean 'getting aroused'. But, despite my ignorance, I was no pushover. What a delicious irony there is in the School Broadcasting Council carefully debating and planning sex education programmes while Frank enrolled me on his own exclusive course of tutorials and practical sessions. Had we been caught, things would have turned out very differently. He took a hell of a risk in doing what he did, but somehow we got away with it.

I'm sorry that my father doesn't come out of the book at all well. I had forgotten how difficult he was in those days and can't explain why he behaved as he did, but I suspect he never came to terms with losing his wife and son. He never spoke about them again. It was only after many years that I realised he was struggling to cope with his own grief while trying to keep life for the two of us as normal as possible. There is a kind of heroism in that, but his reticence appeared to me as indifference so I rejected him. The dual loss left me with a brave face and the ability to crack jokes, but underneath it all I was angry, scared and cynical about the Swinging Sixties' revolution. I didn't want the status quo challenged, and thought the older generation was letting us down by not making a stand for their values, so I holed myself up in my bedroom and poured my teenage angst into songs and poetry. If you wonder why it took so long for me to change my job and move out of that wretched hostel, for me the prospect of coping with new situations or of sharing a flat with a bunch of confident, outgoing girls – or worse still, boys – was terrifying.

You may also have been wondering how I could have become involved with a man who was so much older than myself. When Frank asked me why I fancied him, I couldn't answer – I didn't know. Now it seems obvious. He and my father had both, to some extent, 'lost' their wives, but there the similarity ends. My father was middle class, tall, anxious, socially awkward and often taciturn; a man whose emotions were strictly controlled until he exploded in fits of anger. Frank, although he had his anxious moments too and was quick to act in self-defence when provoked, was working class, short, easy-going and generous, and his Irishness gave him an extra dash of romanticism. Most of all, he gave me the comfort and belief in myself that my father did not provide.

The Langham itself had a significant influence on events. Its sullen magnificence dwarfed us all. It obliterated the differences in class, age, religion and education separating Frank and myself, yet protected me by restricting his scope for manoeuvre. At times it did feel as if I was in Sleeping Beauty's castle with a prince in heavy disguise, needing an inexhaustible number of kisses to be rescued; but once we set foot outside the building together that spell was broken. We became an old man and a girl: companions, but not lovers.

Rediscovering this diary has been fascinating, but also a highly emotional experience. At an early stage of transcription I realised that, if it were to be published, I would have to find out whether Frank was still alive. I was prepared for the answer, which I found online fairly quickly, but not for the effect that it would have on me. There was a real sadness in going through the book, seeing him again quite clearly and laughing at something he had said, only to have to remind myself that he had died more than thirty years before.

I'm now the same age as was Frank in 1971. How fortunate that I didn't throw the diary away, because in it I found something of much greater value than I imagined I would when I lifted it out of the cardboard box, a far better understanding of the other side of the story. For me, the secret of the diary is that I found inside it the love that Frank left there for me. I can't thank him now for that, or for his kindness, passion and patience, but how lucky I was to have known him.